WARREN R. AUSTIN AT THE U.N.
1946-1953

WARREN R. AUSTIN
Portrait by Fritz Werner in the Vermont State House, Montpelier

Warren R. Austin
at the U.N.
1946-1953

GEORGE T. MAZUZAN

The Kent State University Press

Library of Congress Cataloging in Publication Data
Mazuzan, George T
  Warren R. Austin at the U.N., 1946-1953

  Bibliography: p.
  Includes index.
  1. United Nations. 2. Austin, Warren Robinson, 1877-
  3. United Nations—United States.
I. Title.
JX1977.M4   341.23'092'4 [B] 76-52990
ISBN 0-87338-202-1

To my wife Yvette
and
Michael and Kevin
with
Peace, Love, Joy

CONTENTS

PREFACE

This volume studies the United Nations career of Warren R. Austin who served as American ambassador to the world body during the initial, eventful years of the Cold War. He was an interesting character because he represented a type of person who never fit perfectly the Cold Warrior image exemplified by so many of the personalities of the Harry S. Truman administration.

Austin believed sincerely in the concept of the United Nations. He thought that the legal and moral opinion collectively enunciated by the world's nations would be sufficient to resolve any major differences between individual countries. Assuming that the Soviet Union was as devoted to this concept as the rest of the world, Austin undertook to deal with the Russian representatives in an informal, candid manner. His efforts failed to elicit reciprocation. As lines hardened between East and West and the policy of containment emerged from the Truman administration, Austin saw a slow disintegration of his wartime vision of the postwar world, and his moralism led him to the brink of unreality. Nonetheless, he maintained hope that the United Nations eventually could find solutions for fundamental problems dividing the world's major power blocks.

Because he typified the moralist position, Austin was a notable figure in the Truman administration. He was, without doubt, on the secondary level and never was in a major policy-making role. Yet the symbol he represented —

American acceptance of world responsibility and multilateral collaboration through the United Nations — was an important part of the emerging role of the United States in the postwar world. Austin believed that moral purpose should never be divorced from international political action and, as this study shows, his actions at the United Nations always proceeded from that axiom.

I have accumulated many debts in the course of preparing this work. Most rewarding has been my reliance on others for ideas and advice. Oral historian Charles T. Morrissey availed me not only of his knowledge of Vermont history, but offered fine criticism of the total manuscript. Martin Fausold, friend and colleague at the State University of New York, College at Geneseo, provided me with an ongoing dialogue and raised important questions with his criticism. My father, John E. Mazuzan, a sage Vermont editor, reminded me about the basic rules of rhetoric and grammar. Alonzo L. Hamby of Ohio University and Lisle A. Rose of the Historical Office of the State Department offered important suggestions for the improvement of the work. Lawrence S. Kaplan of Kent State University epitomized all those things a major advisor represents; he furnished intellectual stimulation, criticism, encouragement and friendship in the evolution of this project.

I greatly appreciate the services extended by the staffs of the Columbia University Library; Cornell University Library; Herbert Hoover Library; the Library of Congress; the National Archives; Princeton University Library; University of Rochester Library; Franklin D. Roosevelt Library; Harry S. Truman Library; University of Vermont Library; the Wisconsin State Historical Society and Yale University Library. The reference staff at the Geneseo State College Library deserves special recognition for cheerfully putting up with my multitudinous requests for favors.

The following groups contributed to the study through the use of their funds: the Research Foundation of the State University of New York; the Harry S. Truman Library Institute; the Eleanor Roosevelt Institute; the Geneseo Foundation and the Geneseo State Faculty Senate Research

Fund. This financial aid provided me with an unencumbered summer for research as well as enabling me to travel to several archives.

John Buechler, Head of Special Collections at the Guy Bailey Library at the University of Vermont made my research in the Austin papers a most pleasant experience. He extended many favors to me during my several trips to Burlington.

For their thoughtful courtesies, I also thank Henry Berger, Richard Salisbury, Erwin Mueller, Duane and Lucille Biever, Ray and Kathy Bye and Connell Gallagher. Diana Harke typed the manuscript.

Final words remain for Yvette, Michael and Kevin, who watched this project take shape.

Geneseo, New York
August 1976

CHAPTER ONE

THE ANTI-NEW DEAL INTERNATIONALIST

President Harry S. Truman telephoned Warren R. Austin in the early afternoon on June 5, 1946 to offer him a proposed appointment to the new position of United States Ambassador to the United Nations. Secretary of State James Byrnes had made the recommendation to Truman. The Secretary later offered no reason for the suggestion except that Austin's background in the United States Senate prepared him with "extensive knowledge of and keen interest in foreign relations." And, of course, Austin was not unknown to Truman since they both had served together in the Upper Chamber.[1] But questions must have crossed many Americans' minds on learning of the appointment: Who is Austin? Is he qualified for this important post? What is an anti-New Deal Republican doing as a Truman appointee?

At age 68, Austin already had served in a lengthy private and public career although he was not well known in national circles. Born on November 12, 1877 in Highgate Center, Vermont, a tiny, rural community on the Canadian-Vermont border, Austin spent his developing years in that backwater area of northern New England. His early life was influenced considerably by his mother and father. Ann Robinson Austin shaped in the young Warren a disposition to hard work for which he became much admired in later life. Nonetheless, her regimen of work was not without motherly love for him and his brothers, Chauncey, Jr. and Roswell (Warren was the eldest of the three boys; there were also three girls, but all died of childhood illnesses) and there developed in Warren an admiration for, and closeness with, her that he never lost.[2]

Chauncey G. Austin, Sr. was a country lawyer who, over the years, became one of the most successful trial lawyers in Franklin County. More than anyone else, he helped direct young Warren toward the legal profession. The boy spent as much time as possible at his father's office, and at an early age decided that he, too, would become a lawyer.[3]

Warren attended the Highgate district school through 1891 and then was sent off to Brigham Academy, a semi-private preparatory school in nearby Bakersfield. There he did well academically and socially, graduating at the top of his class in 1895. He entered the University of Vermont in Burlington that fall. At the university he again was a popular student, participating in histrionics and the university band, and serving on various class committees. He also gained some notoriety as a member of the Rudyard Tipling Club in which his capacity for beer drinking, combined with his stout physique, earned him the epithet of "Fatty" Austin. Always meticulously groomed, Austin developed a reputation as a clothes horse, something he maintained throughout his lengthy career.[4]

During his busy collegiate life Austin met and courted Mildred Lucas. She was the daughter of the trainmaster in St. Albans and she often traveled to Burlington to visit friends. On one of these occasions, while attending a tea in 1898, she was introduced to Austin. Later, while on his way to St. Albans to conduct business for the yearbook — he was business manager — he met Mildred again on the train. Although she did not attend college, she became Austin's companion at many of the social affairs of the University. They married in 1901, two years after Austin received his Ph.B.[5]

Upon graduation from the University in 1899, Austin returned home and read law in his father's office. In that same year, Chauncey moved his entire practice from Highgate Center to St. Albans — the Franklin County seat — where he had maintained a part-time office. Warren lived at home in Highgate Center until his marriage to Mildred in the summer of 1901. The couple settled into a St. Albans Main Street apartment, where they remained until purchasing a house on Congress Street in 1913.

The two young people loved each other deeply, so that even their differences dovetailed. Mildred was reserved in public while Warren was gregarious. As a dutiful wife, she quietly supported his ambitions, all the while exuberating a fashionable quality of femininity. While Mildred did not possess the formal education Warren did, she was well read and took great interest in his legal and political work. When their children were born — Warren, Jr. in 1902 and Edward Lucas in 1910 — she devoted an increasing amount of time to their upbringing. An unkind word rarely was spoken between Mildred and Warren, and overall, the qualities of these two people meshed into a loving, devoted companionship that lasted through more than sixty years of marriage.[6]

Austin passed the Vermont Bar examinations in 1902, after which he formally associated with his father's firm. Over the course of the next few years, Chauncey, Jr. and Roswell also joined the practice. Business proved lucrative, and besides practice in law, the Austins expanded into real estate, which provided enough extra income to allow the four families to live quite comfortably.

Association with an already established name in law gave Warren an easy entrance into public life and he soon was involved in many activities of the St. Albans community. Never was it a question that the Republican Party was the one with which a young, politically-minded Vermonter should affiliate. He immediately joined the party's local Civic Committee and in 1903 was appointed a Grand Juror. The following year he entered his first elective contest and won the post of State's Attorney for Franklin County. That same year the local party caucus selected Austin as its choice for the seat in the House of Representatives from Vermont's First Congressional District. The selection indicated the reputation he had established with the political power in the area. This was prior to the introduction of the direct primary in Vermont; consequently, the candidates were chosen by caucus-appointed delegates to the state convention. But since Austin had no following outside the St. Albans area, and the district included all the western half of the state from the Massachusetts line to the Canadian border, his bid at the convention proved futile.

Beginning in 1904 Austin utilized every opportunity to place himself before the public and to increase his contacts within the Republican Party. He developed his talent for oratory and was in demand as a public speaker. The young lawyer thoroughly enjoyed this activity, and often was the featured speaker in some nearby Vermont hamlet on several of the holidays that custom required a public address.[7]

Austin combined his hard work at the practice of law with participation in politics. In 1906 the U.S. Circuit Court for the Second Circuit admitted him to practice and in 1907 he was named a United States Commissioner. Through contacts he made in legal circles and his growing reputation as a party worker, Austin became fairly well known in Vermont Republican circles. In 1908, for example, he was elected temporary chairman of the Republican State Convention, and the following year he was elected mayor of St. Albans for a one-year term.[8]

In 1912, Austin again made a bid for the Republican nomination to the House of Representatives as a progressive candidate in opposition to the more conservative, party-backed representative, Frank L. Greene. Austin lost, but unlike many Vermont progressives, who followed the Theodore Roosevelt movement, he refused to break with the state Republican organization. He continued to make appearances in behalf of Republican candidates.[9]

After this defeat, however, Austin devoted most of his time to the practice of law, which now took him into new areas of professional interest. He studied legal reform, and was admitted to practice before the United States Supreme Court in 1914. As a result, not only did Austin become a better lawyer, he also broadened his contact with lawyers and businessmen from other sections of the nation.

Through his brother Chan, Austin made one particularly important business contact that ultimately took him to the other side of the world. The younger Austin left the family law firm in 1913 for a position in Chicago with the Chicago, Wabash and Indiana Railroad. Warren had always been close to Chan, and the latter's departure from Vermont did not disrupt the relationship. Chan introduced Warren to William S. Kies, a Wall Street lawyer and banker who was general counsel for the Chicago-based railroad and vice-president of New York's National City Bank. Kies and Austin developed a friendship through which Kies became thoroughly impressed with Austin's manner and knowledge of contract law. Kies, being an expert in international financing, with a particular interest in American investments in South America, became a major figure in the development of the new American International Corporation — backed by National City — that was designed to open up trade and finance with all parts of the world. He subsequently drew Austin into that organization as a member of the company's China operation.[10]

Founded in late 1915, AIC, under the guidance of old China hand Willard Straight, construction engineer William S. Carey and financial expert Ernest Gregory, attempted to develop railroad and canal projects in China. By the late summer of 1916, preliminary contracts for the projects were signed with the Chinese government.[11]

To assist Carey in the legal details of future negotiations, Straight, on the recommendation of Kies, offered Austin a position with AIC in China. It necessitated a quick decision for the Vermonter, but the new opportunity, even with all its uncertainties, did not cause Austin to hesitate in his acceptance. From Peking, he later wrote to his friend Roy Patrick that he "could be of more service here than at home, and do my family more good financially."[12]

Austin suddenly joined AIC in August 1916, partly because the assignment was temporary. The arrangement did not preclude the possibility of continued work with the company, but the specific terms indicated a stay in China of not more than nine months. Austin hoped to be back in the United States within six months. His departure left many details of his law practice in abeyance, and startled many of his friends. In spite of his earlier defeats, not a few people saw a bright future for Austin in Vermont politics. Now they were convinced that this adventure might develop into a permanent career outside the state.

After spending several months in China and seeing an end to his work there, Austin's ambivalence continued in regard to his future. On the one hand, he foresaw abundant opportunities if his association with AIC continued. Kies had suggested several possibilities to Austin. More inducement was added when Carey offered Austin a lucrative position in China with Carey's own railway and canal company.[13]

On the other hand, a continuous stream of mail from father Chauncey emphasized his desire for Warren's return to Vermont. The law cases left in abeyance, along with the possibility of a future in politics there, were attractive. Although still undecided in February 1917, Austin wrote to Straight requesting his return to the United States as soon as possible. With the specific mission in China nearly completed, Austin wanted to tidy up the unfinished business he left in Vermont before the Chinese venture while commuting to New York to handle AIC matters. Straight consented and after some delay Austin took passage on the "Shinyo Maru" out of Shanghai on June 22.[14] In this way, Austin avoided a clear-cut decision on avenues his future might follow.

Austin used the last six months of 1917 as a time of careful career consideration. He probed various positions with law firms and financial houses in New York while resuming a full slate of legal business in St. Albans. His Vermont friends strongly urged him to remain in the state.[15] Earlier, he was concerned that prolonged stays in China and Europe would tend to divide his family. Even if he remained in the United States, his New York work would almost certainly compel him to seek residence in the city area. These possibilities did not please him, and they proved to be potent considerations in his final decision to remain in Vermont. The established law practice in Vermont was another strong factor. If he remained in the employ of AIC, or in some New York law firm, he would again start from the bottom. While he considered himself an able attorney, he recognized that he would be under great pressure, because of his age, to progress more rapidly than others. By remaining in Vermont, he could readily resume his practice and quickly return to the political activities in which he had formerly participated. In the final analysis, Austin decided to return to Vermont; he never regretted the decision.

In late 1917, Austin decided to discontinue his association with the family practice in St. Albans and begin anew in the city of Burlington, thirty-five miles to the south. He was not discontented. But being ambitious, he reasoned that Burlington would be a more lucrative place in which to practice. The city was the largest and richest one in the state, and a considerable number of his acquaintances lived there. Austin purchased the languishing Burlington practice of Henry B. Shaw and moved in the spring of 1918.

Situated on the eastern shore of Lake Champlain, Burlington had a population that approached 25,000. While the city had some industry, it served more as a commercial center for a wide rural area. Burlington also possessed added prestige as a cultural center since the University of Vermont and several other educational institutions were located there.

Austin moved his family to Burlington in March 1918. After living for six months in the fashionable Hotel Vermont as he and Mildred searched the city to find a permanent residence, Austin finally leased a house at 43 South Williams Street. The place was a rambling structure, located in the city's hill section, a block from the University and amid many other comfortable dwellings with manicured lawns, cedar shrubs, tall oaks and elms. The arrangement gave the Austins an option to purchase the property at the end of their lease. During the period of the lease, the couple decided this was what they wanted. The property remained their home for the rest of their lives.

Austin possessed a green thumb, but he had not lived at his residence in St. Albans long enough to cultivate it properly. At his new homestead, he and Mildred utilized the spacious quarter-acre back yard to develop a garden filled with many varieties of flowers and plants. The sloping back area already had a small orchard consisting of a few McIntosh apple trees. Over the years Austin studied, secured and planted other varieties of apple trees: rough, brownish-skinned russets; pointed, New York-cultivated Spitzenburgs; the late autumn-harvested Fameuse; a bright, red Wealthy along with the more common good-cooking greening; and the hardy, early-winter Northern Spy. As an amateur horticulturist, he gained expertise and considerable local fame with his collection of trees. The proximity of the agricultural college of the University assured horticultural advice when needed. Austin developed his own art of grafting strains of various trees in order to produce new varieties. Quite a few fair-weather hours were spent in that orchard as it became his major leisure-time activity.[16]

Austin began building his new law practice in Burlington through scantly remunerative work such as searching land titles, preparing wills and handling small claims. Soon, however, his many friends and former legal contacts in the state provided an advantage that brought economic advancement, and it was not long before he served a list of clients that produced a lucrative income. His portfolio included such large Vermont enterprises as the Woodbury Granite Company, Eastern Magnesia Talc Company, Burlington Grocery Company, Porter Screen Company and the University of Vermont. Through his college friend, Roy Patrick, who was president of the Rock of Ages Granite Company, Austin served as counsel, director and large stockholder in that firm. By 1920, Austin had a reputation for charging high fees for his services, but this was matched by his reputation as a sound lawyer.

In the twenties, two notable cases gained Austin a statewide reputation for courtroom skill. The first was a bizarre alienation of affections suit brought in the September 1922 term of the Chittenden County Court in Burlington. Austin counseled the plaintiff, Mrs. Doris Stevens Woodhouse, the daughter of a salesman who lived behind the Woodhouse estate in Burlington. She had married into the Woodhouse family without the consent of Lorenzo, the millionaire father of the clan. Because of this, she charged that Lorenzo, through the use of his wealth and influence over his son, Douglas, had succeeded in alienating the affections of her young husband. The trial, more than five weeks in duration, attracted wide attention in New England. Austin won the case, and his client was awarded $465,000 in actual and punitive damages. The settlement was the largest ever granted in such a case.[17]

Austin was in the U.S. Senate for two and a half years before the second case was settled. His legal skill, however, brought the case to a successful conclusion. A boundary dispute between New Hampshire and Vermont was involved. An issue of long standing, the dispute related to the water marks on the Connecticut River boundary line. The State of Vermont brought the case to the United States Supreme Court in 1915 because the State of New Hampshire taxed several institutions and structures on the Vermont bank of the river. At various times New Hampshire made different claims as to where the true boundary lay: first, that the line was the high water mark; next, that it was at the top of the Vermont bank; and still later, that the mark rested at a point on the Vermont side where vegetation ceased.

It was not until 1925 that the State of Vermont engaged Austin as special counsel. Austin's annual retainer fee of $7,000 was indicative of both the importance of the case as well as of his lucrative practice. But the controversy soon demonstrated the magnitude of work needing completion before presenting the case. Austin sifted, compiled and catalogued volumes of evidence. He directed the taking of photographs of the entire disputed boundary. Once he compiled the evidence, he spent long hours developing his argument and considering all the counterarguments. Austin's final brief claimed that the true boundary was at the low water mark on the Vermont side; the Court also reached that conclusion.[18] The experience enhanced Austin's reputation as an astute lawyer.

At the same time, Austin was active in community affairs. Since 1914, he had served as a trustee for the University of Vermont. In 1922, he helped organize a Burlington chapter of Rotary International and he was the club's first president. He held active membership in the Elks and the Odd Fellows and he belonged to the Masons (he rose to the 33rd degree). In addition, his reputation as a successful lawyer gained him places on several boards of directors of Vermont firms. This long period of involvement made his name well known in Vermont circles.

Although he did not stand for elective office until 1930, Austin constructed a political base within Republican ranks during this time. He worked on committees and with the party leadership and was readily available as a speaker at party functions throughout the state. In 1926, a Burlington newspaper suggested him as a gubernatorial candidate. The highlight of his political forays came in 1928, when, as a Vermont delegate to the Republican national convention in Kansas City, he delivered the first seconding speech for the nomination of Herbert Hoover.[19] Obviously there was political value in all these activities and in December 1930, an opportunity presented itself in which Austin could test his popularity and political base.

In that month, United States Senator Frank L. Greene died in office. His official term expired in 1934, so under Vermont law a special election was required to determine his successor because the vacancy occurred more than six months prior to the next general election. Governor John E. Weeks set the primary election date for March 3 and the special election for March 31.

In the meantime, Governor Weeks appointed a friend of long standing, Frank C. Partridge of Proctor, as interim senator. Partridge subsequently sought to keep his seat in the upcoming primary. He was 68 years of age and already had a long career in public life. Born and raised in Middlebury, he graduated from Amherst and Columbia University Law School. He served, for a time, as secretary to Redfield Proctor, the Vermonter who was Benjamin Harrison's Secretary of War. He subsequently received appointment as American ambassador to Venezuela and later acted as U.S. Consul General at Tangier. He returned to Vermont at the turn of the century and served in a variety of public and private capacities over the next thirty years. He assumed the presidency of the Vermont Marble Company and became an influential director of the Montpelier-based National Life Insurance Company.[20]

Before Governor Weeks appointed Partridge, Austin had decided to throw his hat in the ring. Surveying his life from the vantage point of age 53, Austin decided he had reached a time when he could afford to enter public life on a full-time basis. Nonetheless, encouragement was needed. It came readily from Mildred and close friends such as Roy Patrick, Eugene Magnus of the Eastern Magnesia Talc Company,

Guy W. Bailey, president of the University of Vermont, and prominent Burlington funeral director Tom Gurney. Roswell Austin was also an instrumental influence. He had served in the Vermont legislature for a number of terms and helped his older brother size up the statewide support he could expect to receive. After several days of press speculation, Austin announced his decision to run on December 22, 1930.[21]

An analysis of the short campaign shows three areas in which Austin capitalized. First, he presented himself as a party man but without any strings attached (he campaigned as a representative of the "young guard" of the Party), while Partridge was portrayed as a standpat candidate. Second, Austin emphasized that he was not influenced by any corporations (he successfully played down his contact with Rock of Ages); he suggested that Partridge had such unsavory connections through his association with Vermont Marble and National Life. Third, Austin faced the important prohibition issue in an ambiguous way so that he could attract both the wet and dry vote. Partridge was a declared dry. Austin's prohibition statements emphasized that if elected he would vote to have the question submitted to the people. In this way he took the issue of the public's confusion as to what he really believed (he was a wet) out of the campaign.[22]

But perhaps the most critical factor in the race was the absence of Partridge. He remained in Washington because of a continuing session of Congress, and his campaign was run by surrogates. In the meantime, Austin toured the state, making over sixty appearances and spending considerable money on campaign literature and advertising. On the eve of the primary, the election was declared a toss-up. The next day's count found the Burlingtonian the victor by over eight thousand out of the seventy-eight thousand vote total.[23]

The following special election, like most in Vermont politics, was typically anticlimactic. The Democratic candidate, Stephen M. Driscoll of St. Albans, waged only a token campaign against his Republican opponent. Privately, Austin showed disdain for the Democrat's political power; he noted several days before the election that he planned to move to Washington very soon afterwards. The major concern of Austin and the Republican leaders was voter turnout — not in the sense that the leaders were worried Austin would lose, but rather that the Republican plurality might not be all that they hoped. Their fears proved well founded when a small vote carried Austin to victory by less than a two-to-one margin.[24]

As a freshman Senator, Austin worked with caution as he learned the intricacies of his new position. He found the routine there entirely different from anything he had faced in the past. It is not surprising to find Austin's early years in the Senate characterized by boundless work in committees (Judiciary and Military Affairs were his major assignments) and rigid adherence to an avowed plan not to talk excessively on the floor.

The Vermonter supported the policies of the Herbert Hoover administration because he feared federal encroachment on the power of state and individuals. His conservatism was unabashed even when on the short side of a vote in the Senate, for he believed that he could accommodate principle to politics on any issue short of abrogation of the Constitution. But he sensed that the nation lacked the leadership to move it out of the Depression.

After the defeat of Hoover in 1932, considered by Austin as "a crushing blow to the country," the Vermont Senator remained perplexed by the arguments and the actions of the lame-duck Congress on questions of economy and relief. He thought that the lack of leadership that characterized the interregnum, coupled with the deteriorating economic conditions of the country, caused Congress to take a destructive and contradictory position. In attempting to effect economies and at the same time provide relief from unemployment, Austin noted that Congress cut appropriations which, in turn, created unemployment. Then the legislature reversed itself by appropriating funds to create doles. Regretfully, Austin privately conceded he could offer no solution to this problem.[25]

To understand Austin's stance as an anti-New Dealer, it is necessary to fit him within the characteristics of an American conservative in the 1930s. The Senator's consistent suspicion of executive power was the most striking feature of his conservatism. Very early he denounced the Democratic administration for its abuse of power and would hammer away at this theme throughout the decade. Austin coupled this with a strong belief in the separation and balance of power at the national level. He utilized "liberty" and "independence" — favorite words in the Austin rhetorical vocabulary — to uphold an anti-statist mood. He sought a return to an earlier America — with a small government that provided a minimum of restraint on its citizens.

Austin glorified that type of citizen who exemplified the "rugged individual." As one of the few parts of the nation not attracted by Roosevelt's electoral magnet, Austin's Vermont constituents generally continued to view themselves as part of America's last group of rugged individuals. And they wanted a senator who represented that model. But at the same time, even in Vermont, the thirties produced concern for social and economic stability that offered no haven for a pure form of that type of individualism. This seemingly contradictory position subtly forced Austin and others like him to compromise. They expressed the nostalgic tenets of individualism — independence, liberty, smallness — while at the same time they advocated some form of cooperation designed to bring about stability.

Finally, traditionalism marked the conservatism of Warren Austin. He resorted to the past to uplift his own spirit and to assure, at least himself, that his course followed in the footsteps of the Founding Fathers. In public debate this produced a negative assault on the opposition. Optimistically believing in an idyllic world of the past, Austin thought that, by leaving matters alone, that past might be regained.[26]

The "hundred days" of the Franklin Roosevelt administration left Austin wary of the new President's leadership and fearful of abuse of power. "I am very apprehensive of the arbitrary powers which are being placed in the hands of one man," he wrote to his mother. Three weeks later he again criticized departure from "American liberty" by the Democratic leadership. He expressed a fear that "we are headed for a dictatorship which will make Mussolini blush." Consequently, Austin opposed the majority of first New Deal draft bills sent to the special session of Congress by the President.[27]

This opposition, which continued into 1934, placed Austin in a risky position as the off-year elections approached. The early success of the Roosevelt New Deal increased the Democrats' desire to improve their party strength at the expense of the anti-New Dealers. As early as January, Austin was aware that a stronger than usual Democratic effort would be directed against him in Vermont.[28]

Austin was particularly concerned because the Democrats in Vermont could best concentrate on him. The November election would fill other statewide offices, but the issues at the state level were not subject to attack as was Austin's consistent anti-New Deal position.[29] Nationally, the Democrats looked forward to a big year, and it seemed likely that if Vermont were ever going to repudiate its traditional allegiance to the Republican Party, this would be the time.

As early as June, newspaper writers were predicting that the Vermont Democrats, spurred by Washington support, would run their strongest man against Austin. The Democrats subsequently chose Frederick C. Martin, a native of Bennington, whom President Roosevelt had appointed in 1933 as Collector of Internal Revenue for Vermont. Formerly President of the County National Bank in Bennington, Martin maintained a long and active career in Democratic politics. He was a candidate for governor in 1920 and 1924, and for United States Senator in 1928 and 1932. In the 1932 senatorial campaign, running against the Republican incumbent, Porter Dale, he polled one of the largest votes ever given a Democrat in the state, although still running far behind his opponent. He often was a delegate to Democratic National Conventions, and in 1932 he was chairman of the Vermont delegation. Unlike Austin, Martin was not known for his oratorical ability, but he was recognized as a successful businessman with a winning personality.[30]

The Vermont Democrats opened their campaign headquarters in Rutland, and held an unusually loud convention in Montpelier on September 25. As expected, the major plank in their platform was an unqualified endorsement of the New

Deal program, and early indications were that their campaign would not suffer from a lack of funds. Money from the national Democratic war chest allowed the Vermont party to utilize such techniques as publication of an eight-page news-sheet, *The Vermont Democrat,* and to bring help from outside the state to assist the campaign. Unaided by advertising, the Democrats sent the news-sheet primarily to rural districts. The *Democrat's* main slogan read: "Back Roosevelt — Help Vermont," and it pointed out the programs for which Vermont received money from the federal government through such New Deal enactments as flood control and the AAA.[31]

While Austin was attacked by several state Democrats, Fred Martin carried the full force of the campaign to him. He continuously brought out Austin's anti-New Deal stands. At one point, Martin charged that Austin voted for only one New Deal measure — the National Economy Act — and that vote was favorable only because the Vermont state legislature passed a resolution asking each member of its Congressional delegation to vote for it. Martin's hard-hitting tactics intensified as the campaign continued. While newspaper opinion could not pinpoint the reasons for which the Democrats coveted Austin's seat, most believed that a Democratic victory in rock-ribbed Republican Vermont would have a tremendous psychological effect on the entire nation.[32]

The state Republican organization took no chances as it prepared for the challenge by an all-out organizational attempt. By the middle of October, Republican headquarters announced it had organized nearly every town in Vermont. Republican leaders particularly stressed that new town committees were much larger than before. Fear that voter apathy might prove detrimental to the Senator's re-election motivated this intense Republican activity.[33]

Austin also waged an aggressive campaign. In person or on the radio, he made many speeches throughout the state. His overall theme suggested a return to the development of individual opportunity and incentive. He chided the Democrats for their experimentation program on the ground that it lacked stability. He stood on his conservative record which stressed recovery through normal business practices and fundamental economic laws rather than experimentation, a return to constitutionalism, and an appeal for rugged individualism and the independence of Vermont.[34]

Austin sensed he knew Vermonters and aimed his whole campaign at their grassroots traditionalism.By stressing individualism and the independence of the state, he knew he could appeal to them. He claimed that the Democrats totally ignored the cautious outlook of Vermonters by trying to sell the New Deal, an experiment of unknown quality. He constantly criticized the program for brushing aside the sovereignty and independence of the state. In good campaign rhetoric, Austin maintained that if Martin were elected, Vermont would surrender one of its Senators to the White House and only one Senator would remain to represent the people of Vermont. He thus decried the rubber-stamp attitude of Martin. Austin pointed out again and again that outside political interests were active in Vermont. The reasons were clear enough to him: the national Democrats could not tolerate exposition of their measures. Austin claimed that he spoke for Vermonters who resented the attempts by the administration to inject "foreign doctrines and socialistic ideas" into American life.[35]

On November 6, Vermonters trudged to the polls and demonstrated that Austin's early fear of defeat was well founded. By only a slim 3,514 vote margin was he able to defeat Martin, 67,146 to 63,632. Austin lost six counties to his opponent, and five of them, Bennington, Chittenden, Franklin, Rutland, and Washington, accounted for over half the votes cast. In comparison, the two other Republican candidates running for major office won by the usual large Republican plurality. Charles Plumley of Northfield handily defeated Carroll E. Jenkins of Orleans in a race for Vermont's lone seat in the House of Representatives, 73,500 to 55,005. In the gubernatorial race, Charles M. Smith of Rutland, the former Lieutenant Governor, easily won over the Democrats' James Leamy, 73,521 to 54,083.[36]

Any assessment of the campaign must account for the emphasis placed by the Democrats on Austin's Senate seat compared to the other posts up for election. The Democrats thought that 1934 was their year. Even in traditional Republican-dominated Vermont they believed they had a chance through an appeal for endorsement of the New Deal against Austin's anti-New Deal stance. Bolstered by a popular vote-getter such as Frederick Martin, they considered it worth the all-out effort to turn the trick.

The issue of support or opposition to the New Deal was more important than personalities in the race. Like the rest of the nation, Vermont suffered economically. Because of its smallness, however, the state survived better than many areas of the country. Vermont citizens, then, refused to repudiate their allegiance to the anti-New Deal principles on which the Republican candidate stood.

Psychologically, Austin knew he possessed an advantage. He was a Republican in a thoroughly Republican state. And he stood on a record that favored rugged individualism, frugality and the independence of the Green Mountain State. He emphasized these points at every opportunity. Austin proclaimed himself as his own man, representing his own state against practically the rest of the nation. Thus he wisely capitalized on an appeal to a strong Vermont tradition of conservatism. At a time when change was taking place rapidly, Austin remained within the mold of the conservative Vermont political tradition.

Nonetheless, Austin's close victory demonstrated the impact the New Deal had on the Vermont voters. Nearly half of those who voted were willing to abandon old ideas of frugality, independence and rugged individualism in favor of New Deal experimentation. But in the face of the Democratic attempt to deprive Austin of his Senate seat in 1934, he gained his political tenure. Re-election would never seriously concern him again.

"We Republicans are but a thin line of defense. Our courage is good, but we know that our efforts will be ineffectual," Austin wrote in January 1935. His statement was as depressing as it was pithy, for a mighty mandate from the electorate to support Roosevelt's New Deal left the GOP with only 25 members in the Senate. Even among those few, ten considered themselves progressives who sympathized with the Roosevelt domestic policy.[37]

Historians have not agreed on the differences between the "first" and "second" New Deals and some dispute the whole concept of two distinct New Deals.[38] But Austin's position on legislation followed a consistent course during both sessions. As one studies his voting record and stands on issues, a markedly undistinguished record appears. Without offering alternatives, he adhered to his conservative philosophy and opposed nearly everything the Democrats advocated.

On only one noteworthy domestic issue in the thirties does Austin emerge as a leading protagonist. On February 5, 1937, FDR announced his intention to reorganize the judiciary. Austin's role in the subsequent political fight exemplifies the conservative commitment that made him an anti-New Dealer.

Angered by the Supreme Court's reversal of segments of his New Deal, Roosevelt perpetrated a serious blunder by proposing to alter the membership of the Supreme Court. He sought authority to add a new member to the Court, up to a maximum court total of fifteen, for every justice who did not retire at age seventy. Roosevelt's special message underscored judicial efficiency and the need for new approaches from the bench. But his main objective was obvious — an ingenious attempt to undercut the conservative justices on the Court.

The Court issue unified the Republican ranks as it split the Democrats. Credit goes primarily to William Borah the progressive, Arthur Vandenberg the conservative, and Charles McNary the moderate. Meeting on February 6, the three planned the strategy Republicans would follow. They agreed that a "conspiracy of silence" among Republicans, at least for a week or ten days, would allow vocal Democrats time to split from Roosevelt supporters without fear of being charged with close Republican association.[39]

Austin was aghast when Roosevelt presented the court reorganization bill. The court, after all, was one of the remaining pillars of his conservative philosophy. While Republican leaders planned their strategy of silence on February 6, Austin's initial reaction carried in the press. The President's message, said the Vermonter, was "a most ostentatious request for power to pack the Federal courts."

Austin would not cool down. He wrote the following Monday that the plan "aroused a storm which beats up from all sides" and he gave assurance that he would stand against it. His son Edward, in Washington at that time, observed that the proposal considerably "heated up" his father.[40]

While Austin followed his Party's leadership and remained in quiet opposition to the bill, a *New York Times* interview publicly disclosed his position. He denounced the plan as one that sought to reduce the Court to an instrument of "party policy and political action." He described the established independence of the judiciary as a "barricade of the people against injustice, force and tyranny" and charged that the plan would tend to destroy free government by violating that independence.[41]

The Vermonter, along with Borah and Frederick Steiwer of Oregon, formed the Republican membership on the important Judiciary Committee, where the bill would be scrutinized in public hearings. As he prepared himself for the work ahead, Austin conceded that it was like "sitting on a safety valve" to hold his fire against the plan. He indicated his personal annoyance for the Republican muzzle and hoped the hearings would justify more open opposition by GOP members.[42]

Senator Henry F. Ashurst of Arizona, the chairman of the committee, opened hearings on Wednesday, March 10, at 10:30 a.m. in the Marble Room of the Senate Office Building before several hundred spectators. Between that day and April 23, 1937, when the public hearings concluded, the committee heard eighty-one witnesses, while seventeen additional individuals or organizations submitted written statements. With the exception of two days, when business of other committees detained him, Austin was present for the thirty-one days of hearings.

The Democratic opposition's first objective was to disprove the Roosevelt assumption that members of the Court were senile and unable to do their work. While Democrats supplied the leadership, Republicans joined on several occasions to lend subtle support to this opposition. From the first day, Austin persistently prodded administration witnesses. After Attorney General Homer Cummings opened the hearings with a statement favoring the legislation, Austin, as well as George Norris, Borah and the Democrats, exchanged seemingly endless banter with the chief law-enforcement officer.

Austin attempted to secure from Cummings an admission that the Court was not competent to render enlightened interpretations. Cummings refused. With further questioning, Austin zeroed in on the Attorney General's claim that the unconstitutional decisions of the Court were, in fact, legislation. The Senator asked whether a justice must exercise his own mental honesty and independence in regard to a doubt about the constitutionality of a law. Cummings replied that a justice who voted a law unconstitutional in spite of its approval by Congress, the President and a majority of the Court, was not acting in a reasonable manner.

Austin pressed Cummings further. He asked how the Attorney General could pass judgment on a justice's decision merely because he voted the "wrong way." Cummings replied that was not the case. He cited the rule of the Court that no law should be voided unless it is unconstitutional "beyond a reasonable doubt," and then quickly turned the question on Austin: "Now, how in good conscience, Senator, can a minority say that a law is unconstitutional beyond a reasonable doubt when five or six distinguished brethren on the bench say the law is constitutional?" Austin shot back, "I can be one of a small minority standing by my convictions." "Yes," replied the caustic Cummings, "that was indicated in the last election."[43]

Austin interrogated other administration witnesses. He not always used the same thrusts. For example, the Vermonter questioned William Green, president of the American Federation of Labor, on the necessity of changing the Court in order to place the stamp of constitutionality on social and economic acts. Austin endeavored to commit the last administration witness, Ferdinand Pecora of the New York Supreme Court, on whether free government meant unlimited power for the executive and legislative branches. The Senator implied that the Court bill would do that, but Pecora's rebuttal evaded the implication by stating that neither should the judicial branch have unlimited power.[44]

With jabs, questions and criticisms, Austin violated the planned strategy of silence more than the other two Republican members. Steiwer asked few questions, while Borah, absent from most of the meetings, said little when he was present. Austin, however, employed a subtle approach to avoid a strong Republican identification with the opposition. In that way he actually conformed to Republican strategy. It is noteworthy, too, that the hearings also functioned as a safety valve for him. He happily struck at the administration while allowing the main thrust to come from the Democratic side.

Austin asked few questions as the parade of administration witnesses reached an abrupt end on Saturday, March 20. The administration's initial strategy meant to move the bill quickly through the committee where the leaders hoped to take no more than two weeks. With Pecora's testimony, only half the scheduled administration witnesses had been heard, but sensing that more delay meant trouble, the administration closed its case. The following Monday, and throughout the remainder of the session, the committee heard from opposition witnesses. Senator Burton K. Wheeler of Montana, who led the Democratic opposition in the Senate, was the lead-off witness.

Wheeler's testimony included a damaging blow to the administration's case. He presented a letter from Chief Justice Charles Evans Hughes which countered, point by point, the procedural arguments used by Roosevelt and his Attorney General as grounds for reorganization. Austin had visited the Chief Justice on March 18, along with Wheeler and William H. King of Utah, the ranking Democratic member of the Judiciary Committee, in an effort to convince Hughes that he should lend his support against the bill by appearing before the committee. After conferring with Justice Louis D. Brandeis, Hughes declined to appear. But over the weekend Brandeis and Wheeler convinced Hughes that a letter from him, presented by Wheeler in his opening testimony, would have great impact.[45] So Wheeler detonated his bombshell.

The opposition witnesses, many of whom traveled to Washington at the expense of the Republican Party, proved anticlimactic after Wheeler's appearance. Yet the opposition would not let down its guard. Austin continued to support the case through thorough research and presentation of evidence on one of the major arguments of the administration concerning writs of certiorari. The administration had attempted to prove that the Supreme Court displayed inefficiency by denying numerous writs. On this score Austin questioned one administration witness and then proceeded to delve deeper. On March 19, he requested the committee to ask the clerk of the Supreme Court for evidence on the number of cases on the docket at different times.

Wheeler's presentation of Hughes's letter to the committee on March 22 had alluded to the administration's argument. Austin added support on April 5 by presenting evidence from the Court's records which proved that a large number of denials of writs were requested by the Attorney General's office. Austin closed his attack by charging deception on the part of the administration: "Year after year the Attorney General has been boasting in his annual report of the department's success in getting the Supreme Court to deny writs of certiorari. Now he comes forward and makes those denials a ground for attack on the Court."[46]

Austin appeared more optimistic as spring came to Washington and the committee went into executive session. The President's decision to insist on the bill without amendments encouraged the Senator. Late in April he noted that ten members of the Judiciary Committee would probably vote the bill out adversely. On the floor of the Senate, he counted fifty senators whom he thought would vote against it as it stood. However, Austin placed doubtful marks against eight of that total if the bill were amended.[47]

In late March and early April two new Supreme Court decisions changed the complexion of the controversy. On March 29, the Court upheld a minimum wage law in the State of Washington. Even more important, on April 12, the Court upheld the National Labor Relations Act. Now the battle shifted from one between the New Deal and a conservative Court to one between Roosevelt and his intransigent Democratic Congress. As a result, the Republicans continued to remain generally silent. Still confident he could win, Roosevelt spurned any compromise.

Four days before the committee voted on the bill, Austin optimistically wrote that he thought they had the "President's bill whipped." Furthermore, he believed that strong support was developing against any compromise. He admitted the difficulty for him to remain silent, but that, if a floor fight did ensue, the Republicans probably would vocally join it.

On May 18, the bill received an adverse committee vote by a ten-to-eight count. It would be nearly a month before the committee's report would go before the full Senate. The report closed with a strong statement denouncing the bill's purpose and recommended that the measure should be "so emphatically rejected that its parallel will never again be presented to the free representatives of the free people of America."[48]

Throughout late June and July, Austin received a deluge of correspondence from many parts of the nation. Other opposition senators likewise were inundated. Most of Austin's letters encouraged him by denouncing Roosevelt and urged the Senator to stand firm in his opposition to the Court-packing measure.[49]

The final debate before the full Senate, while bitter and heated, was anticlimactic compared to the earlier committee struggle. The administration attempted to compromise in early July, but the timing was too late. The death, on July 14, of Joseph T. Robinson, the bill's chief lieutenant in the Senate, added a touching aura to the dramatic final vote on July 22. By a 70-to-20 margin, the Senate recommitted the bill to the Judiciary Committee. Austin noted with jubilation from his Senate seat: "No more important service to the country has been made in my lifetime than this. The Court Bill is not only dead; it is interred."[50]

By the conclusion of the next year's session, Austin's anti-New Deal days were behind him. Foreign affairs and national defense then were among the leading issues of the day and they captured the headlines thereafter. Austin turned more and more of his attention to those matters. Almost ironically, he began to draw on his intellectual interest in internationalism, which in turn often placed him in company with the administration on foreign policy issues.

While on domestic matters he had remained mostly in the background, in foreign policy he was to develop his greatest interest and success.

Late in his career, Austin recalled an event that he claimed inspired and shaped his thought on international affairs over the years. In 1913, he attended a meeting of the American Bar Association in Montreal at which Viscount Haldane, Lord Chancellor of Great Britain, was the main attraction. The Lord Chancellor appealed for a widening of courtesy between nations and a strengthening of the values of international law. He hoped there might arise a higher ethical conception of the duties and mutual responsibilities of nationhood. In other words, he proclaimed a sense of moral obligation, in which the self-discipline of nations would assure peace.[51] Austin adopted Haldane's thoughts as his own philosophy, since they dovetailed with his acceptance of law as the only rational solution to problems among men and nations. Haldane's ideas likewise fit Austin's sense of moral righteousness, which was ingrained in the Vermonter from his early years.

Austin's ideas identified him in the context of the later labeled "Eastern Republican Establishment," whose brand of internationalism was compatible with the Vermonter's philosophy. Intellectually nurtured by such minds as those of Elihu Root, Charles Evans Hughes and Nicholas Murray Butler, this school of thought inclined toward a judicial rather than political settlement of international disputes. These "limited internationalists" acted as a middle road between Woodrow Wilson's concept of a universal alliance for the creation of a "concert of power" and the ever-present and politically strong isolationist group characterized by rabid nationalism and nonentanglement on all issues.

The limited internationalists held a world view. They appreciated the study of international affairs and were convinced that the foreign policy of the United States rested on an educated view of America's place in the world. They placed faith in reason as the source of world order and believed that reason, in turn, manifested itself through international law. The internationalists opposed any authority based on force; they believed America should lend its prestige and moral suasion to the resolution of world conflicts. Quite correctly, some scholars have labeled the attitude the "legalistic-moralistic approach to international problems."[52]

Austin fit the mold of a limited internationalist. He saw importance in the development of a foreign policy based on an educated public opinion. There could be no program stronger than that which the people supported. In this way, Austin hazily envisioned a missionary role for every American. A study of world problems and democracy would cause citizens to make the democratic way of the United States meaningful not only to themselves, but also "competent to the demands of mankind."

Much of what Austin said about American policy and international affairs in the World War I and postwar periods reflected this moral-legal position.[53] But his discussions on foreign affairs were purely academic, for he was not in a position where he could do much about implementation. Nonetheless, his thoughts formed a basis for his later involvement as a Senator.

The threat of another war was on the distant horizon when Austin assumed office in 1931. As that possibility grew through the thirties, he exerted his effort to prepare the nation for a conflict he hoped would not occur. At the outset the Vermonter found himself out of line with the public opinion of the nation, even with his limited internationalist position. As the world crisis deepened, his advocacy of a strong defense, combined with a flexible foreign policy, was still initially contrary to the Roosevelt administration's hesitant policy.

For the most part, however, the domestic situation occupied Austin's time and prevented him from dealing with international matters. In addition, Austin's junior position in the Senate determined his limited role in foreign policy. He was overshadowed by the well-known isolationists William Borah, Hiram Johnson, Arthur Vandenberg, and Gerald Nye. Nonetheless, his interest showed again in 1935, when after his successful re-election he sought a seat on the Foreign Relations Committee. Austin attempted to trade his position on Military Affairs for this appointment. But his requests then and in subsequent years were denied until 1944. This lack of a committee base, such as a Foreign Relations slot provided, blunted Austin's input on foreign policy matters until later in the thirties when he became involved through the overlapping work of his Military Affairs Committee with foreign policy.[54]

Austin's general silence on international issues in the early thirties — both public and private — indicated also his awareness of public opinion. For example, he voted for the Neutrality Act of 1935 for no other reason than that the measure reflected the mood of the nation. Other than casting that affirmative vote, however, he did not openly side with the tide of opinion running toward legalized neutrality and isolation.[55] Two explanations account for his position. First, he felt that foreign policy was only as effective as public support of it. Second, Austin's lack of leadership in this area was apparent. Unwilling to speak out when it was not necessary, he made no attempt to lead public opinion, but was content to follow it. In the long run, however, he developed a negative position on neutrality legislation.

Austin's interest in other aspects of foreign affairs quickened later in the thirties. As world events started competing with domestic affairs for American headlines late in 1937, the Senator's private and public record began to disclose a fuller position on foreign policy. It conformed to his long-standing internationalist philosophy and moved him out of the mainstream of Republican thought on foreign affairs. He soon found himself a lonely Republican Senate spokesman for his position.[56]

When the new "permanent" neutrality law was brought to the Senate floor for debate on March 1, 1937, Austin was absorbed in Judiciary Committee work relating to Roosevelt's court-enlargement scheme. The bill was considered an improvement over the earlier versions of 1935 and 1936 in that the president's discretionary power was increased. He could list commodities other than munitions that belligerents could purchase on a "cash and carry" basis. But the proposed law, like the 1935 version, relinquished American claims to freedom of the seas in wartime.

Austin wanted no legislation that might prevent the nation from pursuing a flexible foreign policy. He confessed he had no special knowledge about the bill, but to him, the measure looked like "running before we are attacked." While initially undecided on how he would vote, he leaned against the bill as he listened to Senators Borah and Johnson. The two isolationists opposed the "cash and carry" feature; they wanted a tougher bill with no discretionary provisions for the president. Austin, however, differed from the isolationists although he stood against it. He believed there should be no neutrality law at all. America, thought Austin, could not remain safe from world dangers by passing neutrality laws. So ironically, for opposite reasons, Austin found compatibility with Borah and Johnson along with Senators Styles Bridges, Peter G. Gerry and Henry Cabot Lodge, Jr.; they cast the only negative votes on the measure.[57]

The summer of 1937 saw the Chinese-Japanese war start anew. In the midst of that ongoing Asian situation Roosevelt's "quarantine" speech in Chicago on October 5 was like a fire bell in the night. If the President engaged in "metaphoric oratory," as one historian concluded, and was not serious about changing the course of America's involvement, the speech affected Austin.[58] He took a cue from Roosevelt to record his attitude on the subject.

"Peace cannot be preserved by mere declarations," Austin said in a talk three days after Roosevelt's Chicago speech. He claimed the first line of defense for the United States stemmed from the nation's moral responsibility to condemn aggression. Should those pronouncements prove ineffective, Austin favored independent sanctions by his country. He threw aside the question of neutrality in favor of a national security.[59]

Flexibility became a clearer key to Austin's view on foreign policy. As he observed the world situation, he saw the major question facing the United States as a choice among "isolation on one hand, alliance on the other hand, or a position in between them." He thought the Rome-Berlin-Tokyo pact subsequently would cause the communist governments to join together in a race for military supremacy. In this event, Austin asked, should the democratic governments form an alliance to preserve their own integrity? He was not willing to allow America to proceed that far, except as a last resort. But he also opposed isolation.

Rather, he advocated that "position in between": independent sanctions placed in effect "currently with similar sanctions by allied democracies" as well as temporary alliances suited to the circumstances. Thus the nation would follow what he labeled a true spirit of neutrality: "not the so-called neutrality of a statutory quarantine which really assists one combatant against another — but neutrality which is free from obligations arising within or without the country."[60]

Austin disagreed with the isolationists because he saw the inevitability of American involvement in world affairs. In 1938, he continued sounding an evangelical tone and inculcated a sense of American mission to the world. He wanted a foreign policy which would make the "American way of life ... more secure for ourselves and more possible for other people who desire it." He viewed world peace as the paramount objective of American policy. But the nation could not accomplish this through sanctions of force; good example was the course to follow: "judicial poise, Christian kindliness" and the recognition of the right of every state to follow its own beliefs. While Hitler savored his appeasement victory of Munich, Austin called for the "interchange of things of the higher value." The Senator cited ideas, knowledge, art, science, hospitality and friendship as valuable areas in which to cultivate "the ultimate good — peace."[61]

At the same time, Austin favored strengthening of the nation's defenses because it would increase flexibility. He thought the nation should have a "respectable defense posture" but should not join an arms race with the rest of the world. He liked, for example, the President's message to Congress in January 1938 asking for additional monies for naval expansion. The subsequent Vinson Naval Expansion Act, which encountered a rancorous debate on the Senate floor, confirmed Austin's original intention to vote in favor. "Big navy," he noted, "sounds more like peace for us than war."[62]

From mid-1939, Austin became more directly involved in the neutrality revision fight. His role indicated the growing reputation he was developing as a Republican internationalist.

Revision had bogged down in the Senate. Apprehensive Key Pittman, Chairman of the Foreign Relations Committee and selected to pilot the revision through the Senate, was not the man for the task. That fact, combined with a lack of strong presidential leadership, shifting public opinion and fear of reaction from the Senate isolationist bloc, caused postponement of hearings before the Foreign Relations Committee until April. Then Pittman failed to get the measure out of committee. In May, Roosevelt and Secretary of State Cordell Hull turned to the House for revision. There Sol Bloom, chairman of the Foreign Affairs Committee, was optimistic about passage of a bill. After lengthy debate, the House passed a curious measure on June 30, 1939 which continued an embargo on "arms and ammunition" but allowed shipment to belligerents of "instruments of war." The spotlight swung back to the Senate where, on July 5, the Foreign Relations Committee reopened hearings. A week later the Committee voted, 12 to 11, to postpone further consideration of the bill.[63]

The postponement initially made Roosevelt angry. But he listened to Secretary Hull, who urged a conciliatory approach toward the Senate in a last attempt to secure revision. On July 14, Hull delivered a special message to Congress that reiterated the need for flexible action and asked for repeal of the arms embargo. Austin doubted the message would change the vote for postponement, but he agreed with the administration position. Moreover, he saw the issue as a storm warning for himself in the future. "I regret," he wrote, "to be separated from many of my fellow Republicans on this subject."[64]

After consulting with Democratic Congressional leaders, Roosevelt decided to meet with a bipartisan group of Senators to push his revision appeal. Austin was invited because of his position in the Senate as Assistant or Deputy Minority Leader. Since 1933, at Minority Leader McNary's request, Austin had served occasionally and informally in that capacity. Since the Republicans numbered so few in these years, the position was not of much importance, and in some sessions Austin's service went unused. But since neutrality revision was a maneuver that required floor action, he was extended an invitation. He predicted the occasion would be memorable but was pessimistic that FDR could get the desired action.[65]

The widely recorded mid-summer meeting of July 18 included Roosevelt, Vice-President John Garner, Hull, Senators Alben Barkley, McNary, Borah and Pittman. Upon entering the White House, Austin encountered a battery of newsmen and photographers on the portico. He told them that his participation was with a bipartisan attitude. In recording this event the following day, Austin recalled that he said this to forestall any suspicion that might characterize Republicans as the obstacle to action. The meeting confirmed that representatives of both parties agreed that the time was inopportune for revision.[66]

The President, sitting on a sofa behind a table covered with "pads, gadgets and smoking materials," opened the gathering with characteristically humorous remarks. Then he quickly moved to the issue and expressed his conviction that he had averted imminent war on two previous occasions through appeals to Hitler. Austin quoted Roosevelt as stating that he had now been "deprived of my last cartridge by the failure of Congress to act." Secretary Hull then described the world situation in bleak terms. Austin recorded that Hull "showed much emotion," a comment coinciding with Hull's own recollection of the moment. Austin made only slight reference to the much-publicized verbal encounter that occurred between Hull and Borah over the gravity of the situation.[67]

The discussion turned to consideration of the statement that the President had exhausted his "ammunition." Austin reminded Roosevelt that Congress passed his entire national defense program. The Vermonter contended the new provisions gave the President more power than he recognized because it served notice to the world that America was strong, so much so that "no country would voluntarily make an enemy of her." Discussion brought out that public opinion ran counter to suggested revision; consequently, the administration must make best use of the present law until a more favorable atmosphere developed in the country. Vice-President Garner then polled the senators. All agreed that no revision could take place at the session.[68]

The White House press statement on the meeting charged that failure to secure a new neutrality law rested squarely on the Senate. Austin's memo, written after issuance of the White House statement, underscored the Vermonter's irritation at Roosevelt's attempt to make the Senate appear as the scapegoat. Austin would not forsake Senate loyalty despite agreement with the administration on the need for revision. He noted that the Senate was entitled to some credit for preventing a sharp split in the nation if the issue was debated at that time. He viewed the postponement as beneficial to future agreement on revision at the January session of Congress. Then, he thought, tempers would have cooled, and the legislators would have had an opportunity to sense the opinions and feelings of their constituents. Current debate on the subject, Austin noted, would prove productive only if some crisis occurred "which outweighed in import-ance the diverse interests and inclinations now dominating different legislators."[68]

Hitler's blitzkrieg against Poland on September 1, 1939 started a chain of events which backed Austin's July 19 analysis. Roosevelt issued neutrality proclamations under the 1937 law, sent out feelers on Congressional opinion for revision, and then acted to bring the Congress into special session on September 21 to repeal the arms embargo. To plan strategy, Roosevelt invited Republicans Austin, McNary and House Minority Leader Joseph Martin to another bipartisan White House meeting on September 20.[70]

The participants at that meeting agreed that nonpartisan-ship was important in the upcoming issue. Roosevelt, with Austin's support, initially stressed repeal of all neutrality legislation and a return to former status under international law. Key Pittman was antagonistic: "If you try that," the chairman said, "you'll be lucky to get five votes in my committee." Both Roosevelt and Austin then accepted the fact that, while they might obtain repeal of the embargo, some form of cash-and-carry law would continue.[71]

Through the subsequent Senate debate, Austin listened carefully, but did not join the fight until the last day. Earlier, he had sent a special letter to his Vermont constituency, asking its advice on his position, which advocated total

repeal. Response was favorable, but he knew from the drift of
the debate that repeal of all neutrality legislation was not
possible. The Senate revised the law, repealed the embargo,
but still maintained a cash-and-carry provision.[72] Austin
had to be contented that it was the best that could be
obtained at that time.

The intensification of the European war in the spring and
summer of 1940 brought Austin closer to the administration.
He supported the administration-backed defense appropriations and the controversial Burke-Wadsworth bill which
gave America its first peacetime draft. When FDR announced his destroyers-for-bases deal, Austin again gave his
consent. In doing so, he noted privately that America's line
of defense was on the other side of the Atlantic.[73]

Two particulars are noteworthy regarding Austin's
support of defense legislation. First was the bipartisan
nature of the Vermonter's position. For example, he
attempted, through an amendment to the national defense
bill, to establish a nonpartisan authority to plan the
acceleration of production of war material. When it met
defeat, he was angry but not discouraged. In May he
chastized both Democrats and Republicans because they
allowed "the spiritual and physical means of national
defense to die with rust." In July he pleaded with Americans
to stop bickering and renew their faith in government. That
same month he told his Military Affairs colleagues that his
support of the Burke-Wadsworth measure was bipartisan,
based on convictions backed by strong constituent support.[74]
Knowledge of the world situation, combined with an ardent
personal patriotism, explained Austin's bipartisan stand. In
addition, he was acutely aware of the nation's lack of
preparedness. He admitted that he was out of step with many
of his Republican colleagues, but the strength of his own
convictions enabled him to hold a divergent view.

Second, in light of Austin's previous apprehension
regarding Roosevelt's strength in the domestic area, the
Vermonter's defense of executive power appears entirely
inconsistent. However, in areas of foreign policy and
national defense, he recognized a need for a strong executive.
For example, while debating the National Guard bill in

August, opponents charged that Roosevelt would bring the nation closer to war through the provisions of the proposed legislation. Austin defended the measure. The President would not send troops to a foreign land without just cause, he believed, but the government must maintain a free hand in its foreign policy. Unwise restrictions on the President would prevent the needed flexibility.[75] Austin was more realistic than most Republican senators and a large number of Democrats. Moral and physical preparedness continued as the basis for his positions on national defense and foreign policy. But Austin coupled that with an interpretation of constitutional flexibility that allowed the President to direct America's foreign policy as the national interest dictated.

Austin barely had to campaign for re-election in 1940. His Democratic adversary, Ona S. Searles, offered only token opposition that was quite common in highly Republican Vermont. The vote gave the incumbent more than a two-to-one majority, larger than any of the other Republican candidates in the state.[76]

After the election, the Senator quickly returned to the related problems of national defense and foreign policy. In late November, he commented that, while he had always favored American aid to England, he favored it "more so now than ever." In December Austin suggested changes in the combat zones under the neutrality laws so that American vessels could legally carry goods to the British Isles. At the end of the year he supported Roosevelt's "arsenal of democracy" plea because he throught it kept the President's "hands untied," and in early 1941, he vigorously supported the lend-lease bill since he viewed it as a bulwark in the nation's defense preparations. His strong, independent stand in favor of the measure was not overlooked. Secretary of War Henry Stimson courted Austin's vote and Roosevelt showed his appreciation by sending him a pen used in the signing. He was the only Republican so rewarded.[77]

Throughout 1941, Austin continued as an embattled Republican on the side of administration measures. He supported the successful draft extension in the summer and lobbied long and hard for further neutrality law revision. That effort was successful on November 7, 1941 when Austin and only five other Republican Senators joined the majority in favor of a liberal revision.[78]

Once America entered the war on December 7, 1941, Austin quickly became one of few Republican Congressional leaders publicly calling for planning for the postwar world. The State Department seized on this and utilized his support for its own bipartisan approach toward postwar planning. Secretary Hull selected Austin as a charter member of the Department's Congressional foreign policy advisory group when it formed in 1942; he later became a member of the Committee of Eight, composed of prominent senators who favored some form of postwar international organization. When Austin played an important role in directing the internationalist Mackinac Declaration of the Republican Party in 1943, the State Department used him as a key contact to assure bipartisan support for an international organization plank in the 1944 Republican Party platform. In addition, Austin supported other administration internationalist actions ranging from the United Nations Relief and Rehabilitation Administration to the Dumbarton Oaks recommendation for a postwar international organization.[79]

Austin's Republican Senate colleagues noticed this activity. In spite of his staunch membership in the informal Republican conservative coalition dating back into the 1930s, the powerful Republican isolationist bloc, wielding power far out of proportion to its numbers, ostracized him for his strong support of the administration on foreign policy issues. In 1943, they purged him from the Assistant Minority Leader's position he had held since 1933, and despite his continued requests, he was not given a committee assignment to Foreign Relations until 1944.[80]

Austin's moving force continued to be internationalism, embodied in the creation of a peacekeeping organization based on major power cooperation as well as military muscle — and, of course, with American participation. He viewed isolation as a negative alternative; thus he recognized and practiced bipartisanship as a tactic that would bring his internationalist hopes to fruition. In retrospect, there were strong indicators by the mid-point of the war that bipartisan support for some form of postwar international organization had already won out over isolationism. In fact, in the broad context of American political thought, by 1944-45, the issue of isolationist versus internationalist was no longer a formidable one. Yet within Senate Republican ranks, the struggle had been real and uphill.[81]

In early 1945, Austin did not see the task finished. He attacked the remaining work with the fervor of a crusader: "I have a consecration to the objective (international cooperation through a world organization) which I have never had to any other," he publicly told his Senate colleagues in late January 1945. "It is so great that it overshadows any other duty I have in the office of Senator of the United States." While he recognized that the recently discussed Dumbarton Oaks plan was not perfect, Austin considered it as a marked improvement over the League of Nations. He told every audience he encountered that the proposed international grouping was important because it would "terminate unilateral actions which seem to be necessary because we do not have any organization." Yet he hedged his internationalist argument to convince die-hard isolationists that the plan would preserve American sovereignty. Austin was willing to give the organization "limited force in dealing with the preservation of the peace," but he categorically denied "abandoning this country to a supra world organization."[82]

Cooperation among the great powers held Austin's faith. When questioned by Senate critics about the possibility of the Security Council coercing a major power into accepting a Council decision, Austin replied candidly that the organization would fail. Major power cooperation, Austin said, "is the oaken beam that supports the whole superstructure of this building. Without faith, anything that we put into a treaty will fall, no matter whether we have the peace force of military kind in it or not. If we have to suppress by armed force, one of the great powers, we are at war already."[83]

The death of Roosevelt on April 12 saddened Austin. He had opposed the President on many issues, but he deeply admired the man's courage. Although Austin knew Harry Truman from their Senate days, he was, like many Americans, wary of the new President's lack of experience. When Truman came to Capitol Hill on April 13 to lunch with several former Senate colleagues, Austin was among them. The Senator hoped the event marked a continued congenial relationship in the formulation of foreign policy such as he experienced with the FDR administration.[84]

In those momentous months of mid-1945, when the Senate debated and reached its anticlimactic decision to approve the United Nations Charter, and the Pacific War drew to its dramatic close, Austin recognized more than ever that the new peace was not the final victory over the problems facing the United States and the rest of the world. As early as 1942 he had seen a long period of time between the end of the war and the actual accomplishment of postwar objectives. He predicted then that the postwar era would be a period fraught with difficulties and sacrifice.[85]

One of his concerns in 1945 involved the economic policies of the United States. Austin's thoughts and action in this area were based on his premise that economic peace, led by America, was necessary to insure political peace in the world. In writing to a correspondent in 1945 about his decision to support the Trade Agreements Act, Austin stated that he had no choice but to favor that and other economic measures because of his own belief that such acts would prevent future wars. He supported the Bretton Woods Agreement in July 1945. As author of a favorable report of a sub-committee of the Foreign Relations Committee on the drafting of a constitution for a permanent international organization on food and agriculture, he reported that it was time to lay the groundwork for such an organization while the rest of the world was willing to cooperate with the United States. In late summer, Austin wrote that the need for continued efforts to gain an economic peace involved the rehabilitation of Europe and the Far East. American aid must accomplish this, Austin insisted, even at the possible expense of retaining into peacetime some wartime restrictions on the economy.[86]

The Senator supported the British loan, negotiated in December 1945, and revealed more of the same economic philosophy. In February 1946, Austin told his Senate colleagues that politics should not enter into the consideration of the loan. He argued that the United States must increase its production and develop new markets. The loan would help Britain bolster its economy and it could become one of America's best markets once again. But perhaps even more important was the fact that Austin agreed with the administration that the loan was a step toward the larger objective of an expanding world economy. He privately made it apparent that the United States was in a position of superiority and, if it followed a proper course, it could remake the world along American lines. In other words, Austin recognized that the United States possessed the initiative.[87]

Austin's statements and actions on these various aspects of economic foreign policy could easily be construed as evidence of conscious support for an imperialistic American policy. But to so construe them would be a misinterpretation. The support he gave to economic policy was more in line with his missionary character that America had a role to play in helping the world recover from the war as well as in support of the new international order he saw through the United Nations. Missionary zeal and naivete characterized Austin in his economic outlook as they would in many of his other tenets of foreign policy. To assign him credit for deeper thought or planning on the subject would be ahistorical.[88]

Overall, Austin's effort to convince his Republican colleagues as well as the nation that the United States must play a leading role in the postwar world was the highlight of his Senate career. By successfully pursuing his beliefs, at times against seemingly overwhelming odds, Austin also satisfied himself that a better world was in the offing only if the United States pursued an active part. There was no place for isolationism in his thinking, and his bipartisanship underscored that belief. Thus this combination of internationalism and bipartisanship allowed him to accept easily the United Nations job in the Truman administration.

CHAPTER TWO

KEEPING FAITH IN A NEW CAREER

Austin was a dedicated supporter of the United Nations, and his devotion to its principles inspired his earnestly idealistic representation at the "town meeting of the world." But to Truman, the fact that Austin provided a logical bipartisan choice was probably more important. The Vermonter fit well the format that one scholar of bipartisanship in Truman's foreign-policy development recently judged to mean "acquiescence by the other party in the administration line and hopefully public agreement and active support of foreign policy objectives and tactics determined in advance by the White House. The administration sought to guarantee these results by choosing as collaborators Republicans whose previous positions had demonstrated adherence to its ideas."[1] So as a Republican, Austin could effectively blunt any criticism against America's United Nations policy.

Edward R. Stettinius, Jr.'s abrupt resignation as the first United States representative to the United Nations prompted the Austin appointment. Reports had circulated that the former Secretary of State was irked because he believed the position was not one of importance. And confidentially, he told Byrnes that he found himself in a limited role as a figurehead carrying out decisions made in Washington. But officially, Stettinius claimed he quit because his major objective — helping to establish the United Nations — was completed.[2]

Others could have served in the post as well as Austin. Two internationalist senators, Vandenberg and Thomas Connally, immediately come to mind. The former, then at the helm of the Senate Republicans in foreign policy matters, was more valuable to the administration if he remained in the Senate. Since Connally was a Democrat, bipartisanship was not a consideration, but like Vandenberg, he was a powerful influence as leader in the Senate Foreign Relations Committee and undoubtedly was a greater asset there than at the United Nations.

Ernest Gross, a legal advisor in the State Department at the time of the Austin appointment and a future colleague in the permanent delegation of the United States Mission at the United Nations, later recalled his belief that the appointment was not one of mere political expediency. He thought it was part of Truman's deep conviction that internationalism and bipartisanship should characterize America's foreign policy. Gross noted that there were no other Republican senators who would have resigned their position to accept the United Nations post. Austin, however, regarded the job as an opportunity to serve a greater cause and so was willing to move out of the Senate. His Senate term was up that fall and while there is nothing to indicate that he could not have won re-election easily in his Republican constituency, his career as a political leader was behind him. Austin realized that and saw the United Nations position as a fitting culmination to his public career.[3]

The appointment required a confusing arrangement. Congress recently had granted full ambassadorial status for the United States representative to the United Nations. But since the Constitution forbade a member of Congress to accept, during his term of office, a position created by the legislature during that period, Truman appointed Austin as a Special Representative and Advisor to the Acting Representative of the United States in the United Nations (Herschel Johnson). Austin served in that interim capacity until the conclusion of the second session of the 79th Congress. He then officially resigned and assumed the new position with full status. So technically, his permanent assignment did not begin until January 13, 1947[4]

The appointment elated Austin and generally brought laudatory comments. Filled with optimism, Austin exclaimed that he would not have accepted it if "I didn't have faith in the possibility of making progress." Senate colleagues Connally, Barkley and Vandenberg praised the selection. James Reston called Austin an "advanced progressive in external affairs"; one whose "diligence and intellectual ability have placed him above the political and ideological struggle on Capitol Hill." Arthur Krock reviewed his record as one of boldness and daring; he saw Austin as a conscientious public servant who was willing to put his office on the line for what he believed was right. Austin's hometown Burlington radio station commended the appointment as outstanding compared to some earlier Truman selections for key positions. Another editorial expressed confidence in Austin and stated that any other Republican appointment would have brought fire from the Democrats.

However, there were doubters. For example, the *Miami Daily News* commented editorially that Austin was not known well enough internationally for the appointment. The paper also stated that Austin's Republicanism could backfire on Truman. Citing the speculation on Stettinius's reason for retirement from the United Nations post because he was being submerged and not consulted on policy decisions, the editorial asked what will happen if Austin gets the same treatment. Cedric Foster, speaking on the Mutual network, was not concerned with that. He thought that Austin could stand alone and Byrnes and Truman would accept his advice and opinions.[5]

So at the age of sixty-eight, Austin embarked on a new career. Fifteen years in the Senate had provided him with experience in negotiation and debate. His internationalist fight in those years raised his enthusiasm for the ideal that men and nations could carry out their affairs on a high, moral level. He conceded that it might take a long time and that many hazards were ahead. He built his hope on a belief in cooperation, hard work and perseverance. Very soon he found his personal conviction on international affairs meeting its sternest challenge.

The United Nations post was unlike any other ambassadorial position in the foreign service. The United Nations Participation Act that established the position virtually bestowed prestige on it. A direct link was provided between the president and the ambassador as well as through normal State Department channels. In addition, a strong symbolism already was attached to the job, for the post represented the triumph of internationalism through the long American struggle to join a world organization. Furthermore, President Truman set a precedent which lasted into the 1960s in appointing ambassadors backed by national prestige and political background.[6]

Until 1951, when the completed United Nations complex along the East River in New York City was occupied by the international community, United Nations meetings were held first at Columbia University and then at Lake Success on Long Island. Austin moved from the Shoreham to New York in the fall of 1946 and settled in his new government-provided residence on the forty-second floor of the Waldorf-Astoria Towers. His office at the United States Mission was initially located at the Hotel Pennsylvania, but in 1947 the government rented several stories of the Waldorf-Astoria office building at 2 Park Avenue. The Mission remained there until 1961 when it moved to quarters at First Avenue and East 45th Street directly opposite the low-styled General Assembly building.

The remainder of 1946 tried Austin's flexibility since the move from the Senate to the United Nations demanded a considerable adjustment. Just administering the United States Mission posed a challenge in itself. A New York staff for the American Mission was first established in March 1946 and was known collectively as the United States Delegation to the United Nations. The Delegation gathered personnel and took on new duties as the United Nations permanently established itself. Stettinius and later Austin saw the need for a reorganization of the Delegation to provide more uniformity and control. Very early Austin discussed this problem with officials in the Department and with the President. Under an executive order in April 1947, a unified diplomatic mission under one administrative head was established. The American representative at the seat was the administrator and the Delegation was renamed the United States Mission to the United Nations. As chief representative, Austin coordinated the Mission's activities.[7]

Under this organization, the Mission became the formal medium through which the United States government maintained representation in the various divisions and activities of the world group. Besides Austin and his deputy, Herschel Johnson, the Mission consisted of representatives to the permanent committees of the General Assembly, the Security Council, the Trusteeship Council and the Military Staff Committee. With the exception of the latter, which reported to the Joint Chiefs of Staff, all representatives reported through Austin to the Office of Special Political Affairs in the State Department. That office had been established in 1944 and was later changed to the Office of United Nations Affairs. Then under an overall State Department reorganization in October 1949, the office was elevated to the Bureau for United Nations Affairs and headed by an Assistant Secretary. This, however, did not affect the structure of the Mission.[8]

When the General Assembly was in session (the regular sessions met in September and tried to finish before the end of the year), the American representatives to that body (specially designated by the President for each Assembly session) functioned as a delegation rather than as an integral part of the Mission. Thus Austin wore two hats when the Assembly met. As Chief of Mission, he received instructions relating to the conduct of the permanent Mission activities. As a representative to the General Assembly, he was instructed as a member of the delegation. Normal practice soon developed to appoint the Permanent Representative (Austin) as the "senior representative" of the Assembly delegation. However, when the Secretary of State participated in the Assembly, the title was relinquished to him. None of this affected Austin's position as Chief of Mission.[9]

Austin initially directed a staff of over one hundred people, which handled many of the everyday details and problems. To assist him, John C. Ross, a senior advisor, planned and coordinated the Mission's daily activities. The Mission's

Secretary-General, Richard S. Winslow, a career State Department official, supervised essential clerical and maintenance services. Also directly responsible to Austin and attached to the Mission was an Office of Public Affairs, which performed multitudinous informational and publicity functions. Porter McKeever headed this unit and was assisted by Chester S. Williams. All these people worked closely with Austin.

Unlike the personnel in his small Washington office, most of the individuals on Austin's staff were selected by the Department. However, he brought his legislative aide, William H. A. Mills, and his long-time secretary, Josephine V. Thompson, with him to New York. Both were designated Special Assistants. The large size of the function eliminated much of the informal personal relationships to which Austin was accustomed in his Senate operation and he was forced to rely much more on his assistants to administer the office. Nonetheless, the Mission gained a reputation for operating in a congenial, informal atmosphere.[10]

Eleanor Roosevelt, a member of the 1946 Assembly delegation, recalled the first meeting chaired by Austin. The Senator (he retained use of that title rather than his new designation of ambassador) made a "sensible little speech," she wrote in her memoir, about efficiency in each delegate's work to avoid overtime and night work. The new appointee thought in that way everyone would be "fresher and will have better ideas of how to achieve our goals." Mrs. Roosevelt correctly speculated that in a few months Austin would probably recall the difficulty in being well organized in United Nations work.[11]

The weight and complexity of the workload at the United Nations taxed both the physical and mental capacities of Austin. Just understanding the variety of issues before the various organs of the United Nations was intensified by the seemingly never ending flow of written words. Position papers, memoranda, public opinion surveys, press digests and personal correspondence were processed to Austin through evaluation and by assignment of priorities. The Mission staff showed its value in absorbing much of the routine work. This permitted Austin to apply himself to

important issues. Nonetheless, this division of labor provided little leisure time. Long working hours were the rule,
and often they were extended by both official and unofficial
weekend duties. As a consequence, Austin remained close to
the Mission, but occasionally, he and Mildred retreated 300
miles to their Burlington home. There Austin found
relaxation in his beloved backyard apple orchard and quiet
study in his spacious library. But those days were few.

Austin attempted participation in as many Mission
activities as possible, but he found the burden increasingly
difficult. For example, in the fall of 1947, Thomas Powers, the
acting Secretary-General of the Mission, informed Austin of
some trying negotiations in which he was involved with the
management of the Waldorf-Astoria hotel. It was a touchy
racial issue related to the hotel's accommodating the
Liberian Delegation at the upcoming General Assembly
meeting. According to Powers, the Waldorf management
considered "the situation a rather bitter pill." Use of Austin's
name, however, as well as stress on the possibility of adverse
criticism for both the United States government and the
Waldorf, settled the issue in favor of the Liberians. Powers
said he informed Austin of the matter in the event that the
Waldorf management "were ever to refer to it."[12]

Austin utilized much of his time from his June appointment to the opening of General Assembly session in the fall
of 1946 to continue marshalling public opinion in support of
the United Nations. He wrote in June that his convictions
remained strong that all nations, regardless of ideology,
would strive for methods other than war to settle controver-
sies. He had confidence in his own ability to share in
developing such a procedure.[13]

In late June, Austin elaborated on his ideas. He stressed
United Nations goals for peace and the responsibility of all
members in collaborating to reach those goals. To keep the
faith, the world organization had to concentrate on specific
objectives. Resolutions and principles were not enough.
"People cannot act unless they see clearly where they are
headed and what is required of them," Austin said.

Once the United Nations outlined those objectives, Austin
saw the development of vague large-scale plans based on

mutual self-help. He mentioned no specific programs, but he obviously had in mind the use of the United Nations agencies. Yet he cautioned about the danger in expecting the United Nations to spread itself over too wide an area in the formulation of such programs. The problems, he realized, were many, and risk, sacrifice and persistence were needed for success.[14]

Austin fully understood the importance of the United States to the rest of the world if only because it was the major nation that came through the war relatively unscathed. Unrealistically, he saw his country channeling its nonmilitary resources through United Nations agencies such as the International Labor Organization and the Food and Agriculture Organization of the Economic and Social Council. At the same time he spoke favorably of the loans the United States made to many of its former allies in lieu of the termination of lend-lease. Austin advocated both types of aid to other parts of the world if that provided the best means to solicit cooperation.[15]

Austin's abounding optimism for success is best shown through his emphasis on public opinion in the success of the United Nations. Fresh in his memory was the overwhelming ratification triumph of the Charter of the United Nations in the United States Senate. Austin thought that achievement was due to the work of civic organizations, churches, schools, press, radio and public speakers in providing knowledge of the Charter and its potential. Likewise, he believed the business of the United Nations rested on a worldwide audience that was informed and interested.

At this time and throughout his tenure at New York, the Senator frequently consulted with various patriotic, internationalist and peace groups that maintained an interest in the United Nations and were constantly seeking to strengthen it. The American Association for the United Nations was the most prominent supporter of the world body. Hard-working internationalist Clark Eichelberger, former national director of the defunct League of Nations Association, headed the American Association. Other groups also supported the United Nations, but often advocated more idealistic plans for a supranational government. Included were such organizations as the United World Federalists, led by its youthful, idealistic, national president and war hero, Cord Meyer, Jr.; Clarence Streit's Federal Union; and the Citizen's Committee for United Nations Reform. While these groups made valuable contributions by maintaining public awareness of the work of the United Nations, they were, to a large extent, handicapped by their own disillusionment with the world body.

Talking to the United Nations Association in October 1946, Austin said that when national delegations formed their plans and proposals for the upcoming General Assembly session, each of those nation's citizens must make sure that their wishes were presented. Likewise, when recommendations of international bodies reverted to the national governments for ratification and support, public opinion was essential to make implementation effective.[16] In other words, Austin thought the world's varied governments would rely on common opinion to the degree America's system permitted. While he wanted as much support as possible for the new organization from the people of America, his enthusiasm to bring about the result appeared to have clouded his view of how to gain support for the United Nations in other countries that lacked similar public-oriented bases. Austin merely applied his American values to a worldwide situation. In doing so, he revealed his own determination to utilize open diplomacy as well as the United States' program at the United Nations to legitimatize the nation's foreign policy.

Austin had spent a major part of the war years campaigning for an international organization; furthermore — and this is important in understanding Austin — he believed in the system. His public statements and private communications revealed this concept. Now as a leading spokesman for United States policy at the United Nations, he supported an internationalist approach with total honesty and sincerity. Ernest Gross, after watching Austin in action at the United Nations for four years, could frankly comment, "There was something almost old-fashioned about Warren Austin's conviction of the spiritual foundations of the United Nations."[17] Austin never considered his enunciations of

American positions as merely lip service to the objectives of the United Nations.

To understand Austin's role at the United Nations and the institutional nature of the post he occupied, recognition of the global body's relationship to American foreign policy is necessary. National interest, often in conflict with the ideals of international organization and cooperation, underscored United States relations with the United Nations. Because of its preponderance of power and influence during the initial postwar years, the United States had a distinct, though not easy, advantage in pursuing its own national interest through the United Nations. Of the organization's initial membership of fifty-one nations, the United States could generally rely on forty-two of those to support important resolutions. Or viewed from a different angle, the United Nations could be used as a public forum where the United States could muster support for the legitimatization of its policy, no matter what it was in terms of national or international interest. As the membership increased over the years, more members voted an independent line than in those early years. But it was not until long after Austin left the United Nations that America's overwhelming majority on most issues was seriously threatened.[18]

As Cold War tensions mounted, the United Nations became a battleground. The United States used the world group's functions to discredit America's major adversaries — the Soviet Union and the countries within its bloc. This helps to explain the Soviety Union's frequent use of the veto — an issue that highlighted the early years of the United Nations. Consistently outvoted in both the Security Council and the General Assembly on matters which it considered in its national interest, the Soviet Union found the Security Council veto its only means to achieve a semblance of parity.[19]

To most Americans, and especially to Austin, the predominant theme of immediate postwar foreign policy incorporated the concept of a global community. Memories of a Wilsonian idealism that proclaimed a world system which could maintain peace combined with the long-established notion that the United States must provide the leadership to accomplish such an ideal, were powerful motivating forces. The evolution of the United Nations, then, was more than a mere symbol; many Americans saw its success as an ongoing national mission.[20] So the dichotomy of a global community versus national interest was present when the United Nations was established. By 1946, many American officials and policies disclaimed the idealism of the United Nations; nonetheless, it was inadvisable to abandon either the ideal or the organization even if it became a difficult arena within which to operate.

Several items brought before the Security Council in 1946 resulted in clashes on the East-West diplomatic battleground. In January, Iran's new postwar government charged Russia with interference in its internal affairs. At that time the Security Council took no action other than to encourage negotiations then in progress between the two countries. But in March, at the urging of the United States, the matter was again brought up by Iran, which charged that Russia maintained troops in northern Iran beyond the time limit stipulated in the Tripartite Treaty of 1942. The United States kept public pressure on the Soviets by insisting that both sides present all the facts. The Soviets attempted to block this, without success, and walked out of the Security Council. However, in late March, Russia and Iran reached an agreement which provided for withdrawal of Soviet troops and the establishment of a joint Soviet-Iranian oil company. The matter seemed resolved, but the friction it produced affected Soviet-American relations tremendously.

Also in January, the Ukrainian Soviet Socialist Republic demanded an immediate Security Council investigation of the situation in Indonesia, where it reported that British and Japanese troops were fighting the Indonesian population. The United States voted with the majority against an investigation on the basis that an inquiry was warranted only if the continuance of the situation endangered peace. The Security Council took no further action on the case and the Soviets were stymied.

The Lebanese and Syrian governments complained to the Council in February that the British and French were maintaining armed forces in those Middle Eastern nations after the close of hostilities. The United States attempted to pacify the situation with a resolution that the concerned nations undertake direct negotiations to resolve their differences. The Soviet Union vetoed it.

Outside the United Nations, the Paris peace negotiations attended by the Foreign Ministers of the United States, Great Britain, France and the Soviet Union discussed terms of treaties with Axis satellites. While the Big Four reached agreement on some issues, major differences were not compromised. This added to the hostility between the Soviets and the Western nations. Obviously, the people of East and West wanted to live in peace, but their leaders could not agree on the terms.

By September 1946, the conduct of American foreign policy produced trouble within Truman's cabinet. Secretary of Commerce Henry Wallace, the only major critic of a "get tough with Russia" policy, was not ready to abandon wartime collaboration just because postwar agreement did not come easily. At a Madison Square Garden speech on September 12, he stated support not of appeasement but of sympathy for the problems of the Soviet Union and he criticized American policymakers' lack of patience and understanding. Truman subsequently asked for Wallace's resignation and the matter signaled the administration's move toward an unofficial hard-line policy against the Soviet Union.

In this context, Austin's hopes appeared out of touch with what had developed as government policy toward the Soviet Union and its allies. Certainly if American policy were to prevail in the world, a firm position was the order against the Soviets. Proponents of cooperation with the Soviet Union, including Austin, lost practically any base of strength they held in their advocation of an accommodating policy.[21]

Yet the United Nations remained a useful diplomatic tool for both those who advocated a hard-line approach toward the Soviets as well as for those who sought cooperation. For the hard-liners, the world organization was an arena in which, rhetorically, the United States could strongly advocate internationalism. At the same time, the Soviets were held up before the world as opponents of international cooperation. This set the stage for an evolving, public denunciation of Soviet motives, ideology and intransigence that, in turn, brought an increasingly uncompromising policy by the United States. For the cooperationists, the United Nations was an evolving organization. They admitted it possessed apparent weaknesses. But they hoped that, with continued United States support and the world body's own perseverance, the United Nations could become a vigorous organization capable of fulfilling the fondest hopes of any internationalist.

Probably no other single issue related to the new activities of the United Nations aroused more sustained public controversy in the early years than the veto question. By the time of the opening of the delayed 1946 October General Assembly meeting, the Soviets had cast eleven vetoes in the Security Council.

Particularly acute was the question of to which substantive and procedural matters the veto applied. The four sponsoring powers at San Francisco had stated that, if a matter was defined as procedural, only a simple majority of the Security Council was necessary to take action on it. However, the four-power statement precluded such a decision on the preliminary question of defining a matter to be procedural or substantive. On that point, unanimity of the permanent members was required. This led to what became known as the "double veto." A permanent member would cast the first veto to prevent designation of a question as procedural; it would then use the second veto to block action on the measure as a substantive question. The Soviets particularly utilized this maneuver, and it underscored what the Western nations called "misuse of the veto."

While Soviet use of the veto militated against issues supported by the West, the United States position, as well as that of the other permanent members, did not include any proposal toward elimination of the veto. Throughout 1946, complex negotiations took place in the Committee of Experts of the Security Council, a group designated to draft permanent rules of procedure for the Council. In its discussions, the United States attempted to narrow the usage area for the veto. The meetings failed to reach their objectives.

Since the problem threatened future work of the Security Council, both Australia and Cuba placed the veto question on the October General Assembly agenda. Australia's innocuous resolution merely asked members of the Council to consider the general rule of unanimity on matters before the Council. The Cuban proposal was more basic. It suggested calling a general conference with a view toward amending the Charter and eliminating the veto.[22]

Austin was faced with handling the American positions related to this problem. Through a series of meetings at the State Department in September and early October he learned the intricacies of the situation. As head of the delegation, he would direct the day-to-day maneuvers on the question in the General Assembly. He would work closely with Senator Connally, the main United States representative in the First Committee — the Political and Security Committee — where discussion of the veto proposals would take place. In addition, Austin directed the daily delegation meetings where various committee's assignments and positions were discussed and coordinated.[23]

The American position on the veto was formulated in the Department in September and Austin contributed his ideas. He opposed amending the Charter at that time. Rather, he thought — and others in the State Department agreed — that a broad expression of the Assembly's view was necessary to accentuate the positive elements with respect to unanimity and voting in general. Austin commented that the draft position paper discussed at the meeting presented an unduly pessimistic view of present procedures. He preferred to see accomplishments emphasized. The revised final position paper underscored this idea.[24]

Later this position was discussed at the first meeting of the United States delegation in New York. Austin stressed again that the United States preferred not to change the Charter in regard to the veto. He realized this placed the nation in an awkward position, as it appeared that the United States was running counter to world opinion in light of the Soviet misuse of the veto. To offset this, Austin advocated a positive position by suggesting rules, regulations and definitions that would clarify the voting procedure. Delegation member John Foster Dulles questioned Austin on the American procedure. Why should the United States defend the veto if the purpose of the General Assembly discussion was merely to air the grievances of the smaller states? Austin replied that the United States had a responsibility to assume leadership to "revive the spirit of our people" toward the United Nations. He thought that Americans had lost sight of the fundamental conception of the United Nations because of the attack on the misuse of the veto.[25]

The discussion continued a few days later. Austin announced to the delegation that he would formally speak to the plenary on the veto subject and declare that the United States' position had not changed. Delegation members Connally, Arthur Vandenberg and Charles Eaton expressed their dismay as they saw the United States cast as a defender of the veto and thus implicated in its abuse. Austin hoped that his speech would eliminate that concern.[26]

Soviet hostility against the West erupted before Austin delivered his first major position speech. On October 29, Foreign Minister V. M. Molotov blistered the United States in an address that struck directly at American motives in the world organization. He dealt with a wide range of issues, but his main thrust demanded a discussion of total disarmament. Molotov concluded with the introduction of a proposal on the general reduction of armaments, including atomic weaponry.[27]

American planning did not call for Austin to discuss disarmament. Austin's speech planned to stress the flexibility of the United Nations through its specialized agencies. With this approach, Austin could favorably present a positive United States position on voting in the Security Council. While there was concern in the delegation that some other nation might take the initiative to discuss atomic energy proposals, Austin thought that he could not change his thrust unless he received new instructions. But the Molotov proposals forced swift revision of the speech. A new draft attempted to defuse the Soviet challenge and regain the initiative for the American proposals by taking a positive approach.[28]

Within the context of hardened East-West attitudes, many officials already disregarded the United Nations as a place for the resolution of international conflict. While Austin's maiden speech appeared highly rhetorical, it was significant because it embodied the liberal-internationalist principles he strongly favored and it symbolized the faith Americans maintained for the United Nations. Although the final draft was a composite production of the Office of Special Political Affairs, it encompassed Austin's words and the position in which he believed. As far as he was concerned, accommodation could be reached with America's antagonists and he was convinced that open diplomacy through an international system was the best means to gain that end.

This was the General Assembly's first session in the United States and the American delegation capitalized on the attention the affair received. Austin opened his remarks to the plenary with a plea to Molotov to stop recriminations. He stated that he would not participate in any exchange of that nature. Then, speaking directly to Molotov's resolution on disarmament, Austin accepted the Soviet challenge by agreeing to full discussion of the proposal.

Austin moved quickly to his main point — unanimity of thought and action. Acknowledging the deliberative nature of the United Nations, he saw agreement forged from disagreement through frank discussion. Potentially, Austin noted, the General Assembly was the most important branch of the United Nations. Backed by the moral forces of the international community, it wielded power "as the voice of the conscience of the world." No nation would disregard its recommendations since it represented the agreement of "aroused world opinion." As time passed, the Assembly would expand the areas of activity undertaken. Only the base had been established. Austin saw functions not specifically covered by the Charter entrusted to the Assembly as it made the ambiguous language of the Charter take on substance.

Austin believed in unanimity. That principle, he said, reflected "the realities of the world as it is today." The abolition of war depended upon the cooperation from all nations competent to wage war. The permanent members of the Council, by the fact that they were the strongest nations, possessed the ability to keep peace. The Charter, Austin said, did not give them that power; it merely recognized it as a fact.

But the Charter placed the moral responsibility for its correct use upon those nations. Austin defended the unanimity formula from critics who said that it legalized aggression by a permanent member because that member could, by veto, prevent enforcement action against itself. Falling back to a legalistic-moralistic position, Austin referred to those Charter articles that required all members to settle their disputes peacefully. The permanent members of the Council had a moral obligation to follow that rule even though they were equipped with the veto. Austin admitted that if one of the permanent members committed aggression and the Security Council decided to take military measures against that nation, war was inevitable. But that would occur, he argued, despite the legalized unanimity principle. Consequently, the only peaceful policy to follow was for all nations to live up to their moral commitment made when they joined the United Nations.

Austin hoped to reconcile the differences on the Council without amending the Charter. It was too early, he stated, to build a case for amendment. Many of the problems facing the Security Council were the direct result of the war. The United Nations was not designed to deal with the peace settlements and until those were completed, problems would exist for the Council which the original plan did not envision. Austin thought that reduction in those areas of disagreement would occur as settlements were made. In the meantime, Austin's remedy was the employment of self-discipline to "avoid doing anything contrary to the letter or spirit of the Charter." He closed his address by stating that the United Nations offered the greatest potential for peace that the world had yet known. But it would take a long time. There was no magic formula. Man must rely on fundamental principles to give the Charter "a living spirit in the moral sense of nations."[29]

If response to Austin's speech was an indication of the general attitude toward American policy at the United Nations, he had followed the correct line. Truman congratulated him the following day. The President thought the speech "hit the bull's-eye" and he expressed complete accord with Austin's words. The Senator's colleagues at the United Nations found his speech reassuring after the Molotov denunciation. Alexandre Parodi of France said the speech showed there was a willingness to discuss and negotiate. Even Poland's Oscar Lange praised Austin's argument for unanimity. The *New York Times* editorially cited Austin as being wise in remaining away from the "reckless charges" Molotov aimed at the United States.[30]

Radio commentator Cedric Foster asked how the Soviets, with justification, could reject the appeal for unity which Austin projected throughout his speech. Erwin D. Canham, editor of the *Christian Science Monitor,* commented over the American Broadcasting Company network that he thought Austin had placed his finger on the key to the veto problem; it was not the existence of the veto that was the problem — it was its misuse. *The New Republic* described Austin as the first voice America had used which really felt "the pulse of the people." Truman and Byrnes, the author chided, failed to enunciate this attitude; but Austin did. The article went on to say that he was neither brilliant nor profound, but was entirely honest in portraying "a sense of the true and the great in the American republic."[31]

The warm response was heartening to Austin. He believed that his speechmaking was an important aspect in presenting the United States as a peaceful, cooperative nation. Ernest Gross noted later that Austin employed emotionalism as little as possible in his presentations. Austin thought it advantageous to present the clearest and most logical arguments and he followed this tactic throughout his United Nations years. Nonetheless, his approach also met with disapproval by some on the grounds that it enabled the Soviets to command the headlines through their own use of sensationalism.[32]

After much discussion and maneuvering in the First Committee, a compromise resolution on the veto question passed the Assembly on December 13. That day Austin spoke to the plenary in favor of the First Committee report. Based on the earlier Australian proposal, the report made the suggestion to the Security Council that it utilize a consulta-

tion procedure before taking votes on issues. It was hoped
this would ensure that the use of the veto would not impede
the prompt decision-making process of the Council.[33]
Naturally, a number of states were unhappy. On the one
hand, several advocated either amendment of the Charter or
fundamental changes in the practice and procedures of the
Security Council. On the other hand, the resolution was
stronger than a Soviet proposal that merely expressed
confidence in the Council. But since the final resolution was
only a recommendation, in reality, it meant little.

Austin feared the results of the veto problem. He was irked
at what he considered undue criticism directed at the faults
of the organization. He wished more people would realize
that the Security Council was only one of many elements
within the United Nations and believe that the General
Assembly and the Economic and Social Council played
important roles in building groundwork for peace. Those
organs possessed an added advantage through lack of the
veto problem. His own sincerity in the United Nations
caused him to look to these other agencies to avoid disaster
due to impasse. In time, this approach became more and
more important to him.

Criticism on the basic Charter and hope for its immediate
review also upset Austin. He advised those quasi-supporters
who wanted to see the idea of a world government
immediately put into practice that they continue support of
that ideal. But at the same time, they should withhold their
attempts to convert the United Nations to world government
until the organization was strong enough to bear the strain
of a drastic change.[34]

Nonetheless, Austin's optimism remained high as he
assessed his first General Assembly session for President
Truman in December. He thought that when the session
began there was a definite air of bitterness toward the United
States on the part of the Soviets. Slowly, wrote Austin,
"without appeasement, but with reasonable consideration
for each other's points of view, the United States and Russia
came to agreement upon practically every great issue." He
believed that a "strengthened confidence and faith in the
United Nations" was apparent at the end of the meetings.[35]

Containment was not the official policy of the United States in late 1946 and early 1947. Nonetheless, men with gloomy expectations on future relations with the Soviet Union dominated State Department thinking. Byrnes, Undersecretary Dean Acheson, George Marshall, who replaced Byrnes as Secretary in January 1947, Soviet experts George Kannan and Charles Bohlen, and Ambassador to the Soviet Union Averell Harriman were the most prominent. These men hardened in their attitude toward dealing with adversary nations as they realized that the stage was set on many fronts for the time when they might present a fresh statement of policy and action. Within this context the Department's Office of Special Political Affairs appeared to go against the trend. One student of the early Cold War analyzed the situation: the "so-called 'U.N. boys' appeared as a major internal roadblock to a firm stand against the Soviet Union."[36] The main thought prevailed both at Special Political Affairs and at the United States Mission in New York that if the nation remained generous toward its adversaries, solutions to major problems were in the offing. Austin was a leading believer in this approach. Not ready to take a hard-line stand, his guide was a liberal policy, based on fair play, moral righteousness and justice.

There can be detected, however, a measure of realism from Austin's first encounter with the Soviets. When he emphasized that the other organs of the United Nations were as important as the Security Council in finding solutions to problems of security, he cautiously admitted that the unanimity principle probably would not work in the end. It was a signal in his own mind that a search must start for other alternatives to preserve security. He saw some possibilities through the various agencies, but he was not yet willing to admit that a direct confrontation might be the solution — within or without the United Nations.

Confirmation of this position came later in the month. While spending the Christmas holidays in Vermont, Austin drafted some thoughts on the role of the United Nations in the world. These were responses to questions in preparation for an NBC radio interview in early January. Austin found grounds for optimism in sections of the Charter pertaining to

functions of the General Assembly. He saw that body
expanding its operations in the area of international peace
and security. He continued thinking that the Soviets had met
the Americans half-way during the recent General Assembly
meetings in a mutual search for understanding and based on
this, he expressed faith for the future. But he also admitted
that the Security Council, with its unanimity rule, would
pose the toughest obstacle to overcome. Austin used this
theme on the broadcast when he spoke in Chicago in mid-
January.[37]

Special Political Affairs continued its ambivalent attitude
in instructions to Austin. It opposed consideration of the veto
problem by the Security Council in January 1947 as
premature and fruitless. The office thought that some of the
ramifications arose because of various approaches to a
problem rather than basic policy differences. It instructed
Austin to consult with other members of the Council on these
differences in an attempt to reach the broadest possible
agreement. The instructions indicated continuing hope for
unanimity despite the course of events of the past year.[38]

Given the attitudes of leading State Department officials,
it becomes apparent that Austin's role as a significant
contributor to American policy would be limited. Lack of use
of the United Nations for formulation and conduction of
significant American policy greatly circumscribed Austin's
role. In addition, his personal faith in the role of the United
Nations, while respected by other Department members, was
out of line with their attitudes toward the development of
actual policy. Nonetheless, the selling of the United Nations
as a cornerstone of American policy was something which
the United States could not abandon. So support for its
principles was an area in which Austin was well suited and
could continue to play a leading and useful role. At the same
time, he would not be involved in major policy development.
In other words, while the institutional nature of the United
Nations would symbolize and be supported by the United
States as the world's "best hope," it was not compatible with
the unilateral trend of American Cold War policy. Austin
would become a microcosm of that situation, and his
continued support of the United Nations underscores the
trend.

The Soviet Union's use of the veto as well as its representatives' frequent diatribes created an increasing public demand in the United States to revise the Charter in order to eliminate pitfalls already encountered and to move toward a more idealistic world government organization. Several bills were presented in both houses of Congress throughout 1947 that indicated this increasing dissatisfaction with the United Nations. In their various forms, these proposals sought revision in the Charter in order to establish a limited world government. Their advocates contended that national sovereignty was too dominant a force within the United Nations Charter. Their remedies generally called for greater sovereignty for the international body at the expense of the sovereignty of the member states. This movement disturbed State Department leaders as well as Austin and his staff.[39]

Austin constantly defended the organization in its present form. He believed this was a significant part of his function as representative. He was well equipped to handle such an assignment. His knowledge through long study of United Nations functions, precedents and legalities, combined with his dedicated belief in the organization, classified him as an expert. In addition, the subject gave Austin a platform from which to voice his belief in the cause of peace as well as confidence in American leadership at the United Nations.

By fall 1947, Austin had held the job for more than a year and he regretted public disillusionment with the United Nations. He thought the organization needed new energy and spirit. Proposals for world government appeared impractical to the Senator when he considered the previous long, difficult path in organizing the United Nations. But he wished not to alienate those groups who supported revision, nor to discourage consideration of the hope of a future world government.[40]

Austin regarded the Charter as the most realistic and practical vehicle for agreement among the major powers in the postwar world. He did not view the document as an infallible instrument, but he saw it had advantages over the proposals to try something even more obligatory and specific in its operation. Austin wanted the organization to retain flexibility so that it might develop majority opinions and positions despite opposition and noncooperation. He thought the Charter's present form allowed for that and that premature or ill-conceived changes might disrupt the organization and destroy what it already had accomplished.[41]

Charter revision reached a climax by early 1948 when the House Foreign Affairs Committee scheduled hearings to determine methods of strengthening the United Nations. In public sessions, the Committee sought the views of both laymen and public servants in response to the number of pending resolutions in Congress.

Austin would testify before that group, but, in the meantime, he continued to discuss the question of change. Privately, since he advised against amendment of the Charter, the Senator checked the Security Council's four other permanent members and also found them opposed. Under those circumstances, he could see little benefit gained by arousing the American public in favor of Charter alterations. Austin was realistic. He realized the United States could not propose a ready-made constitution in the form of an ultimatum to other nations. Developing practices and procedures within the present Charter which eventually crystallized in rules was his alternative. He thought this approach would produce effective results.

Austin believed the United Nations was currently strengthened through use of all its councils and standing agencies. But he recognized that the American public expected immediate results, and because of the organization's slow progress it was difficult to show a developing strength. In looking ahead to possible congressional action, he hoped that any resolutions seeking to strengthen the United Nations would be positive and express the vigor of the organization. If not, the public would receive another false impression of the United Nations. The attempt to move toward a world government was fine as an ideal. But Austin thought such a goal was unattainable in his lifetime. Still, he considered a discussion of the subject valuable because it might inspire the public to take an interest in possible improvement of international relations.[42]

Austin was one of two star witnesses before the House Committee hearings on May 5. George Marshall preceded

him as an administration witness. The Secretary's statement was a blunt exposition of American policy toward the
United Nations. He said the United States would continue to
aid noncommunist countries through the recently passed
Marshall Plan and in other ways, but it would not support a
policy to seek revision of the Charter which would change the
structure of the organization. Rather, American policy would
work toward bringing about evolutionary change.[43]

Austin designed his subsequent testimony to subdue the
passion for change in the United Nations Charter. To do so,
he contended that the United Nations continued as the best
hope of the world for peace and cited some of the achievements of the Food and Agriculture Organization as an
example. That group established a World Food Council
which helped allocate exportable food surpluses and fertiliz-
ers and also focused attention on dangerously low food
resources. The FAO dispatched agricultural experts to
Greece and Poland to advise on plans for increased
agricultural development. It helped Near Eastern countries
begin deep-well irrigation and swamp-drainage projects. The
organization was aiding Peru in establishing refrigeration
and storage facilities for that nation's fishing industry. It
continuously advised the International Bank on loans for
agricultural and industrial machinery purchases. While
these were all positive contributions of that organization,
Austin testified, by their nature they did not make the
headlines. A Soviet veto always gained much publicity, but
Austin thought the long-range collective efforts to remove
the causes of war through such agencies as the Food and
Agriculture Organization were of far more significance.[44]

Austin turned to the seemingly obvious impasse in the
Security Council. There he admitted a certain lack of
achievement but he still believed that the United Nations
had not failed in its mission. He cited a number of Council
accomplishments. That group helped induce the Soviet
Union to withdraw its troops from Iran in early 1946. Later
that year the strong views of the Council helped to bring
about the withdrawal of British and French forces from
Syria and Lebanon. The Council also succeeded in arranging
a truce between the Dutch and the Indonesians and
subsequently established a good offices committee to help

the opposing sides reach agreement. At the time of Austin's testimony, Security Council recommendations for a truce and plebescite to settle the conflict between India and Pakistan over Kashmir were awaiting acceptance by the parties concerned. These last two achievements, Austin testified, were not challenged by the veto.

In citing Greece and Korea, Austin mentioned two areas in which Soviet and American interests were directly involved. Despite three Russian vetoes in the Greek case, United Nations service for peace still remained a force, Austin stated. The General Assembly had taken up the issue and proceeded to call on Yugoslavia, Albania and Bulgaria not to furnish assistance to the Greek guerilla forces. On the Korean issue, the Senator noted that a United Nations Committee was in Korea, with the hope of bringing about unification of the country after Soviet-American disagreement resulted in an impasse.[45] He saw these as positive performances.

Even when the veto stopped action, it could not suppress the examination of evidence. Austin noted the recent coup in Czechoslovakia, where the Soviets threatened to veto any Security Council action to investigate the incident's circumstances. Even if a veto occurred, evidence was spotlighted for public scrutiny because Council members would record the facts they possessed.[46]

Of course, Austin's arguments were fallacious. The United Nations was not successful in handling issues directly involving the Soviet Union and the West. Accomplishments came about only when the issues were between second-class powers or a major power and a second-class power. For example, the United Nations was not successful in resolving the situations in Greece and Korea, where major power interests collided. While Austin cited the maintenance of an open record in the Czech case, it had not prevented the Soviets from dominating that nation. Austin deceived only himself in assigning United Nations achievements in these dreary events. He desperately wanted to show progress made by the United Nations; but in so doing, he was not entirely guileless in trying to convince the committee of the success of the United Nations.

Austin was on more solid ground when he spoke of other merits of the United Nations. Most important, the organization formed at least a shaky bridge between the East and the West in providing a common place for discussion and negotiation. As a result, some collaboration did occur in all activities of the world body. Austin noted that if this universality of membership was lost, a complete break might take place between East and West.

Finally, Austin noted that the United States needed an open forum for explanation of policies and the mobilization of public support for them. The United Nations provided this forum and proved to the world's countries that America needed their assistance as much as they needed American help.[47] This testimony reflected Austin's preoccupation with the value of public opinion in the conduct of international affairs. Even more important, it was a frank acknowledgment of America's utilization of the United Nations for foreign policy legitimatization.

Pressure to amend the Charter finally resulted in a weak paragraph in the Senate's famous Vandenberg Resolution passed in June 1948. That compromise document, worked out in consultation between the administration and members of Congress, focused public attention on paragraph 3, which proclaimed American association with European regional and other collective security agencies. But numerous references to the United Nations were inserted throughout the resolution. The last paragraph, in particular, stated that the United States should call for a review of the Charter, if necessary, after making adequate efforts to strengthen it, including a major one to obtain agreement on restricting the use of the veto. Since no radical revision was publicly advocated, the administration, and particularly Austin and the United States Mission, claimed victory.

Austin remained on guard against radical change throughout his United Nations tenure. Later he conceded the weakness in his earlier basic assumption of cooperation among nations, but he thought this was not dangerously disruptive to the world organization. By 1949 he was fully convinced that any new organization would upset the cooperation which already prevailed. Speaking to the

Vermont legislature in February 1949, Austin observed a lack of reality in proposals for a world federal government. He described them as a "far vision" not suited to the context of the current world situation. He opted for gradual but continuous change.[48]

Austin never asked for a halt in the criticism of the world body. Rather, he sought constructive criticism which would help the organization grow and mature. He wanted wide public scrutiny and debate on issues which were before the various United Nations organs. For example, he asked how many critics knew of the work of the United Nations in connection with the World Health Organization or the accomplishments in promoting peaceful solutions in Palestine, India and Pakistan? He thought better understanding of these activities would enhance the United Nations' image. He criticized the advocates of world government for failure in helping to offset the indifference and cynicism then prevalent in the nation by including such public information activities in their programs.[49]

To gain support and initiate better liaison with some of the revisionist groups, in September and October 1949, Austin directed his staff to arrange a program of meetings with the leaders of the United World Federalists. It was one of the most vocal in advocating radical change in the United Nations. Establishing a world government was the Federalists' ultimate goal. So the meetings were called to underscore the danger that the energetic idealism of the Federalists might have in discrediting the United Nations. Austin was pleased with the outcome. He hoped the meetings had moderated the Federalists' stand and would bring renewed support for the United Nations from them.[50]

In a continuing effort, the Mission staff studied various position papers on the question of world government and conferred with Department officials in Washington. All agreed that the way to strengthen the United Nations was through an evolutionary process. Mission members were convinced that despite idealistic fallacies in the plans of the revisionist groups, the government should take a positive approach toward them because their membership included an intelligent group of internationally-minded citizens. A defense of the status quo could not meet the revisionist's challenge to the United Nations. The United States must reaffirm the central place the United Nations occupied in American foreign policy. And coupled with this was a need for clarification of the objectives the free world hoped to attain through the United Nations in the next few years.[51]

Austin subscribed to this approach. In a way, it reflected both his naivete and that of his staff. By this time, the central thrust of United States foreign policy certainly was not through the United Nations. Nonetheless, although the Mission's appraisal of United States foreign policy was not realistic, it was the only approach to follow in discussion with the revisionist groups. But for Austin, the theme continued as a belief, and reflected his earlier vision of prominence for the United Nations in the affairs of all nations of the world. He maintained his faith.

CHAPTER THREE

THE BALANCE OF POWER
AND THE UNITED NATIONS

Austin's optimistic outlook on world affairs combined with a naive appraisal of Soviet conduct came into bold relief when two new weapons of the expanding Cold War were utilized by the United States in 1947: the Truman Doctrine and the Marshall Plan. In bypassing the United Nations with these issues, the Truman administration forced Austin to rethink his own internationalist philosophy if he was to remain consistent with his earlier principles as well as to continue to support the administration's foreign policy.

The Senator's thoughts about Soviet-American relations dated back to 1945. One of the first public signs of noncooperation came at the San Francisco conference and many interested Americans viewed that development with dismay. One friend of Austin wrote to the Senator for his opinion on the responsibility for the United States' attitude. He asked if the State Department followed a hard-line policy, as it appeared to him. Austin's confidential reply defended the Department, but for the first time, he showed some apprehension about his own belief in international cooperation. He wrote that the organization would fail if it were not "founded upon continuing peaceful feelings among the great powers." Later, in August 1945, when Secretary Byrnes met privately with Austin at his Shoreham Hotel apartment, Byrnes informed the Senator that he learned at Potsdam that the way to deal with the Russians "is to hit them hard, and then negotiate." The Secretary portrayed Stalin as a crafty diplomat who would take advantage of any situation.[1] The fact that Austin thought it important enough to record this conversation in a memorandum is significant, for it revealed Austin's as well as Byrnes's concern over future Soviet-American cooperation.

In several letters to Vermont acquaintances, the Senator appeared wary of continued cooperation and hinted about other necessary measures to maintain peace. He stressed that he was not giving up on the United Nations, but saw continued vigilance for the victors "not alone with the vanquished, but among themselves." Additional strength, he wrote, would come from development of a regional self-defense group rather than relying solely upon the United Nations. The Russians would not like that, he conceded. In addition, Austin thought that United States possession of the atomic bomb would have a "benign influence in the whole world."[2] He did not elaborate on that point. However, it is apparent that his operating philosophy was now tempered with a decidedly American internationalism that incorporated a wariness about continued cooperation.

Yet Austin was not ready to regard the Soviet Union as completely opposed to his concept of international coopera-tion. While debating, in March 1946, in favor of extension of the draft, he used the Senate floor to disclose publicly his own observations on Soviet foreign relations as well as his continued fear of an American return to isolationism. He thought the unilateral action pursued by the Soviets in Eastern Europe was an unnecessary but logical step for Russia to take. Rather than viewing the Russian situation as one of aggression, he maintained that it was in the form of a defensive maneuver aimed at thwarting a German revival. Austin's lack of analysis showed, however, when he went on to state that it was a natural step for Russia because the United States was shirking its worldwide responsibility and was retreating toward isolationism. Consequently, the Senator said, Americans should not totally criticize Russia. Instead, Austin suggested, the United States must maintain a position of strength to support the new United Nations organization. In that way, he believed the Soviet Union and any other security-conscious nation could develop faith in both the United States and the United Nations.[3]

Two weeks later Austin took a stronger line against the Soviet Union. He admitted to a Vermont audience that Russia had not cooperated and was pursuing an unwise pattern of action "quite similar to that of Hitler." After listing events of intransigence on the Soviets' part, Austin proposed a policy for the United States which took into consideration "the situation in the light most favorable to Russia." He again stressed his simplistic assumption that Soviet policy in Eastern Europe was primarily due to the lack of faith in American promises. "Should we not," Austin asked, "promptly give evidence of our capacity to support the United Nations effectively, to successfully occupy and pacify our portion of Germany and Japan, to garrison island bases, and to maintain general security of the United States pending successful establishment and operation of the United Nations?"

Austin also saw American possession of the atomic bomb as vital to backing this policy of internationalism. He expanded on this theme the following day in addressing the Middlebury College Cultural Conference when he declared that American military preparedness was not meant for the destruction of the Soviet Union. "In the warfare of nerves now in progress," Austin said, "we have the choice between appeasement of Russia and neutralization of Russia's fear." He thought the former was unrealistic but accomplishment of the latter was possible through possession of the atomic secret until the United Nations could establish effective international safeguards. That, in turn, would give Russia faith in the world organization.[4]

Soviet-American relations continued to occupy much of Austin's thinking. A few days after his Vermont speeches he wrote in a draft radio message that only a nation with "effective military power" could make headway in "negotiations with Russia for peace and for a strong U.N.O." Concerning the atomic secret, Austin contended that to give it up "would mean appeasement at the cost of U.N.O. development." He did not use this line in the actual radio discussion. Instead he drew an analogy between the United States and the Soviet Union. Both countries, he said, had their internationalists and their isolationists. He saw Russia as "working both sides of the street — supporting a collective security program through the United Nations, but hedging against the possibility of its failure by trying to consolidate her position in every country" on her borders.[5]

Austin's view of Russian conduct as defensive and security-conscious in nature was certainly an oversimplification. He lacked the analytical framework within which to place Soviet motives. While he viewed American power as a direct countermeasure to the Russians, he saw it more as a means to tell the world that America was ready to assume its responsibilities through the United Nations. Once that organization asserted its authority, the Soviets could see there was nothing to fear from the West.

The first nine months of Austin's United Nations appointment did not change his thinking on Soviet-American relations. He continued his strong support of action through the world group even though the Soviets displayed a recalcitrant attitude. During this same period, Austin's superiors moved toward a tougher public position with the Soviets.

Spurred on by George Kennan's and Presidential Assistant Clark Clifford's analyses of Soviet conduct and foreign policy combined with encounters with Russian officials at the United Nations and at the Foreign Ministers conferences, American leaders in early 1947 believed that the Soviet Union was inevitably hostile toward the United States. Thus, a short intellectual jump provided them with a view of Soviet hostility which resulted not merely from Russian insecurity, but was synonomous with what Arthur Schlesinger, Jr. later described as "the intransigence of Leninist ideology, the sinister dynamics of a totalitarian society and the madness of Stalin" all combining to plot the overthrow of weak areas outside the Soviet orbit.[6]

Government leaders perceived that up to that time, American power had not been utilized successfully. Somehow the United States must employ its strength to bring more favorable conditions in the world. The Greek-Turkish aid crisis, precipitated by Britain's memorandum announcement to the State Department on February 21 that it would withdraw its financial and military support from those two countries by March 31, was the catalyst that moved American leaders to action.

Until recently, most accounts give the British departure as the beginning of a turning point in American foreign policy. In fact, however, leaders in the State Department already took this as a foregone conclusion and had moved "to prepare the necessary steps for sending economic and military aid" to Greece. What created a crisis was the British memorandum's announcement of such an early date — March 31 — for the British abandonment. Working within a limited time, the Department immediately formulated a policy that not only incorporated an aid program for both Greece and Turkey, but it also became a basis for other actions the United States saw fit to take in the future to maintain a balance of power in Europe and the Middle East. Frequently quoted Department speechwriter Joseph Jones has made an overstatement that "All . . . were aware that a major turning in American history was taking place." Rather, more appropriately, the government hammered into final form an evolving piecemeal policy of the previous two years, which called upon the total experience of American foreign policy to justify its being. Right or wrong (the question is still debated), the policy incorporated both a sense of mission and the preservation of the balance of power which long were associated with the American national interest. In its use of unilateral rhetoric, however, the policy ran roughshod over those extremes of the American ideological spectrum — isolationism and internationalism.[7]

Administration leaders quickly formed a consensus that any course decided upon required "bold action at the top." They assumed — correctly so — that the nation, including members of Congress, was unaware of the gravity of the situation. Consequently a program was designed by the Marshall-Acheson team and approved by the President. Congressional leaders were informed, and the plan was initiated.[8]

Throughout the next two weeks' planning, no consultation took place with the Department's Office of Special Political

Affairs which handled United Nations matters, or with Austin and his staff. Acheson, never a strong United Nations supporter, later wrote that this "fortunate error" was his. He explained that "since time was so short," the President was not advised to go "through the futility of appeal to an organization in which the Soviet Union would veto action and where in any event help must come from the United States."[9] The Department's major concerns were Congress, from whom appropriations must come, and the public, whose support was needed for any new policy.

Acheson was probably strengthened by the reticence of congressional leaders at a February 27 White House meeting, as well as in a larger gathering there on March 10, which disclosed that the United Nations was not an area of concern. An indication of this was given by at least one key senator — Vandenberg — who considered the question in the interim between those first and second White House meetings. Representative John Bennet had written to him about referring the matter to the United Nations. Vandenberg's reply indicated his lack of confidence in the world body, tempered with an appraisal of how to handle such a bypass. "I think Greece could collapse fifty times before the U.N. itself could ever hope to handle a situation of this nature," he wrote. But he thought it advisable to attach the world body collaterally.[10] However, Vandenberg made no mention of the issue at the March 10 meeting.

Much the same nonchalant attitude developed with regard to possible public reaction to bypassing the United Nations. At a meeting of the State-War-Navy subcommittee on foreign policy information on February 28, practically every aspect of the situation was discussed fully. But a United Nations role was not discussed. A brief comment was made that the Soviet Union might bring before the United Nations the question of United States political influence over Greece. No further discussion took place. That group formed a strong consensus that the upcoming speech by the President should underscore the theme of selling the public the necessity of holding the line in a struggle between Communism and Democracy.[11]

Austin knew little about those preparations. When he was consulted on March 6 about his upcoming Security Council reply to Soviet Representative Andrei Gromyko's remarks on atomic energy, he became aware that Truman was to give a strong public statement on Greece. But neither he nor his staff were consulted or briefed on how any contemplated action might affect the American role at the United Nations. The implication is clear as to where the United Nations group stood in the eyes of Department planners. More remarkable, however, is the fact that Austin never inquired further about the content of the President's upcoming statement. Perhaps the Senator was too busy with his pressing Security Council work, but probably he was so isolated from the Department's decision-making channels that a clear indication of what was happening was never hinted strongly enough to arouse his curiosity. Under either circumstance, Trygve Lie, Secretary General of the United Nations, corroborated the fact that Austin was neither consulted nor informed in advance. Consequently, Austin routinely received his first complete statement on the new policy on March 11, the day before the President delivered it to Congress. The covering letter from Acheson accompanying the final draft copy of the address merely stated that Truman would deliver the speech the following day.[12]

Austin penciled some interesting observations in the margins of the speech. He was concerned, and justifiably so, with the paragraph about the United Nations. Acheson later described Truman's United Nations reference as "minimal obeisance." The speech noted that the United States must supply Greece with assistance and while the United States government was considering how the United Nations might assist in the crisis, the situation was urgent and required immediate action. According to the text, the United Nations was not "in a position to extend help of the kind that is required." Austin's marginal note read, "This is *not* the right answer. We need better ones. U.N. is *already* assisting through border commission. This is a supplemental stick to strengthen *U.N.*"[13] In Austin's mind, this was a policy conflict, for his government was pursuing unilateral action in bypassing the United Nations. The world organization had a team in the field investigating the Greek situation as Austin noted. Although not specifically stating it, Austin broadly hinted that the logical procedure to follow would be to wait for this report and its recommendations. Then if the recommendations showed it necessary, the United States could deliver aid to Greece. In this way a doubled-barreled policy would result because it would also strengthen the position of the United Nations.

The President's summary paragraph opened with the statement, "This is a serious course upon which we embark." Austin cynically noted in the margin: "Wrong word — we embarked on collective security when we became a member of U.N." At first glance, it appears that Austin questioned Truman's semantics, but careful study of the document reveals more. Coupled with his earlier observation, this notation leads to the conclusion that Austin did not see the speech as a dramatic shift in United States policy. Or at least, if he did, he did not want to believe it as such for to do that would shatter his own faith in the organization. Rather, he saw aid to Greece and Turkey and the whole concept of the Truman Doctrine as another step toward collective security. He accepted the general lines of the administration's course of action: continued symbolic support of the United Nations backed by a unilateral containment policy.

The administration sensed immediately that it had blundered in not considering the public reaction to its lack of concern about the possible role played by the United Nations in the situation. Acheson and the Senate Foreign Relations Committee, meeting the next day for two hours in executive session, discussed the already immediate negative reaction to the U.N. issue and attempted to formulate some way to alleviate the public concern. It marked the beginning of an Acheson-Vandenberg rescue operation in the Congress.[14]

Austin, in the meantime, issued a carefully worded explanation at his New York headquarters. A spokesman announced it was only an interim statement and that the Senator planned later to give a full accounting in the Security Council. The document appeared as Austin's personal article of faith in the United Nations. He reaffirmed his nation's hope in that organization. He thought that American support of Greece and Turkey was essential to the principle of collective security and that it would prove to be a new and effective action. The statement closed by emphasizing the aid as supporting United States policy in the United Nations. In the meantime Austin immediately left for Washington to receive new instructions.[15]

The initial public reaction soon became a floodtide. The Gallup Poll reported that two out of three persons interviewed thought the United Nations should handle the Greece-Turkey problem, but at the same time a majority of those held reasons for not doing so. All who opposed the policy agreed that it bypassed the United Nations. Trygve Lie later commented that the United States, already committed to the principle that the United Nations was a "cornerstone of its foreign policy," should have at least announced to the Security Council its intention of undertaking such a program.[16]

Commentators deplored the action without notification of the world body. Walter Lippmann, for example, advocated some action which would "rehabilitate the moral authority of the United Nations and would reaffirm our loyalty as a member of the organization." Four days later he wrote that if Acheson had the time to inform Congress, "there is time for Mr. Austin to inform the United Nations." Anne O'Hare McCormick viewed as absurd the charge that the Truman Doctrine bypassed the United Nations, but she thought that the United States could bolster the world group by wisely using the reports of the United Nations commissioners who were studying conditions in Greece. She advocated that the United States should include United Nations observers in the mission America proposed to send to Greece and Turkey. She thought that the United States had an obligation to act as a member of the international body until the time came when the United Nations could function by itself. In his syndicated column, Marquis Childs recommended working through the United Nations Food and Agriculture Organization which recently issued its own report on the rehabilitation of Greece. In that way, Childs asserted, the United States "would make plain that our action in Greece was not a personal and private adventure."[17]

Support was forthcoming in Congress, but not before questions were raised about the United Nations. Representative Thomas L. Owens of Illinois told reporters that the United Nations died as a result of United States unilateral action. Virginia's Senator Harry F. Byrd asked where the next American intervention would come if the United Nations was bypassed this time. He cautioned that unilateral movements would destroy the United Nations. Senator Carl Hatch of New Mexico said he would support the new program, but deplored the trend toward balance-of-power settlements through bilateral and multilateral treaties. A strong United Nations supporter, Florida's Senator Claude Pepper urged handling of the case in the United Nations with United States financial aid extended to Greece and Turkey until the world organization was able to function fully.[18]

Republican Foreign Relations Committee chairman Arthur Vandenberg rescued the issue in the Senate. In private notes he stated that the administration made a colossal blunder in ignoring the United Nations. He himself, of course, had passed off this concern earlier when the policy was in the planning stage. Now much to the delight of Acheson, Vandenberg zeroed in with what was by a now a familiar pattern: direct public attention to the issue; make a great deal of it; then propose a solution through amendment, with, of course, the Vandenberg name attached to it.[19]

Vandenberg opened his strategy by compiling questions gathered from the legislators which were forwarded to the State Department where they were answered and later published. While some of the questions submitted were direct and pointed, the answers often were an exercise in verbal gymnastics.[20]

In the House and Senate hearings on the aid bill, Acheson, substituting for Secretary Marshall who was in Moscow attending a conference of Foreign Ministers, presented the administration's attitude that the United Nations was not, at that time, in a position to render aid to Greece and Turkey. He stated that, even if Soviet bloc opposition was not present in the United Nations, debate and action on the situation would have taken too much time. And in this case, time was the important factor. Acheson stated the realities the nation must face. He said, "it would be a tragedy, and a travesty

upon logic, if an overestimate of the immediate powers of the
United Nations should succeed in preventing this country"
from using its power to establish economic and political
stability. In later questioning, Acheson was asked if it would
not have been wiser to announce the policy through Senator
Austin. The acting Secretary brushed this aside as a matter
of opinion but conceded it was one way to proceed.[21]

Austin, meanwhile, had to defend his nation's policy
against expected charges from the Soviets and their allies.
But perhaps even more important, what he said in the
Security Council would, it was hoped, convince Americans
that their leaders were not abandoning the United Nations.
He had asked for time on the Security Council's agenda for
March 28. Prior to that he met with Acheson, Secretary of
War Robert Patterson, Secretary of the Navy James Forres-
tal and the President to discuss his position. The task
assigned him was similar to Vandenberg's. According to
Acheson, Vandenberg's amendments — "window dressing
that must have seemed either silly or cynical or both in
London, Paris and Moscow" — greatly pleased Austin.[22]
Certainly they complemented the position planned for him
in the Security Council. There Austin was to relate the
United States' aid program to the principles of the Charter
and reconcile it with the work of the Security Council
through its Commission of Investigation.

Austin opened his remarks on March 28 by stating that the
belief of his government was that "the whole world should be
fully informed of the acts, motives and purposes of the
United States." So in accordance with the Charter, the
United States would register all agreements made with
Greece and Turkey. He emphasized that there would be no
secret treaties.

He moved quickly to his main theme that the action of
America meant "to strengthen the United Nations and to
advance the building of collective security under the United
Nations." Like the Security Council's Committee of Investigation in Greece, Truman Doctrine aid was directed toward
the same end. He said the disruptions by armed bands in that
country created economic chaos. American aid would
sustain Greece while that nation stopped those intruders.

But he also insisted it was a responsibility of the United Nations to take further action to stop the aggression.

The Senator's next point was one he had enunciated previously and would continue to pursue. Undoubtedly, he was convinced more than American leaders that the United Nations one day would assume the responsibilities for assistance to nations such as Greece. But he emphasized to his Council colleagues that the organization had not yet matured to that stage. Consequently, America temporarily shouldered the burden. Austin regarded it as an emergency action. He argued that since America was one of the most powerful nations in the world, it must assume a great share of responsibility for events in the world even though it appeared to usurp some of the power of the United Nations. But in reality, Austin said, the United States supported the basic principles of the United Nations. And when the United Nations was ready to take on the task of providing financial support and aid, America willingly would relinquish the obligation.

With the Soviets obviously in mind, Austin stated that the United States did not intend to "dominate, intimidate, or threaten the security of any nation, large or small." Rather, his country respected the right of any nation to follow whatever way of life or system of government it chose, insofar as it did not interfere with the same right of other countries.[23] So in a more subtle manner than that employed by President Truman, Austin restated the ideological challenge of the Truman Doctrine for his international audience.

This official announcement of the Truman Doctrine in the Security Council attempted to appease the many who said the United States had bypassed the United Nations. The favorable reaction to his remarks that Austin received particularly pleased him in view of the fact that he had asserted in the Council that the United Nations should complement the American program.[24] He apparently feared that his speech may have too strongly challenged the United Nations.

What is revealing about Austin's position is his unwavering support for unilateral American policy in light of his known commitment to multilateral cooperation through internationalism. Nonetheless, his conduct appears logical, for what alternatives were open to him? After-the-fact protest through normal channels would have amounted to little. The possibility of resignation appeared at first as an effective alternative as far as emphasizing his discontent with the bypass issue, but it would have eliminated him from any future attempt to build something solid from the fledgling world organization. He always considered that a long time was needed to adjust to postwar difficulties. So Austin now presented this belief as the reason the United Nations could not react quickly to situations like that in Greece. He faced reality squarely: the organization was not at a stage of development to handle such a crisis. He had seen fissures develop in his postwar ideal of unanimity and negotiated settlements of world problems, yet he still refused to abandon that ideal. But in order to work with the realities of the present, he sought solace in another pattern of thought flexible enough to remain consistent with the times: he accepted a postulate of evolutionary growth for the United Nations. Under its guise, he could adequately defend any United States unilateral action just as he had done in the matter of aid to Greece and Turkey. At the same time he could rationally continue to trust that the United Nations, at some future date, would stand on its own. Determined and confident, Austin continued to believe in the United Nations' principles and optimistically anticipated their future employment throughout the world. The Truman administration could not have found a better spokesman for the American view of the United Nations' task.

Vandenberg pursued much the same philosophy in the Senate. On March 31, he introduced another amendment to the aid bill which included a provision that the President would withdraw the aid if the General Assembly or the Security Council found that action by the United Nations made the aid "unnecessary or undesirable." *Time* correspondent Frank McNaughton reported that Vandenberg proposed this amendment because he wanted to "submit the morality of our position to the judgment of an international jury." Vandenberg had told McNaughton that the amendment's adoption "will automatically force all fair-minded men in every nation to compare our willingness to abide by a majority decision with that of the Soviet Union which has ten times used the veto to frustrate the will of the majority."[25] This was a tougher line than Austin preferred, but the moral aspect meshed well with his philosophy. The amendment also provided Austin with more verbal ammunition to beat back any Soviet charge at the United Nations.

Austin clung to his optimistic beliefs while working for a government managed by extremely skeptical leaders. For example, Austin was a member of the administration's Executive Committee on Disarmament, owing to his position on the United Nations Atomic Energy Committee (he replaced Bernard Baruch in January 1947). Other members included Austin's deputy on the Atomic Energy Committee, Frederick Osborn, the Chairman of the United States Atomic Energy Commission David Lilienthal, Acting Secretary of State Acheson, Navy Secretary Forrestal and Secretary of War Patterson. In a meeting on April 3, Austin impressed Lilienthal with a remark that it was harmful to accept an attitude of defeatism as to whether the Soviets would agree to United States proposals on atomic energy. Austin thought it wrong to discredit the Russians because they would not agree. Rather, he advised the group toward an approach of optimism and hope. "It is a mistake to take the position," Austin said, "'Here it is; take it or leave it.'" Lilienthal considered himself very unlike Austin as he was skeptical about Soviet motives. Yet in the gloom generated by a lack of evidence for agreement in the predictable future, Austin drew responsive, almost sympathetic, applause from Lilienthal. The following day the AEC Chairman noted in his journal: "This attitude of determined confidence, so obviously sincere and deeply felt, seems to me quite right. The United Nations represents a great step forward, a very great step, he says, and it is our only hope for peace." Skeptic Acheson was never so kind. It was precisely this Austin attitude that caused him to remark contemptuously in January 1947: "Senator Austin terrifies me. 'I can handle the Russians.' God! Famous last works."[26]

Armed with this sanguine attitude concerning the future, Austin was ready to continue to fight for agreement on any issue that arose in the United Nations. But the Greek-Turkey aid bill still was under fire. In the Security Council on April 8, Gromyko attacked the American move with charges that the proposed aid constituted interference in the domestic affairs of those Mediterranean countries, and it was thus inconsistent with the purposes and principles of the United Nations. At the next meeting, Austin refuted the Soviet charges. He contended the bill before the Congress contained built-in safeguards against usurpation of the authority of either of the two countries. As far as consistency with the United Nations was concerned, Austin explained that his nation would register the matter with the world organization in compliance with its regulations. Thus the United Nations would have the opportunity to determine if the United States interfered in the internal affairs of Greece and Turkey.

Austin quickly resorted to his new approach in explaining why the United Nations was not the primary agency employed in the crisis. Claiming the world group did not represent the "infallibility of perfection," Austin said this explained why the United States was obligated to fulfill the requests of the Greek and Turkish governments.[27] These nations could not have turned to the United Nations for quick help and so the United States was the only alternative open to them.

In his earlier denunciation, Gromyko charged that the Truman Doctrine was a cover-up to gain control over smaller nations under the guise of peace and security. Consequently, it threatened international peace and that called for Security Council action. On April 18, Austin replied to that charge with a farfetched argument that nothing of a security nature was involved. He downplayed the Soviet complaint as nothing but an innuendo, certainly not of enough significance to permit the Security Council to take action. He said the whole world could view United States action in behalf of Greece and Turkey and he closed with a jibe at his antagonists: "If it should occur . . . that these funds were being used for a political purpose, we should not need a police force to discover it: the press and the radio of the United States would announce it to the whole world the same day it was discovered."[28]

The next day Austin delivered a speech in Washington at a gathering of the nation's newspaper editors. Again he used the same theme to legitimatize the controversial course on which the United States had embarked. Acheson, who had spoken to the group the day before, favored use of a direct economic course of action over one diplomatically oriented. The Undersecretary explained the reason for this lay in the fact that recent attempts at open diplomatic negotiations — through the United Nations and at Foreign Ministers meetings — had failed. Austin's remarks dovetailed with Acheson's views. The Senator charged that too many people regarded the United Nations as a ready-made ultimate solution for postwar problems. Instead, he wished people would view it as "the first in a long campaign to establish permanent peace by building a system of collective security." Ironically, Austin described as idealists those who claimed that the United States should turn its new aid program over to the United Nations.[29]

Reaching back into the recent history of the United Nations, Austin used the example of the postwar peace settlement to make his point. Authority to negotiate the peace treaties intentionally was not given to the United Nations. Austin emphasized it as a good example of not saddling the organization with the immediate task of settling terms of peace treaties, but rather giving it time to develop and prepare itself to assume responsibility following the peace settlements. Austin noted that because those treaties were not concluded many related problems continued to affect United Nations development and so its growth was not as rapid as some advocates had hoped.

Similarly, the specialized agencies of the Economic and Social Council were still in formative stages. Austin spoke of advisory groups that were functioning in the fields of labor, agriculture and civil aviation. But they could not adequately carry out a major aid program, he contended. Also not ready to operate were organizations such as the International Bank for Reconstruction and Development and the International Monetary Fund. Because of their state of evolutionary growth, economic aid and reconstruction of the still war-devasted areas of Europe was not possible through those agencies. But Austin was not annoyed with the United Nations; rather he espoused a positive major theme — the developmental process of the world body. This view dovetailed with the government approach, countering the charge that the United Nations was being bypassed.

In characteristically zealous and missionary terms, Austin argued that the United States pursued this course of action because it was a rich and powerful country cognizant of its responsibility to both the United Nations and the world. The nation marshalled all its resources in full support of the Charter and toward the goal of collective security. While aid to Greece and Turkey demonstrated that responsibility, Austin suggested that in the future the United States might find it necessary to aid other nations.[30] The Senator was not privy to the initial work then taking place on the larger plan of aid to Europe. However, he was aware of the serious economic conditions facing that continent through his frequent contacts with Western European representatives at the United Nations.

In January and February 1947, public and official reports from Europe convinced many United States officials and commentators of the need for American aid. General discussion in the country was widespread. Columnists Anne O'Hare McCormick, Hanson Baldwin, Walter Lippmann and James Reston all favored American leadership and responsibility in the situation. In its winter program, the Council of Foreign Relations emphasized the need for European reconstruction. In early 1947, the Congress considered and later passed an administration-proposed emergency appropriation of $350,000,000 for Austria, Greece, Italy, Hungary, Poland and China that underscored the continued need for long-term planning in foreign aid. In Europe, pro-Western governments in Italy and France were fending off strong communist political organizations that gained much support from the economic chaos. Germany was producing twenty-five per cent of its food, a drop from eighty-five per cent in 1936. Both occupied and unoccupied Eastern European nations were in difficulty.

In the United Nations, the Economic and Social Council still was attempting to undertake programs essential to the creation of conditions of stability and well-being throughout the world. Progress was made, but not quickly enough to grapple effectively with Europe's economic chaos. The

General Assembly had recommended in December 1946 the establishment of two regional economic commissions — one for Europe and one for Asia — and at its March 1947 session the Economic and Social Council established the Economic Commission for Europe. The commission had no executive powers, but it could make recommendations to member governments of the United Nations.[31] Willard L. Thorp, an experienced State Department economic advisor, was the United States Representative on the Economic and Social Council, and William L. Clayton represented America on the Economic Commission for Europe.

Although Austin was not directly involved with the problems of the Council and the Commission, he was naturally concerned with their development. He often had stated that the specialized agencies were an important part of the long-range development plan of the United Nations. Now, as other top American officials were delivering talks on the role of the United States in the world economic situation, Austin also took the stump to speak to an important business group, the United States Associates of the International Chamber of Commerce, to explain the role of the United Nations in international economics.[32] It highlighted his evolving attitude about the United Nations and its place in American foreign policy.

Austin's talk cited what he termed misconceptions of many Americans. Most citizens, the Senator said, favored rejection of political isolationism but "still cling to economic isolation." He thought much of this was due to an emphasis on political order and security. But he wanted to underscore "constructive measures of cooperative economic action." Because the United States was the only nation in a position to lead the way, it must "pull its own weight." Although the United States supported the United Nations, it could not rely totally on the organization's infant international economic branches. While there were those who saw this as bypassing the United Nations, Austin would not subscribe to the theory. The important objective was to guarantee that agreements concluded always coincided with principles of the Charter. He went on to define a nation that bypassed the United Nations as one which opposed those principles.

Austin saw no reason for fearing a recurring depression if
the American business community and the government
invested sufficiently and wisely in development abroad. He
cited the many needs of the world as offering America a
constant market for its rich productivity — as long as
leadership and action was provided to ensure those markets.
Immediately, he saw three areas in which the United States
must play a leading role — emergency relief, investment in
the reconstruction of war-devastated industrial nations as
well as underdeveloped countries, and the creation of trading
conditions to meet an expanded American productivity.
Because of its resources the United States must act primarily
and initially in the first two of these areas. The United
Nations, Austin emphasized, was doing its part in the third
area through the creation of such agencies as the Economic
Commission for Europe and the Food and Agriculture
Organization. In each instance, however, whether it be a
unilateral or multilateral action, Austin emphasized that it
would not bypass the United Nations as long as the
approach conformed to the Charter.[33] While this theme could
be viewed as window dressing and a rationalization for
American action, it also expressed a subtle continued faith in
the United Nations. And considering the thrust of this
economic speech, the Marshall Plan announcement came as
no surprise to Austin.

The Senator was scheduled to make several commencement appearances at New England schools in June. Much
time was spent on planning the themes of any speeches he
would deliver. At one preparatory conference at the State
Department on the development of foreign policy, he noted
widespread concern regarding United States participation
in the United Nations. Earlier, staff member Chester
Williams had suggested that Austin utilize his position as
chief delegate as well as his strong belief in the United
Nations to point up the American commitment to the United
Nations. Williams wrote, "your personal conviction on what
it takes to make a success of the U.N." would make any
speech effective. This idea, incorporated in his June
speeches, meshed nicely — albeit coincidentally — with the
content of Secretary Marshall's Harvard speech. At the

Massachusetts Institute of Technology and in two addresses at Bates College and at the University of Vermont, Austin emphasized his continued faith in the United Nations. At MIT he stressed, "We should never permit ourselves to be driven into inaction or despair by apparent stalemates." America, he said, possessed decisive power to create the conditions for a permanent peace through collective security.[34]

Austin conceded that the United Nations had problems, but considering the scope of the objectives people sought from the organization, he thought it had made progress. After all, he argued, it was still in its formative stage. And while it was necessary to continue support of the United Nations, the United States must utilize other channels to preserve peace and uphold the principles of the United Nations. Thus the United Nations would gain the time needed to develop into a functioning institution.[35]

In those pessimistic months of mid-1947, Austin appeared unrealistic in delivering such optimistic statements. Never losing faith in the goal of the United Nations, he viewed the policy of the United States as a supporting function of the United Nations rather than as a direct, primary approach to the balance of power in Europe. And in sticking with this outlook, he remained within a minority in the State Department. Nonetheless, his personal enthusiasm remained at a high level even while American policy shifted toward the publicly elaborated containment thesis. But with his optimism, Austin reconciled that approach in his own mind and still believed in the United Nations as a primary instrument in the conduct of American diplomacy.

Truman's March 12 speech to the Congress that emphasized an ideological division between the United States and the Soviet Union also clouded the connection between the Truman Doctrine and the later Marshall Plan proposal. Truman's stress on ideological differences was missing in the Marshall speech and his lack of continuity caused widespread questioning about the exact policy of the government. Did the Marshall Plan mean that the government abandoned the Truman Doctrine? Policy Planning Staff director George Kennan's anonymous article, "The

Sources of Soviet Conduct," in the July issue of *Foreign Affairs* somewhat cleared the air by placing United States foreign policy in the context of a schematic, historical Soviet framework. But it also raised again questions relative to emphasis on incompatible ideologies and the effect they would have on continuing relations between the United States and the Soviet Union.[36]

An examination of Austin's attitude toward the Soviet Union through a study of his reading of Kennan's article is quite revealing in the light of the gloomy prognostication of future relations between the two nations. Out of it is provided a basis for his continuing optimism. Remember that Austin had made no marginal comments on the key phrase in Truman's March 12 speech which declared the "policy of the United States to support free peoples who are resisting attempted subjugation by armed minorities or by outside pressures." Undoubtedly at that time, he was more concerned with what Truman said about the role of the United Nations. But his lack of notation adds confirmation to his own later deemphasis on ideological differences.

Lack of agreement on fundamental issues such as use of the veto, disarmament and control of atomic energy had not diminished Austin's faith in the United Nations. In his April talk to the newspaper editors, he declared that the Soviet Union was "ideologically the same today as it was during the war" and that differences between the two countries "were as wide then as they are today." Recognition of this fact did not change his belief that there could be agreement. He thought that as long as the United Nations existed it provided a forum which could contain and conciliate the disagreements and rivalries of the two powers. He saw only one alternative if that forum failed: two or more rival camps, possibly setting a course of war.[37] Austin recognized that frank discussion would not necessarily mean a reconciliation of the ideological division, but it allowed both sides to air their views and gain different perspectives on problems. It was hoped that it would also define the outstanding issues and result in greater efforts by all sides to seek remedies. Naturally, he believed that remedies were possible.

In May, he inserted a section into his speech to the International Chamber of Commerce group that again portrayed his optimism. He cautioned Americans to free themselves from the fear of "differing economic ideologies." All systems and ideologies must stand the "practical test of meeting conditions." It made no difference whether they were "capitalistic, socialistic or communistic," Austin contended; because they were man-made they were subject to change. Austin thought the hope of the world lay in patience and understanding — "using our strength on the side of reconstruction and development, cooperating in the United Nations with men of all faiths and ideologies."[38]

Austin was spending some leisure time in Burlington when he received from his aide John Ross a copy of the July *Foreign Affairs* magazine with Kennan's "X" article clipped in it. Ross's covering letter highly recommended to Austin that he read the article and noted that it had "been rumored in the press that "X" is George Kennan." In later reading the piece, Austin had his own insight in regard to the author as he penciled in the word "Kennedy?" — a reference to Joseph P. — beside the article's by-line.[39] This notation is evidence that Austin knew nothing of the February 1946 "long telegram" Kennan sent to the State Department even though it had received wide circulation. The *Foreign Affairs* article embodied that document. Moreover, the notation is another indication of Austin's position within the mainstream of the Department's policy planning channels. When one couples this article with the lack of consultation on the Greek-Turkish issue, it provides further evidence of the framework within which Department leaders considered the United Nations.

While it is difficult to assess the article's effect on Austin's idealism, it is interesting to note the points he emphasized. The essay apparently received thorough study because many parts were underlined. No notations appear, however, with the exception of Austin's surmise regarding the author's identity.

The Kennan article's stress on the insecurity of Stalin and his cohorts within the sphere of power they coveted impressed Austin. He underscored Kennan's point that Soviet insecurity was created by the impact of the Russian-Asiatic world and caused Russian skepticism toward the "permanent and peaceful coexistence of rival forces." On the following page, Austin also noted how Kennan continued to speak of Stalin's desire for security without consideration for the comforts and happiness of his own people.

Back in 1946, Austin had stated that the security factor that ruled Soviet reasoning explained why this Eurasian nation pursued a unilateral policy in Eastern Europe. At that time the Senator said that Russia was extremely security-conscious because the United States failed to maintain its responsible position in the world. It appears Austin sought further support for this thesis in the Kennan article. He did not, however, underline any parts of the Kennan analysis of the Soviets' hostility toward the outside world. Probably he realized it would undermine his own simplified view, for Kennan stated that Soviet policy was based not on objective analysis of the outside world but on the compulsions of internal politics.

In writing answers to a United Press questionaire a few months later, Austin touched again on the source of current Soviet conduct. He stuck to his primary analysis that Russia was security-conscious. He wrote that the Soviets would not recognize any program of collective security becoming sufficiently effective to guarantee protection for their country. Consequently they established a fifth-column movement to create buffer states; they maintained the military spirit of the Russian people and the skill of the Soviet armed forces as a principal part of their national program. But Austin did not see in this an ideology directed against capitalist nations. In his view the East-West division was not widening because of ideology; that division was always there. The emphasis was merely more pronounced. Rather he continued to see Soviet action as defensive measures because of the failure of the world to establish adequate collective security. To Austin, Soviet actions indicated a return to reliance on national sovereignty, but since the cleavage was due to mistrust rather than ideology, he saw hope for a *modus vivendi*. Once the United States convinced the Soviets it sought only peace, the breach would narrow. In a year-end report on the accomplishments of the United Nations, Austin concluded that the United States and the Soviet Union were not "hopelessly divided." He wrote that as the "Soviet Union perceives that collective security is as valuable, or more valuable, to her than national security alone, she will begin to collaborate more fully."[40]

Returning to the reading of the Kennan article, Austin stressed the author's paragraph outlining the containment policy the United States was following. This fit Austin's own analysis as it emphasized his ability to take what he wanted from the policy to fit his own conceptions of what his government was doing. He realized there was no short route to peace and security in the world and that a long evolutionary course was the only possibility. Although he saw the United Nations as the means to that end, he was able to accept unilateral action by the United States as a temporary means to support the principles of the United Nations while the world body strengthened itself. Eventually, he believed, the United Nations would fulfill totally its obligations.

Austin also noted Kennan's summary. The fact that America could not expect to see a close relationship develop with the Soviet Union was reason enough for the policy of containment. Likewise, he recognized that American policy should not merely maintain the status quo. Kennan's statement helped convince Austin that the United States had a responsibility to show the world that it recognized its goals, could cope successfully with both its domestic problems and the responsibilities placed upon it as a world leader, and could compete with other ideologies on its own merits.

Meanwhile, the United States Mission staff sought assurance against its anxiety that the Marshall Plan might be interpreted as bypassing the United Nations. Austin aide John Ross searched for the extent of this attitude in conversations with several people. Byron Price, an Assistant Secretary-General of the United Nations, related not only his own concern over the American plan but also that of Trygve Lie. James Shotwell of the Carnegie Institute, a leader in the important American Association of the United Nations, hoped that the development of the Marshall Plan would not lose sight of the work of the United Nations' European Economic Commission. He told Ross that he was aware that the Soviets could delay action through a United Nations group; however, he thought that the United States should work "directly to the extent necessary, but to do so within the orbit of the United Nations." Nonetheless, Shotwell saw no evidence that fear of bypassing the United Nations was a top issue. Clark Eichelberger, director of the Association, told Ross that there was strong feeling at least within the membership, that the United States had deemphasized the United Nations by utilizing a unilateral approach through the Marshall Plan.[41]

To alleviate these concerns, Austin was a chief public spokesman for the plan to legitimatize American action within the context of the evolutionary growth of the United Nations. His statements underlined the world organization as a means to the end rather than the actual end. He claimed that those who persisted in the bypassing argument did not really understand how the organization worked. He stated that the United Nations need not involve itself in everything in order to secure peace in the world and as long as the United States adhered to the principles of the Charter, it helped secure the objectives of the organization. Austin stressed that a nation which really bypassed the United Nations was one that used its strength against rather than for the principles of the Charter.[42]

The American public did not charge the Marshall Plan with bypassing the United Nations to the extent it had at the announcement of the Truman Doctrine. Most informed citizens recognized that the Soviets would nullify any action through the United Nations and so an American unilateral course was necessary. Nonetheless, while the administration focused on convincing the Republican Congress of the need for such a plan, it also was concerned with American public opinion vis-à-vis the United Nations. The Truman Doctrine bypassing issue was too recent to forget. The administration's tactics were to keep Austin informed of Marshall Plan progress and to publicize this action so that Americans were aware that consultation was taking place with the nation's United Nations representative. Obviously, the leaders were not concerned with Austin's position; they were concerned with positive public opinion.[43]

Charges from the Soviets were not immediate. The Soviet Union participated in the exploratory European meetings of Paris summoned by Britain's Ernest Bevin in late June to work out a European initiative called for by Secretary Marshall. After five divisive sessions, Molotov, on orders from Moscow, abruptly departed. Russia feared subordination to the West under the Marshall Plan and felt it had no choice but to leave the conference. It signaled a clear East-West European division and placed the responsibility for the split on the Soviet Union. Likewise, the walkout doomed any hope for constructive work coming from the United Nations' Economic Commission for Europe.[44]

Soviet attacks on the Marshall Plan came at the Second General Assembly session in the fall of 1947 under the guise of an overall charge by the Soviet Union of use of war propaganda by the United States and its allies. Andrei Vishinski led this verbal onslaught. He said the United States wanted war and used the United Nations for its own purposes rather than for worldwide interests. When the United States failed there, it resorted to such unilateral measures as aid to Greece and Turkey and the proposed Marshall Plan. The Soviets attempted to gain world sympathy for their minority position through this resolution directed against war propaganda. The measure raised tensions considerably at the United Nations, but the Soviet effort failed as the United States continued to muster the needed votes for its position. The Soviets salvaged something of their original resolution but it came out of the session considerably weakened in tone owing principally to United States maneuvering. With Austin leading the debate, the United States sought total defeat of the original Soviet resolution.[45]

The intransigence and inflammatory outburst by the Soviets at that fall General Assembly played into the hands of administration planners, who still had to gain Congressional approval for the European Recovery Program. For by the time Senate hearings on the Marshall Plan opened in January 1948, the lack of a United Nations role, which had earlier concerned the administration, was no longer a consideration. Soviet intransigence at the United Nations eliminated that.[46]

Public reaction concerning the role of the United Nations in giving aid to Europe evoked such little anxiety among the policymakers by the time the hearings opened that no one from the United Nations section was even scheduled to give testimony. The planners could easily have arranged for Austin or some lesser American United Nations official to testify in support of the compatibility of the Marshall Plan with United Nations principles. The few questions which were raised in the course of the hearings were quickly answered by sympathetic Marshall Plan witnesses.[47] This indicated not only the framework of futility within which American leaders viewed the United Nations; it also provided evidence of a growing disillusionment on the part of the American public with the effectiveness of the United Nations in the conduct of major United States foreign policy.

The wartime ideal about postwar nations living peacefully together, protected by a powerful United Nations organization, was almost completely shattered after two years of frustrations. Quite early, there were many in the government who realistically had seen the schism develop and who advocated departure from the liberal-internationalist tradition espoused by Austin. When the smoldering Greek situation was thrust upon the United States by a financially-racked Britain, the time to act was evident. President Truman's decision to shoulder the burden of Greece and Turkey and to state the Government's containment policy brought a dilemma to Austin. Deeply committed to the principles of collective security and cooperation among nations, he viewed this unilateral policy as a threat to his beliefs on the conduct of foreign affairs. Yet he realized the new approach was necessary.

So Austin accepted the policy as a short-term, emergency measure designed to substitute for the United Nations until that body could develop through an evolutionary process into a vigorous organization. He reasoned that the American policy supported the United Nations. By accepting the containment thesis in that context, he continued his support of both the policy of his nation and the idealistic principles embodied in the United Nations. He regarded the United Nations' evolutionary process as a means to reconcile his ideals with the realities of the day. Thus, he maintained his liberal-international approach, though it was tainted by the distastefulness of the world situation. Because of this innocent simplicity, Austin remained confident that his belief in a moral and righteous philosophy eventually would become established in international affairs.

CHAPTER FOUR

THE CONVERSION YEARS: 1947-50

Important transition years for Austin were sand-wiched between the initial implementation of the official containment policy in 1947 and the outbreak of the Korean crisis in 1950. While he did not totally lose faith in his internationalist concept, the world situation prevented him from seeing his goals realized. Such highlights of the deepening Cold War as the Palestine question, the commun-ist takeover in Czechoslovakia, the Berlin blockade, NATO, and the General Assembly "Essentials of Peace" resolution subtly converted Austin to the hard-line tactics of the Truman administration

Various present day United Nations attempts to solve the Near Eastern question on Palestine have brought frustra-tions similar to those stemming from the same baffling issue that rooted itself in the United Nations in 1947-48. Austin was an active participant in those events as they developed within the larger context of Soviet-American confrontation.[1]

The Palestine question dated back to the time when Britain wrested the area from the Turks in World War I. As the major power in the Near East, Britain was selected as mandatary for Palestine by the League of Nations. The League designated it a "class A" mandate, meaning that Palestine was to gain independence within a short period of time. The Balfour Declaration was closely tied to the mandate. It stated that Britain viewed with favor "the establishment in Palestine of a National Home for the Jewish people." As the Jewish numbers immigrating to Palestine swelled, the leaders of the Palestine Arabs began to fear that the Arab majority's hold on political power in the area would be weakened. This, combined with strong outpourings of Arab nationalism and of Zionism, brought violence to Palestine on several occasions throughout the interwar years.[2]

The strategic importance of Near Eastern oil determined British policy. Because the Arab nations comprised a potentially hostile network of Near Eastern states, Britain curtailed its attempts to resolve the Palestinian problem. In 1939 a British white paper underscored the long-range importance of the oil fields and lines of communication in the Arab Near East. Representing nearly the complete victory the Arabs aspired to in Palestine, the white paper recommended strict limits on, and eventual ending of, Jewish immigration, prohibited or restricted transfer of land from Arabs to Jews and declared that Britain's mandate would cease in ten years.[3]

Britain's policies and the outbreak of World War II further stimulated both Arab nationalism and Zionism. Nazi attempts to destroy the European Jews intensified demands to increase the number of Jews immigrating to Palestine. In 1942 the World Zionist Organization called for a Jewish state and for unrestricted immigration. Later, in 1945, six Arab states organized the Arab League as Britain had encouraged them to do. Pan-Arabist countries, while splintered by many factions, could at least agree on their hostility toward Zionism. Throughout all of this, violence continued sporadically in Palestine and by the end of the world war, the Arab League and the world Zionist movement were ready to demand from Britain an account of its mandate.

While British power and influence in the Near East reached a peak during the war years, it deteriorated rapidly thereafter. Emerging from the conflict victorious but war-weary, and struggling with overwhelming financial problems, Britain was forced into a policy of retrenchment abroad.[4] With no clear solution to the Palestine quandry evident, Britain decided to turn the matter over to the United Nations. Before doing so, however, it made one last attempt to resolve the problem jointly with the United States.

American attitudes and policy toward the Near East and Palestine varied during the late years of the war. Knowledge of German atrocities against the Jews became widespread early in 1943. Zionists effectively appealed to the humanitarian instincts of the American people concerning the plight of the Jews and won consideration of Palestine as a Jewish haven. Both political parties, for example, included planks in their 1944 platforms calling for unrestricted Jewish immigration to Palestine as well as for establishment of a Jewish state there. Public sympathy toward settling the Palestine problem in favor of the Jews grew stronger in 1945 and 1946.[5]

The State Department held a less humanitarian view of Palestine's importance. The larger context of the strategic, political and economic importance of the Near East determined its Palestine policy. State Department planners saw any overt favoritism toward the Zionist cause as detrimental to Arab-American cooperation. They considered Arab goodwill highly important to United States interests. Oil concessions and the strategic military importance of the Near East circumscribed several competing objectives of United States foreign policy. One was to prevent an outbreak of hostilities that could lead to further instability in the area. A second goal was to prevent the region from falling under the control of a power hostile to the United States and its allies. Furthermore, maintenance of air and sea transit routes was deemed a salient objective and to this was tied the continued flow of oil from the Near Eastern fields to Western markets. Although American-owned oil concessions in Arab lands were numerous, maintaining American ownership was given lower priority than continuing the flow of oil. These considerations underscored the Department's insistence on preserving the status quo in Palestine.[6]

As America moved toward publicly committing itself to creating some form of Jewish homeland in Palestine, government officials faced problems in the area, which many of them thought the creation of a Jewish state would only aggravate. Coupled with this was the fact that Britain held ultimate responsibility for the fate of Palestine. It is significant, then, that Britain invited the United States to sit on a committee of inquiry into conditions in Palestine during the fall of 1945. The extending of the invitation symbolized the new importance of the United States as a power in the Near East. American involvement generally increased as British power waned. In addition, acceptance of the invitation indicated that the United States was ready to assume some responsibility toward reaching a solution to the problem of Palestine.

The Anglo-American committee's final report of April 30, 1946, however, cast the issue into doubt. It rejected partition of Palestine into separate Jewish and Arab states and instead suggested federation as a solution, with neither community being dominated by the other. Britain would continue as the mandatary power until the United Nations arranged a trusteeship. During the ensuing year Britain attempted to work out a plan for an independent Jewish-Arab community. Meeting noncooperation from Jewish and Arab groups, she decided to turn the matter over to the United Nations and requested a special session specifically to deal with the question.[7]

Long before the spring of 1947, the State Department anticipated that the Palestine issue would come before the General Assembly and the lack of instructions for the American delegation concerned some State Department officials. Several policies were suggested, ranging from a radical stand favoring creation of a Jewish state to an ambiguous one of marking time.[8] While the question was not raised at the 1946 General Assembly session, the Department's Near Eastern desk continued to work toward a more clearly defined position.

By the end of the year, a loose policy was formed. Independence for Palestine was the ultimate objective, but with the important proviso that the Arabs and Jews must agree to the terms. The United Nations was to negotiate the plan for independence. Since neither the United States nor the United Nations possessed military capability of any size in that area, the Near Eastern desk officers suggested that Britain continue its control of Palestine under United

Nations trusteeship until independence was arranged.[9] The cautious design of this policy gave the United States as much flexibility as possible without further alienating either the Arab or Jewish communities. Since the United States could control events in the General Assembly, the policy would not greatly jeopardize the United States strategic concerns and objectives. With little modification, the United States followed this policy until it was scrapped following the events of May 1948.

Since the 1930s, Austin had maintained an interest in Near East developments. During the war, he had discussed Palestine in the subcommittee of the State Department's Advisory Committee on Problems of Foreign Relations. Austin then found himself in the minority when he advocated a binational state in Palestine. The Senator argued with Sumner Welles, who favored the creation of a Jewish state. Welles connected his plan with agreements and economic developments in surrounding Arab states that would permit the deportation of Arabs from Palestine to those states.[10]

Austin's idea reflected deep study and yet a strange naivete. Interestingly, it had a considerable similarity to the controversial American proposal he later presented to the Security Council in March 1948. In 1942, Austin had wanted the Allies to take over Britain's Palestinian mandate, "so that no selfish motives could interfere with the trusteeship necessary for the inauguration of a government strong enough to maintain itself." He believed the Allies' tutelage would create a strong free government, in which the Palestinians would all have equal opportunity, as Americans do in America." He went on to note that he strongly disagreed with those who claimed the Jews and Arabs would never consent to a binational state. Austin wrote, "I claim that the Jews and Arabs are cousins," and if an example of the maintenance of a free government was shown to them, their fear of each other would dissipate. Referring to his earlier study of the Near East, Austin stated that young Arabs and Jews of intelligence, who would be the future leaders of their people when this issue was decided, convinced him that they had no doubts that they could get along with each other. However, he thought it necessary that a truly neutral third force help build a viable framework. But Austin conceded that few members of the committee agreed with him. This "cousin" solution was broached in secret session. Later, in 1948, while publicly discussing the Arab-Israeli war before the United Nations, Austin showed his continuing simplicity on the subject when he urged the Arabs and Jews to come together and "settle this problem in a true Christian spirit."[11]

These private conversations revealed Austin's concern and that of others in Congress and the State Department over the Near East embroilment. As noted, until late 1947, no overall review of the situation was undertaken nor was a coherent policy developed by the United States. Instead, as the war had ended, public opinion imposed the issue piecemeal on the government. In addition to the party platforms of 1944, showing American sympathy for the plight of the Jews, a congressional resolution was introduced that year favoring creation of a Jewish state. It was stopped only by recommendations from the War Department and the State Department on the ground that Arab reaction might hamper ongoing military operations. Late in 1945, Austin was a member of the subcommittee of the Foreign Relations Committee that drafted a composite resolution offering the good offices of the United States to resolve the trying situation. But privately, he indicated that he was not in favor of the setting up of a Jewish state.[12]

When the first session of the General Assembly opened in October 1946, the general course the government followed was intended to protect similar British and American interests in the Near East. If this meant alienating strong Zionist groups in the United States, State Department officials were willing to take that risk. So when the British decided to turn the matter over to the United Nations, American policy required a cautious position at the special session in April 1947.[13]

Another important consideration justified this stance in the United Nations. The Near East imbroglio was part of the Cold War struggle that had so recently heated up. While Soviet and American attitudes toward Palestine appeared similar, the State Department had no intention of allowing the Soviet Union an excuse or opportunity to exert its influence in the area. Stalin's negative reaction to the Anglo-American Committee of Inquiry, his attempt to seize the Turkish straits and to tear Iran apart in 1945-46, as well as the covert support for communist insurgents in Greece made American officials overly cautious about Soviet overtures in the Near East that might threaten United States interests there. The strategy of containment, enunciated publicly by President Truman in his hard-line speech of March 12, 1947, set the policy the United States would follow vis-a-vis the Soviets, in spite of any possible Soviet agreement with the United States on a proposed course of action. Middle East scholar J. C. Hurewitz has recently noted that containment "gave the United States an inclusive regional interest: that of hemming the Soviet Union in at its Middle East frontier."[14]

Both Austin and his deputy, Herschel Johnson, represented the United States at plenary and committee meetings during the short special session held from April 28 to May 15. The delegates held to a constrained position in the special session, for they were under orders to promote only the procedure for dealing with Palestine. "Substantive policy," the Department instructed, "can best be determined in our view after the ad hoc Committee makes its report to the next regular GA session."[15] The meeting accomplished that objective when the Special Committee on Palestine (UN-SCOP) was established with instructions to investigate the present circumstances and to submit a report and recommendations to the second session of the General Assembly in September 1947.

However, creation of the committee was not easily accomplished because of a controversy over major power representation. Two similar resolutions were introduced. Both requested a special committee and designated its objective. But the resolutions differed over the committee's composition. An Argentine resolution, supported by the Soviets, called for a committee composed of the five permanent members of the Security Council and six other members. The second resolution, proposed by the United

States sought a smaller committee and confined its member-ship to nonmajor countries. The two arguments used by Austin and Johnson in supporting the United States proposal—one, a smaller group would enhance the pos-sibility of unanimous recommendations, and two, Britain, as a party to the issue, should be excluded along with the other major powers—masked the main thrust of the American proposal. The United States was determined to keep the Soviets from intervening. The Department believed such intervention would be inevitable if that nation was permitted representation on the committee of inquiry. Throughout the protracted debate, Austin and Johnson never revealed this motive. A compromise, in part favorable to the United States, finally resulted. It was based on an Australian resolution that established a large committee of eleven members on which the major powers would not be represen-ted.[16]

Austin's report on the special session to Secretary Marshall indicated his optimism toward solution of the Palestine situation. But he warned that little time remained before delivery of the UNSCOP report and in the interim the United States should develop its own tentative position that would aid the next regular session in reaching an early decision on a solution. Austin suggested as a working hypothesis that there should be a unitary, independent Palestinian state — neither Jewish nor Arab. His plan would authorize minimal yearly immigration based on the econom-ic "absorptive capacity of the country." Preparations for independence were to take from five to ten years, during which the country would be administered under United Nations trusteeship, while various agencies of the world organization would furnish economic assistance. Austin told Marshall that he realized the difficulty of implementing the plan, but it was one which "should be the most appealing one of all reasonable people," including the Soviets, Arabs and Jews.[17] Austin's plan indicated that his ideas had changed little from those he held in 1936 and 1942 when he publicly and privately advocated a similar solution.

The special session generated other comments. Loy Henderson recommended a trusteeship solution similar to

Austin's. Special Political Affairs officer Dean Rusk reported his concern about the Soviet position. He indicated the Soviets were left in an "excellent tactical position for the future" because they made "statements adroitly designed to gain credit for themselves both with the Jews and with the Arabs." A Department draft paper favored trusteeship for Palestine because the Trusteeship Council would handle the issue and the "Soviet Union has only one seat out of ten — a seat which it has not yet occupied."[18] Obviously, the Cold War had crept into the Palestine issue and trusteeship would work in favor of the United States.

Marshall answered Austin's cable with encouragement after the Department drafted a working paper on Palestine. Its top secret contents provided a solution that incorporated Austin's ideas as well as those of others. Nonetheless, the position elaborated was tentative; Marshall had not cleared it. By early July, three other plans for Palestine were developed, including one for a binational autonomous state and another one that suggested partition into two separate states. The third one favored a multinational community under a single, unified government.[19]

While the summer planning progressed, official government policy remained one of neutrality. President Truman issued a public appeal to Americans to remain nonpartisan on the subject, and the State Department ordered its diplomatic and consular officers at twenty critical posts to emphasize a neutral view, pending the UNSCOP report.[20]

UNSCOP gathered evidence throughout the summer of 1947 and delivered a report to the Secretary-General in September. While a minority report representing the views of three member nations opted for the creation of a federal state in Palestine, seven members of the committee recommended partitioning the country into Jewish and Arab states with an economic union for both areas. The report further recommended placing the Holy City of Jerusalem under international trusteeship and throughout a transitional period of two years, Britain was to administer the area under United Nations auspices.

To discuss the UNSCOP report, the Assembly designated its total membership to sit as an ad hoc Committee. Three

subcommittees were created to facilitate its work: the first
was to draw up a detailed plan based on UNSCOP majority
recommendations, the second to draft a plan for a unitary
Palestinian state, and the third to attempt to gain agreement
between the Arabs and Jews.

The UNSCOP report created a problem for the State
Department and its representatives at the United Nations.
Should the United States now reverse its unofficial plans
concerning a federal state and support the majority report?
The government had to reach a decision soon as Secretary
Marshall's upcoming major speech to the General Assembly
on September 17 would be expected to include some comment
on the situation. A discussion took place among the
American delegation in New York on September 15 with
Marshall presiding. Other members present were Austin,
Henderson, representatives Eleanor Roosevelt and John
Foster Dulles, Assistant Secretary of State John Hildring
and Thomas F. Power, Jr., Deputy Secretary General of the
United States Mission.[21]

The Secretary pointed out the difficulty of the decision.
Uppermost in his mind was the concern that American
support for partition "would mean very violent Arab
reaction." He believed that the United States "should avoid
actively arousing the Arabs and precipitating their rap-
prochement with the Soviet Union in the first week or ten
days of the Assembly." Yet, he noted, if America did not take
a clear stand, he and the Department would be "severely
attacked for 'pussyfooting'."[22]

Eleanor Roosevelt then asked if it was certain that the
Soviets would oppose the majority report. Marshall replied
that this was assumed since it offered such a "fine
opportunity" for them to gain Arab friendship. Mrs.
Roosevelt was not convinced. She believed the Arabs feared
the Soviets more than the United States. Loy Henderson
countered that he was convinced that the Arabs, for
convenience, would work with the Soviets against their
common enemy.

Eleanor Roosevelt attempted to raise the whole question to
a higher plane. She believed the overriding issue was
whether to support "a report brought in by a United Nations

committee, for the value of such support in promoting the success of the United Nations." Marshall answered her, stating that merely voicing support for the report would not accomplish that objective. Rather, the United States must be prepared to back its support by force if necessary. Henderson supported Marshall and also contended that those nations that signed the majority report were not responsible for its implementation. That burden would rest with the great powers.

Austin also agreed with Marshall. If the United States favored the partition plan, it then must prepare itself to support the position with force. He opposed partition; in prophetic commentary, he stated his belief that such a Jewish state would "have to defend itself with bayonets forever, until extinguished in blood." Nonetheless, Austin believed it wise for the United States to enunciate a clear position in Marshall's speech because the nation would "stand before the world as courageous and wise. . . ."[23]

Marshall's subsequent remarks on September 17 hinted that the United States gave special weight to the partition recommendation, but the final decision to support the majority plan was not made by Marshall until September 24. The timing for announcement of the position was kept secret; it depended on the course of general discussion in the United Nations committee, and the American plan was hedged with a number of reservations designed to maintain flexibility. Marshall also decided that the Department should develop a switch position if a two-thirds vote for partition did not appear likely in the Assembly.[24] Thus the door remained ajar for a future change in policy.

Truman later wrote about the decision to support partition. He said that his purpose was based on the historical consideration of maintaining the pledge made in the Balfour Declaration as well as to relieve the misery of the victims of Nazism. Undoubtedly, the President's concern over the prestige of the United Nations was also a factor, along with the tremendous pressure exerted on him by Zionists. But he stated he was not convinced by the State Department's arguments for maintaining the status quo in the Near East.[25]

Objections within the Department to American support of the majority plan continued but were disregarded. On

October 9, two days before Herschel Johnson officially stated United States support for the plan in the ad hoc Committee, Secretary Marshall met with Austin, Johnson, Mrs. Roosevelt, Hildring, Rusk, Charles Bohlen, Charles Fahey and Paul Alling. While there was a consensus to support the decision to back the plan, most thought a two-thirds vote in the Assembly was not obtainable. But Marshall insisted that the United States not pressure any state to vote for the plan. In the event the majority plan did not secure enough votes, a vague form of trusteeship was discussed as a contingency.[26]

A few days later, American policymakers were perplexed by the decision of the Soviet Union to back partition also. Ambassador Bedell Smith later commented on the shift from his Moscow post. He said he was convinced that the Soviets believed the European and Asiatic areas were considerably softer for Soviet exploitation than the harder Arab Near East. He believed an alliance with the Arab states would gain little for the Soviets in the long run. But support of partition would enable them to secure "appropriate implementing measures" that would prepare the area for future Soviet activity. In addition, approval of partition might hasten British withdrawal, long a Soviet objective. Even more important, according to Smith, partition would allow penetration of covert Soviet aid and would incite both sides, thus threatening American and British interests. Furthermore, Soviet tactics were sufficiently flexible to permit reversal if events dictated it. Smith contended that the Soviets had nothing to lose in supporting the partition plan.[27]

For the Americans, the Soviet decision was unexpected and it considerably influenced the United States position in the subcommittee of the ad hoc Committee which had the task of detailing a plan for the General Assembly. Representatives of the United States, the Soviet Union, Canada, Poland, Czechoslovakia, South Africa, Guatemala, Uruguay and Venezuela made up the subcommittee, which was chaired by Canada's Lester Pearson. Herschel Johnson sat as the American representative while Austin remained in close contact with the proceedings and acted as liaison between the delegation and the Department.

The American position in the subcommittee clearly indicated a perceived Soviet threat to inject itself into the situation. The American proposal sought direct transfer of authority from Britain to the two new Near Eastern states on July 1, 1948. A Soviet proposal called for an early termination of the British mandatary, followed by a one-year transitional period during which a commission authorized by the Security Council would administer Palestine. The Soviets were provided with a significant foothold through their place on the Security Council. Once the Soviet plan was announced on November 3, Department officials formulated a counterposition. The Americans believed the Russian proposal would not succeed because it relied on cooperation alone. Although its wording was nebulous, it gave the Soviets power over implementation through the Security Council. Subsequently, the Americans supported the idea of early independence, although they flatly refused to accept any plan that left the administration of Palestine under control of the Security Council.[28]

After prolonged drafting, a compromise prevailed in the subcommittee. The mandate would end August 1, 1948, and independent Arab and Jewish states would come into existence within two months after that. The Assembly would appoint a five member commission composed of small powers, who would administer the mandate.[29] Acceptance of this solution meant a diplomatic victory for the United States inasmuch as the plan gave the United Nations commission the necessary authority to act. Without that power, circumstances in Palestine might deteriorate and open the way for unilateral Soviet penetration, on the ground that its nearby northern sphere of influence was jeopardized. Moreover, the possibility of direct Soviet intrusion through use of its Security Council veto was eliminated. But the Soviets did not suffer a total loss. Their objective of eliminating British power appeared closer to realization since its mandatary would end in the near future. And since the new United Nations commission would report to the Security Council, the Soviets could also maintain a valuable official contact with the problem.

When the recommendation was proposed to the ad hoc Committee, only twenty-five states favored it; thirteen were opposed, and seventeen abstained. This forecast trouble for the partition resolution should it come before the Assembly, where a two-thirds majority was needed to pass it. With other business on the agenda completed, public attention focused on this climactic November period. Johnson's statements in the ad hoc Committee indicated strong United States support for the resolution. But rumors and charges that the American delegation exerted pressure on several nations to change their votes to favor partition remain unsubstantiated. Truman denied any involvement. In addition, knowledge of the Department's lukewarm support for partition indicated little enthusiasm to lobby for votes. Yet privately, no small pressure was exerted.[30] The dramatic final vote, cast November 29 — thirty-three in favor, thirteen opposed, and ten abstentions — made the principle of Palestinian partition a reality.

Austin's role in this drama was one of behind-the-scenes support and implementation for both the course of United States policy and the prestige of the United Nations. He believed that partition would not work, but, if the United Nations were to exercise any influence in the situation, the UNSCOP plan was a feasible one. Thus he supported that recommendation. Austin provided the day-to-day leadership as chief of the American delegation while the brunt of the public debate fell to Herschel Johnson. However, in the upcoming new year, Austin was destined to move under the spotlight. Although policy was made in Washington, the focus of exposition and implementation remained at Lake Success. Under terms of the November 29 resolution, the newly created commission on Palestine was to report periodically to the Security Council on its efforts to effect partition. So the first three months of 1948 found a weary but optimistic Austin following a seemingly shifting American policy on Palestine.

Even before partition was adopted, many officials believed it would not work and moved to substitute trusteeship. Back in mid-November 1947, Dean Rusk and Loy Henderson questioned whether the plan could be realized without doing "irreparable damage to the relations of the US and the Arab countries, and affording an opportunity to the USSR to infiltrate militarily as well as politically" into the Near East.

In December, the National Security Council discussed a report that assessed the strategic position of the United States in the Near East subsequent to partition. The report recommended that partition be declared unworkable and proposed trusteeship for Palestine before a new session of the General Assembly. That report was a forerunner of a similar Policy Planning Staff recommendation which Defense Secretary James Forrestal, long an opponent of partition, learned about on January 21. By late January the machinery was put into motion that would result in withdrawal of American support for the plan.[31]

These recommendations must be considered in the context of Palestinian developments and in the broader worldwide Soviet-American confrontation. When the General Assembly ended in November, United Nations Secretary-General Trygve Lie made an unsuccessful effort to mobilize a United Nations police force to implement partition; the British announced that they would retire completely from Palestine by May 15 and the Jews and Arabs pledged that each would fight for their respective plans. Of even greater significance to American planners, however, was what they perceived as the near total intransigence of the Soviet Union wherever its influence extended. In those areas of vital interest to the Soviets — Iran, the Balkans and Germany — covert and overt pressures were maintained by Moscow. In Latin America, communism, perceived by Americans as directed from Moscow, made considerable progress among the poor and illiterate of underdeveloped areas. The Chinese situation grew bleaker for America with each passing month as the forces of Mao Tse-tung continued to overcome Chiang Kai-shek's units. And in the United Nations, the spector of a Russian veto continued to loom large, as Soviet spokesmen stated that they would not be intimidated by the votes of mechanical majorities.

Thus American efforts to prevent Soviet intrusion into the Palestine situation continued to underscore movement in the State Department away from immediate partition. Simultaneously, other factors gave impetus to this movement. Domestic political reasons as well as State Department and War Department concern over the level of American forces precluded the use of military force to maintain the mission the British were now abandoning in Palestine.[32] To satisfy the demands of these constituencies and still maintain the containment policy, a very formal, legalistic approach was made through the United Nations. Austin was its spokesman.

Other questions were under discussion before the Security Council when the first report of the newly created Palestine Commission was submitted on February 10; it was subsequently placed on the agenda for the February 24 meeting. In the interim, Austin was in constant communication with the State Department while unofficial reports were circulating at Lake Success that a special session might be called to repeal or to amend the partition plan. On February 20, the State Department announced that Austin would read a statement at the February 24 Council meeting. He traveled to Washington on February 23 for a last minute conference with Marshall and Undersecretary Robert Lovett. By then rumors were flying that the United States was cool toward partition, and the Senator's forthcoming statement was anxiously anticipated.[33]

At the outset of his remarks on February 24, Austin quickly dissipated the rumors. He said that United States policy "would not be unilateral; it will conform to, and be in support of United Nations action on Palestine." But his next words bristled with the legalistic question of whether interpretations of the General Assembly's partition resolution fell within the terms of the Charter. He carefully developed the argument that the Charter did not empower the Security Council to enforce a political settlement. The council's role was directed against threats to international peace. In the reports rendered to the Security Council up to that point, Austin declared that there was insufficient evidence of a threat to peace to warrant action by the Security Council. Furthermore, Austin maintained, if such a threat did exist, then consultations were necessary because United Nations forces under article 43 were nonexistent.

In his statement the Senator suggested that the Security Council should make every effort to "achieve an agreement . . . concerning the underlying political difficulty." He closed his remarks by recommending that the five permanent members of the Security Council establish themselves as a committee to consult among themselves and with agencies concerned regarding the implementation of the General Assembly resolution.[34]

Austin's presentation indicated a subtle shift in the American position toward a policy with greater flexibility. But the statement signaled attainment of a major objective: a check had been made against a possible Soviet effort to implement a political solution through Security Council action. Consultation was almost the only procedure left open to the Soviets, but in that process the United States could safely block any Soviet move toward interference. United Nations observers also saw Austin's statement as a concession by President Truman that left the decision on Palestine to the State Department.

Press reaction was critical of the Austin statement. "A tissue of inconsistencies," pronounced Freda Kirchwey of *Nation*; Felix Morley noted "it all looks like a backtrack;" Erwin Canham of the *Christian Science Monitor* thought the "President really had no choice than to retreat but he is trying to do it as slowly and gracefully as possible." The *Washington Times-Herald* was less kind in reporting that Austin performed "a neat and we think highly dangerous welsh, straddle, backwater or whatever you feel like calling it so long as you don't call it honest or forthright."[35]

The following day, Austin formally introduced a resolution that backed his statement of the previous day. The first paragraph vaguely supported partition and a more specific paragraph provided that the five permanent members consult on the Palestine problem. On March 2, he spoke further on the resolution by declaring that a vote for the first paragraph of the United States resolution was a vote for partition. His statement was clear: "The United States voted for the solution and still supports it." The only limitation, he said, was that imposed by the Charter. Following three more days of debate on the resolution, a paragraph by paragraph vote was taken on March 5. Through lack of a majority, the one paragraph reiterating support for the General Assembly partition resolution was defeated. Five members, the United States, the Ukrainian

Soviet Socialist Republic, the Union of Soviet Socialist Republics, France and Belgium voted in favor. Six nations abstained: Argentina, Canada, China, Colombia, Syria and Britain. The consultation paragraph and an appeal to all governments and peoples to prevent or reduce the Palestine disorders were the only sections that won approval.[36]

Pursuant to the March 5 resolution, consultation among the permanent members took place. Nothing was accomplished. While details describing those meetings are lacking, reports from various sources indicated they were doomed from the start.[37] Meanwhile, chaotic conditions in Palestine contributed to a growing uneasiness in American government circles over whether it was possible to bring about partition peacefully by May 15. The primary concern continued to be over Soviet intrusion into the area. This set the stage for Austin's appearance before the Security Council on March 19 ostensibly to report on the progress of the Big Five consultations.

Austin received new instructions within twenty-four hours of his scheduled appearance before the Council. Wearied by futile efforts to gain agreement on Palestine, he informed the Security Council's other permanent members of his new orders before leaving for the meeting. The United States would no longer support immediate partition; in its place Austin would request a proposal for a United Nations trusteeship. Trygve Lie, present at that gathering, later noted that Austin had cited the willingness of the United States to implement this new proposal if it was passed by the United Nations.[38]

Austin's formal statement proved to be a bombshell. While rumors about the announcement had circulated for some time, few observers believed it would come this soon. However, State Department officials decided no more time remained to execute the partition plan peacefully. It had all the earmarks of a State Department decision although Truman approved it. The President continued to receive strong encouragement to support partition, and he later wrote that was the course he believed best.[39]

The evidence indicates that the decision was prompted by the realization that a workable, peaceful partition plan was not possible by May 15, and this was buttressed by the bugbear of possible Soviet intrusion. A few days later, the press learned that Secretary Marshall gave credence to this view when he told the Senate Foreign Relations Committee in an off-the-record secret session that the United States supported partition, but its implementation under the United Nations would require heavy military forces over a long period. This, in turn, would have brought in Soviet forces serving under the United Nations. Under those circumstances the Soviets could threaten the oil fields that were needed to support the European recovery program so closely linked to United States interests.[40]

In retrospect, it appears certain that the State Department attempted to effect partition at the eleventh hour in consultation with the other permanent members of the Security Council. When the March 5 Security Council vote on partition failed and subsequent consulation gained nothing, the switch to trusteeship was the only alternative to avoid a chaotic situation on May 15 in which the Soviets could intervene. From this evidence, Austin's March 19 Security Council statement on the shift in policy should be taken at face value. "From what has been said in the Security Council and in consultations among the several members of the Security Council," Austin stated at that meeting, "it is clear that the Security Council is not prepared to go ahead with efforts to implement this plan in the existing situation." The trusteeship, Austin argued, would give the Arabs and Jews "further opportunity to reach an agreement," and it would not "prejudice . . . the character of the eventual political settlement." Thus, the way was left open for partition.[41]

Austin was chagrined by the change in policy. Deeply committed to the prestige of the United Nations as a working force in just such situations as Palestine presented, he must have speculated on the detriment such a shifting American policy might prove to the United Nations. But further speculation on what would happen in Palestine after May 15, following the departure of the British, did not enhance the prospects for a peaceful solution. If all but impossibly quick action was not taken by the United Nations to achieve partition, public services would halt in Palestine, and the United Nations would be unable to administer the country.

Such a situation would also prove highly detrimental to the prestige of the United Nations.

The reversal of the American position brought immediate criticism. As expected, Soviet representative Andrei Gromyko vigorously disapproved of the new American policy. He said it was based on the false assumption that partition could not be established peacefully. After brooding overnight on the decision, Trygve Lie visited Austin at his apartment. He told the Senator that the Washington decision was a severe blow to the United Nations and to himself personally because of his great effort to implement the General Assembly resolution. He said to Austin: "You too are committed. This is an attack on the sincerity of your devotion to the United Nations cause, as well as mine." Lie then proposed that both of them resign in protest over the change in policy. Austin appeared sympathetic, but he advised Lie not to take such action and said that he would not resign. Lie later speculated why Austin would not quit: "because he was less attached to partition or was more skeptical of the impact which our resignations would have, or just thought it was not the right thing to do — he did not share it."[42] Lie was undoubtedly correct in his inferences. Austin had always believed that trusteeship was a better temporary solution than partition. He knew that resignation would have little impact and thought more good would come from remaining on the job and reaffirming his commitment to the United Nations.

The State Department instructed Austin to request a special session of the General Assembly to gain approval for its new plan before the May 15 deadline. Austin asked for the session on March 19 and Lie scheduled it for April 16. The issue was referred to the First Committee where it quickly became obvious that there was little support for the American trusteeship proposal. When, in the course of debate on May 14, the plenary meeting received a report that the new state of Israel was proclaimed and that the United States had recognized the *de facto* government, the session was immediately adjourned.[43] It appeared that yet another reversal of policy had taken place.

Austin was not sitting at those special session meetings. Francis B. Sayre, representing the United States on the

Trusteeship Council, and representative Philip C. Jessup argued the United States' position. Austin continued as head of the Security Council where the agenda included discussion of a truce in Palestine as well as the continuing India-Pakistan problem. Thus, embarrassment of the American delegates at the last special meeting was avoided by Austin. He had recently arrived from Washington, where he was informed of the President's decision to recognize Israel. Unfortunately, the information Austin possessed was not received by Sayre and Jessup on the Assembly floor before the Colombian representative asked them for verification of this report of recognition.[44]

On the surface, these changes in policy appear to show an inconsistent, leaderless America. However, if taken in the context of the deepening Cold War between the Soviet Union and the United States, a straighter policy line appears. The basic concern of American policy was prevention of Soviet intrusion in the area.[45] One cannot lightly dismiss the deep moral concern on the part of President Truman and some of his advisors for the creation of a national home for the Jews, but this consideration appears secondary to the Soviet-American conflict.[46] Initially, the fear of loss of Arab friendship and subsequent loss of American influence over strategic oil supplies and military positions was a vital factor. However, even those were secondary concerns, for the problem would become important only if the Soviets were able to penetrate the area.

Clark Clifford, a firm supporter of partition, accurately summarized the situation for Truman in early 1948. He wrote that the "Arabs need us more than we need them. The Arab states must have dollars, and can get dollars only from the United States. The Arab leaders would be committing suicide to accept Russian orientation." He then touched on the key to the problem. Palestinian partition backed by United Nations authority could preserve the security of United States interests in the area. That would "remain so unless a military vacuum in Palestine caused by collapse of UN authority brings Russian unilateral intervention into Palestine." Thus he concluded that "American self-interest, American military security, American interests in Middle

East oil and American prestige in international affairs all demand effective implementation of the UN Palestine decision [partition]."[47]

Since the containment of the Soviet Union was the strategy of the United States, the development of a policy for each geographical area near the borders of Russia and its satellites was made within the larger framework. As the United States/United Nations position on Palestine and the Arab Near East developed in 1947-48, American national interest as well as Jewish and Arab interests were considered compatible within the context of a peaceful solution to Palestinian partition. Yet, by early 1948, due in large part to American concern over Soviet motives toward Palestine and the Near East, the policymakers saw that an immediate implementation of partition under the United Nations was not possible. It made no difference that a realistic assessment of Soviet capability would find that they were not in a formidable position to penetrate the Near East; the overriding perception was that Soviet expansion moved in that direction. So trusteeship became the American tactic, but without a change in the basic containment policy.

When the Palestinian Jews proclaimed the state of Israel, the world was presented with a fait accompli: partition was achieved, though not in accordance with either the United Nations' or the United States' timetable. Nonetheless, the United States maintained some initiative through quick recognition of Israel. It prevented a Soviet pretext for moving unilaterally into the area to support the new state.[48] In addition, official recognition met with general public approval, offsetting somewhat the image of a vacillating American policy. Ultimately, as in other international events in the immediate past, the policy of containment remained as the *modus operandi* against the possibility of a Soviet adventure in Palestine.

These events lowered the prestige of the United Nations. Many member states wondered what support the world organization could expect in the future from the United States. Morale was low in all delegations, but especially in the American. While his long hours of hard work appeared futile, Austin refused to surrender to the frustration. He was

determined to support the principles of the world organization while carrying out his obligations as the United States'
representative.

The continuing work in New York left little time for rest in
the summer of 1948 as Austin prepared for the third General
Assembly session, scheduled for Paris in October. The
Senator enjoyed generally good health, which he attributed
to inheritance from his ancestors coupled with "regular
exercise every morning." But his advancing age and the long
hours demanded by the position were beginning to have their
effect. His personal physician, Dr. Wilfred Raab of the
University of Vermont Medical College, kept a close check on
Austin's condition. According to Austin, on three different
occasions since June 1946, Dr. Raab had found "peculiar"
conditions in his heart actions. The Burlington physician
conjectured that there was some impairment of circulation
but that it was not of significance.[49]

Austin plunged into the work of the fall Paris Assembly
and the Security Council with his usual vigor. In early
November, he developed a persistent cold that defied
treatment, so he entered the American Hospital in Paris
where diagnosis showed an inflammation of the prostate
gland. The attending physicians recommended that he
return to Walter Reed Army Hospital for further tests and the
possibility of removal of the gland. He flew to Washington on
November 16, and the operation was performed on November 30. Not accustomed to such inactivity, Austin made
extensive notes on his hospital experience. On one occasion,
a cardiologist engaged him in conversation about his
smoking and drinking habits. After informing the physician
of the extent of his consumption, Austin asked for the
doctor's recommendation. He received only a vague answer,
with no positive suggestion. Austin was somewhat indig-
nant and he later penned in his notebook: "I might as well
have consulted with Williston's [Vermont] cigar store
Indian."[50]

Austin expected a rapid recovery from his operation and
wrote friends that he would "be back on the firing line by the
first of the year." President Truman showed a personal
concern for Austin by providing him the accommodations of

the winter White House in Key West, Florida for the Senator's convalescence. But in spite of his determination, he was not able to return to his post in New York until mid-January.[51]

By 1948, the Soviets' seemingly indiscriminate use of the veto and bombastic charges against the West seemed more than matched by the American containment policy in Europe and the Near East. But because United Nations members had deadlocked on the issue of providing military forces to the world organization, means had to be devised to effect military containment without jeopardizing the spirit of the United Nations Charter. The combination of regionalism and self-defense was the solution. Austin accepted the necessity of this tactic and in doing so, he speeded his own conversion to the hardline of the administration.

At the San Francisco charter conference, the United Nations' framers had recognized the need for regional groups, but they also knew that on past occasions such organizations often were directed against particular states and had created fear and suspicion. Pressing on them, too, was the knowledge that regional organizations tended to limit commitment in a world where general commitment was necessary to maintain peace. So they carefully worded the sections on regional groups.[52] Article 52 defined regional arrangements as treaties which had a "regional" character. Article 53 stipulated the type of enforcement action appropriate to a regional group. The article's salient feature provided that "no enforcement action shall be taken under regional arrangements or by regional agencies without the authorization of the Security Council." Thus it restricted the action of the regional group.

Even more important was article 51. As a result of the deadlock of the Military Staff Committee and the lack of unanimity among the major powers, this article gained increased stature. It provided that all states had the right of "individual or collective self-defense if an armed attack occurs." Except for the exercise of this right, the Charter forbade any other use of armed force. The word "collective" is a significant part of the article. The framers intentionally incorporated the term so that the right belonged not only to the attacked state but also to other states which may have united through treaty with the attacked state in order to assist in its defense.

Nonetheless, the provisions of article 51 did not remove the Security Council's responsibility to restore order. That article stated that members exercising the right of self-defense must submit to the authority of the Security Council once the latter group decided to take action in a particular case. In other words, the article was originally designed as a temporary measure until the Security Council acted. As one scholar noted: "The framers . . . did not anticipate that the system of collective security would not work, and they certainly did not intend collective self-defense as a substitute for collective security."[53]

In the late summer of 1947 Austin was involved in the first opportunity to test the regional and self-defense articles of the United Nations Charter. He was appointed advisor to the American delegation attending the Inter-American Conference held at Petropolis, the summer capital of Brazil, from August 15 to September 2. Austin's actual role at the conference was minor. Secretary of State Marshall was dutiful in personally seeking out the members of all other delegations in order to gain acceptance of a United States version of the regional treaty for hemispheric defense. Austin's presence merely conferred an aura of United Nations sanction on the American delegation as the Senator advised the Americans on the jurisdictional weave of the treaty with the United Nations Charter.[54]

Austin liked the final treaty. He regarded it as a diplomatic victory for both the United States and the United Nations. The treaty strengthened the United States' position in the Western Hemisphere by transforming the Monroe Doctrine into an American-led multilateral arrangement. Austin wrote in his notebook that the obligations under the pact were "harmonious under the Charter" and he believed the treaty's implementation would give vigor to the Charter and would bolster the United Nations overall. Austin saw considerable significance in formally allowing a regional group to take defensive action until the Security Council "has taken the measures necessary to maintain international peace and security." Yet he still hoped the Security Council would eventually lift the burden from the regional group.[55]

Austin admitted that the United Nations shouldered a heavy burden due to the Cold War impasse. But he thought the world body eventually could control the situation because its charter was not a static instrument. He cited the Rio Treaty as an example of what common determination could do to protect the peace of many different countries and yet remain consistent with United Nations policies. Austin displayed continued optimism: "The deeper the gulf between the Soviet Union and ourselves, the greater the need for the United Nations. It must not be weakened by impatience, discouragement or belief in the inevitability of conflict."[56]

In jotting down his thoughts for an upcoming November 1947 speech, Austin noted again that the Soviets honestly feared invasion of their homeland and this prompted their behavior. He indicated his misgivings that as long as the United Nations could not establish an adequate defense system that satisfied the Soviets, they would withhold their total participation in the world group. Austin thought the Russians were hedging, for at the same time they were in a position to reap the benefit of what the United Nations successfully accomplished.

To counter this Soviet attitude, Austin outlined a positive, flexible program that included many of the steps already taken by the United States. He cited implementation of emergency measures of relief, support of the Marshall Plan, use of leadership through United Nations agencies where no veto applied, and keeping contending parties at the United Nations conference tables where public opinion could focus on the issues. He thought his would demonstrate that the Soviet fear of invasion was unfounded.[57] All this showed Austin still maintained strong internationalist beliefs while at the same time accepting the tenets of the United States containment policy. Austin thought the program would make economic isolation appear unattractive to Soviet bloc countries and cause a breakdown of the buffer states. It would also lessen the fear the Soviets had of the West and would bring them into discussion to resolve some of the outstanding basic issues.

One item missing from his program was any mention of self-defense groups under the Charter. Austin still lived in his idealistic world and probably did not want to see the expanding national security benefits derived from such regional groupings. Certainly that would fit with his rationale for Soviet conduct, for there was no need for such arrangements if other means were available. But his fresh participation in the Rio pact negotiations made it seem logical that he might mention collective self-defense as a general point in any overall program. He undoubtedly did not see the Rio treaty as specifically directed against the Soviet Union or its allies and he also did not foresee any other major regional treaty at that time. There was no reason why he should. Austin's superiors were at the moment deciding on what step to take. Until that decision was final, Austin was not in a position to make any public policy pronouncements.

In many circles, influential Americans were seriously considering regional collective defense. For example, Hamilton Fish Armstrong, editor of *Foreign Affairs*, suggested in the fall of 1947 what became known as the "Armstrong Doctrine." The idea advocated use of authority in article 51 and in the regional chapter to place all members of the United Nations who thought alike into a regional arrangement. At executive sessions of the Senate Foreign Relations Committee in December, the Rio treaty was recognized as a "model type of regional set up" for possible future copying. Also in December, Secretary Marshall discussed with British Foreign Secretary Ernest Bevin the possibility of some form of Western European union. This was pursued further in January through regular diplomatic channels. Late that month, Bevin publicly suggested Western European consolidation in a speech to the House of Commons; furthermore, he hinted that other nations might join. And Austin, writing in *The American Foreign Service Journal,* contended that America must maintain "a strong defense of our own capable of discouraging threats to peace anywhere."[58] This accentuated his sense that military security was a prerequisite for recovery from the war. Certainly, military defense underscored all this talk and events in early 1948 would push the ideas toward more concrete proposals.

The communist takeover of Czechoslovakia, highlighted by the *coup d'etat* of February 22 and the subsequent mysterious death of pro-West Foreign Minister Jan Masaryk, added to an American perception of a bellicose, expansive Soviet Union. The event hastened the movement by the European countries to form the Brussels Pact, a fifty-year treaty primarily designed for collective defense. Great Britain, Belgium, France, Luxembourg and the Netherlands signed it on March 17.

Events stemming from the Czechoslovakian episode dismayed Austin. On March 8, he received a memo of a conversation between staff member Chester Williams and Aake Ording, the Director of the United Nations Appeal for Children. Ording, who was in Czechoslovakia a few days after the takeover occurred, gave his observations to Williams, and Austin's underlining notes his interest in Ording's conclusion. The Norwegian thought that there was no dependable democratic morale in Czechoslovakia. The people were anti-communist and anti-capitalist, but were "not pro-anything." He said that communist propaganda was successful there in selling the notion that the United States was only interested in "stemming the tide toward nationalization as a first move toward rescuing capitalism." Ording also believed that the Russians realized that the Czech debacle had alarmed democratic leaders elsewhere in Europe, but they were uncertain whether those leaders could formulate a common program.[59]

The Czech issue at the United Nations placed the United States in an awkward position. Dean Rusk later cited it as an example of a situation in which, because any nation could bring any matter before the organization, the United States had to argue a case against the Soviet Union "at the wrong time and without evidence."[60] Austin argued the weak American case.

On March 17, the Chilean representative presented a letter authored by Jan Papernek, the Czech representative before the seizure of power, to Secretary-General Lie that requested an investigation of the Czech issue. Lie placed it on the Security Council agenda and that group discussed the merit of such an investigation on March 23. Gromyko argued that the matter was an internal affair; consequently, it was not the business of the Council to discuss such issues. Austin gamely countered the Russian by emphasizing the similarity between the known facts of the Czech development and situations that had occurred in other parts of eastern and central Europe. He argued in favor of gathering all the facts and hearing all sides. This might result, Austin stated, in a case of indirect aggression which the Security Council must handle. So the United States supported further consideration of the charges.[61]

This opened an entangled two-month discussion on the question of authority to investigate the matter. Finally, the Chilean representative proposed formation of a subcommittee to carry out that task. Gromyko blocked that move through the familiar tactic of the double veto. He first raised the question of whether the formation of the subcommittee was a procedural or substantive matter, subject to the unanimous vote of the permanent members. When the vote was taken on May 24, Gromyko cast his veto, thereby making the formation of the subcommittee a matter of substance. When the original Chilean resolution to form the subcommittee was next taken, Gromyko completed the double veto and killed the Czech issue in the Security Council. This highlighted the very position in which the United States did not want the issue placed. If a veto occurred, the Department wanted it on the question of an investigation rather than on the formation of a committee.[62]

The gloomy international situation further dispelled the beliefs of Austin and the most fervent optimists that a world organization could adequately replace the old balance-of-power system. It is surprising how Austin continued his task at the United Nations in such a hopeful and confident manner. He still believed that the Charter provided the greatest measure of agreement for the entire world. Admitting that the problem hinged on the fundamental rift between East and West, and that as long as it persisted, each side would firmly adhere to its sovereignty, Austin maintained that the time was coming "when we can sit down and talk with the East regarding fundamental solutions, such as United Nations ownership and control of these great strategic points all over the world."[63]

That spring of 1948 saw ideas for further implementation of the European military containment policy being discussed in Washington. On March 17, President Truman hinted to Congress that the United States had to take some type of action to help Europe protect itself. While the United Nations expressed the country's hope for the ideal world community, he noted that the challenge of the Soviet Union made that organization appear inadequate.

Congressional hearings in Senate and House committees on a bevy of proposals to strengthen the United Nations provided the opportunity for both executive and congressional leaders to move in the direction of European collective security. Austin, an administration witness before the House Foreign Affairs Committee hearings, helped foster credibility in regional defense when he testified in May. In citing ways in which the United States could strengthen the United Nations, Austin emphasized regional associations. He noted that the Rio treaty, the pact of the Organization of American States recently signed at Bogota, and the Brussels Treaty were examples of this type of strength. These agreements operated within the Charter and were implemented with military defense clauses which the United Nations was not yet able to provide.[64] Austin opposed any revision of the Charter; he preferred to find compensation in what he called temporary alternatives to the existing schisms of the day.

Meanwhile, State Department and Senate leaders utilized the large number of resolutions dealing with the nation's attitude toward the United Nations as well as current discussion of American security relationships with Western Europe to develop a policy for the government. Throughout April, executive sessions of the Senate Foreign Relations Committee allowed a broad exchange of ideas. At the same time, Chairman Vandenberg met frequently and privately with Undersecretary of State Robert Lovett to develop a "starter in the direction of committee consideration."[65]

On April 27, a significant meeting took place at Blair House. In addition to Lovett and Vandenberg, Marshall and John Foster Dulles were present. Discussion centered on American participation in some form of Atlantic regional group. All present expressed concern that the formation of any type of regional alliance might frustrate the work of the United Nations. Vandenberg thought it best to revise the Charter in order to stem the Soviet Union's use of the veto. Apparently, the recommendation was discarded as discussion turned to other aspects. Both Dulles and Marshall thought there was some artificiality about attempting to secure any arrangement under article 51. Marshall commented that he was in the awkward position of criticizing without having the ability to propose anything better.

Realizing that the Charter was meaningless in the face of a Soviet threat to Western Europe and to the security interests of the United States, these policymakers were willing to pay lip service to the Charter in devising a method to counteract the threat. Nonetheless, they were concerned with the prestige of the United Nations. For example, one participant suggested, rather than a regional pact, some form of unilateral statement of intention, coupled with practical military cooperation. Lovett thought, however, that a better approach was through agreement under article 51 since it would come under Charter jurisdiction and would not give the appearance of an attempt to thwart the United Nations. Finally, the men decided to pursue some form of Senate action generally approving the principle of American affiliation with a regional group.[66]

The result of all this bipartisan exercise was the Vandenberg Resolution that passed the Senate on June 11.[67] In its final form, it proved a masterpiece in the art of employing evasive and open-ended language while at the same time containing the sharp rhetoric necessary to make evident that the Senate had committed itself to a new approach. The resolution reaffirmed the United States' commitment to the United Nations. It sought regional arrangements based upon the constitutional process and within the framework of the Charter, and it recommended the drawing up of such arrangements on the mutual agreement of self-help. The resolution also hoped to strengthen the United Nations through future Charter review with a particular regard to the veto.

Next the administration sought assistance in an effort to convince the public of the necessity of military cooperation with Europe. While Marshall Plan cooperation, the completion of the Rio treaty, and apparent Senate willingness to approve a military commitment through passage of the Vandenberg Resolution set precedents, the compatibility of such a pact with the principles of the United Nations loomed as a formidable difficulty. Austin became a helpful figure in that aspect of the treaty's development. His long internationalist record gave a certain degree of legitimatization to the administration's public position on compatibility and the Senator's former Congressional status gave him a bridge to the all-important Senate. In addition, Austin's position as ambassador provided the administration a staunch United Nations advocate to fend off expected Soviet attacks at Lake Success. During the time between the passage of the Vandenberg Resolution and final Senate approval of the North Atlantic treaty in April 1949, Austin was a chief spokesman for the emerging treaty. In doing so, he displayed again his reluctant conversion to a hard-line attitude toward the Soviet Union.

Austin laid some of the groundwork early. In talks before the opening of the Paris session of the Third General Assembly in the fall of 1948, he spoke of free world strength based on the European Recovery Program, the advances in the development of regional defense arrangements and the adoption of the Vandenberg Resolution by the United States. Nonetheless, he continued cautiously optimistic about the future. Later in the fall, at a London meeting, he expressed hope that the economic and political cooperation then underway in Western Europe was the beginning of the movement toward European solidarity in all areas.[68]

One of the most spectacular events of the Cold War was the Berlin blockade, in effect since June 14 with its ensuing airlift and counterblockade by the Western powers. The eventual solution of the problem, through the use of the United Nations, significantly showed again Austin's position in policy-making channels. Shortly after his arrival in Paris for the fall Assembly meetings, Austin was informed that Philip Jessup, a member of the Assembly delegation, would devote full time to the Berlin issue. After a long summer debate among the Western powers, the United

States had decided to place the item on the agenda of the Security Council.[69]

On October 6, Jessup presented the United States' case to the Council based on the illegality of the Russian blockade. Further meetings that month brought out a compromise resolution presented by six Council nations not directly involved in the dispute: Argentina, Belgium, Canada, China, Colombia and Syria. The resolution asked the four Berlin powers to prevent any further incidents that would aggravate the situation in the occupied city. It also called upon the disputing members to lift the blockade and requested that the four military governors hold an immediate meeting to arrange for the unification of the currency. Within ten days of the completion of these measures, the resolution asked for the four powers to reopen negotiations on outstanding problems concerning Germany as a whole. The Soviet Union vetoed the proposal on October 25.[70]

Diplomatic maneuvering then moved away from the Security Council. Action first centered around a committee of experts acting as mediators between the United States and the Soviet Union. The six "neutral" countries on the Council composed the committee, but success was not forthcoming. In February 1949, representatives of the four powers resumed direct and secret conversations. Jessup continued to direct the United States negotiations and Austin was not a party to the final settlement reached between Jessup and the Soviet delegate, Jacob Malik, in May 1949.[71]

While illness in November forced Austin to return early to the United States, it was not before the Soviets displayed their continuing bellicosity. Austin noted a "nasty talk" by Malik in the Political and Security Committee on October 13. The Soviet charged Austin and others with "lies and slander." While the Senator usually discounted such charges with equanimity, the intransigence of the Soviets had started to dissipate some of his earlier optimism. "Last day of 1948," Austin wrote in his notebook while recuperating at Key West. "A year of good direction toward conditions of peace; tho not much distance gained. Thank God for what we did gain."[72]

Austin found morale low at the United States Mission when he returned to full-time work in mid-January. A drop in news coverage of United Nations activities bothered members of his staff. Also apparent was increasing anxiety that the fight against communist inroads in various United Nations agencies was not going well.[73]

In need of reinforcement, Austin searched for brighter events. A prime example was Point Four, the new foreign aid policy announced by President Truman on January 20. Austin cited it as evidence of undiminished administration support for the United Nations. While the fourth point gained the headlines, Austin thought the President's first point — support of the United Nations — equally important. In a note on the proposal, he admitted that the American attitudes at the United Nations were not helpful in the development of a technical assistance program to under-developed countries. But Point Four would change that. In a later draft paper, Austin wrote that the United States' program would strengthen the United Nations to a great degree because it grew out of the recognition that the "instruments we were using to accomplish the objective of national policy prior to the President's address were incomplete." He thought the program elevated cooperation in economic development to a major role. It was not a redefinition of United States foreign policy objectives; it was merely the utilization of another instrument to accomplish existing objectives.[74]

Yet in 1949, Austin's optimistic idealism wrestled with reality as he was utilized by the Department to support passage of the North Atlantic Treaty. Throughout the process, he displayed his toughening attitude toward America's adversaries. Even before returning to his post in January, Austin received a memorandum from the State Department suggesting that continued negotiations in the Security Council on article 43 forces were not beneficial to United States interests at that time. The message noted the Department's concern over adverse propaganda as a result of such negotiations and it also questioned whether the United States could supply the forces if the talks ever reached a point of implementation.[75] Austin had little choice but to seek consolation in some alternative.

In February, the Senator accepted a long-standing invitation from Arthur Peach of the Vermont Historical

Society to address a gathering of that group. His talk showed how the Cold War years had their effect on him. He told the Society he preferred to strengthen the United Nations through the conclusion of the peace treaties, the implementation of an effective plan for the control of atomic energy and the establishment of a United Nations military force. But, he said, "we have to deal with facts as they are, not as we would like them to be." The Vandenberg Resolution reaffirmed America's determination to insure peace by taking an active part in world affairs while at the same time guaranteeing the security of the United States. The task, said Austin, was to implement the resolution in the context of United Nations principles.

Austin tied the proposed Atlantic pact with Truman's Point Four address. The treaty was the most effective contribution the nation could make toward the fulfillment of the President's first point: strengthening the United Nations. He recalled that for four years the Soviets had broken the pledge to refrain from "the threat or use of force." Not only did they violate this against individual nations; the United Nations also had suffered. Austin bluntly said, "The functioning of the organization and the confidence of people in it have been shaken. The time has come when this trend must be stopped. I believe the North Atlantic pact will stop it and I believe it gives us the best hope of stopping it peacefully." He was admitting that his own confidence in the United Nations was disappearing.

But Austin wanted to dispel any misgivings that the proposed pact would bring a return to the old idea of a balance of power. He emphasized the defensive character of the treaty. He thought it extremely important not to misinterpret the treaty's purpose: to discourage aggression by showing a firm determination to resist attack. Sounding like a Cold Warrior, Austin stated: "We should announce now as public policy that an attack in the North Atlantic region threatens our safety and peace. We should express our intention that the security of the United States would be defended should an armed attack occur."[76] This strong language indicated how far Austin had moved in his outlook over the past two years. While still believing that the United

Nations offered the world the best hope for security, he was ready now, almost eager, to adopt an alternate method to maintain peace. In making his conversion, he developed a new balance. By de-emphasizing the long-range goals of the United Nations, he highlighted what he considered the temporary, short-range mission of United States foreign policy.

The proposed treaty and its relation to the United Nations received considerable scrutiny in the New York Mission office. John Ross told Austin about the public attitudes he found in discussions on the subject. While there was much talk about the pact's integration with the United Nations, Ross found little public apprehension about that aspect. But the future direction of the treaty brought out a principal concern. Ross observed that the public did not want the pact to turn into an old-fashioned balance of power alliance which was designed merely to checkmate the Soviets and then stop there. Yet there was considerable worry that the military aspects eventually would predominate and convert the whole treaty into a military alliance. Ross noted the treaty's potential in programs for economic recovery drew considerable interest as well as the possibility that it might aid in strengthening the United Nations.[77]

Austin carefully studied these attitudes. He knew he would have to help sell the treaty to the American public as well as defend it against almost certain opposition from the Soviets. He needed answers and assurances for friend and foe alike.

The State Department scheduled Austin as a witness before the Senate Foreign Relations Committee hearings on the treaty in late April. The Department considered him important because he could assure the Senators that the treaty was in line with the United Nations Charter. He went to Washington in late March to discuss the treaty with Department officials. They urged Austin to demonstrate that the treaty covered both the self-defense provisions under article 51 and the regional arrangement under articles 52 and 53. In that way, no question would arise on whether the treaty was either a regional or a self-defense arrangement. Specifically, the Department wanted Austin to point out to the Committee the paragraph in the treaty which vested the

North Atlantic organization with functions that fell under articles 52 and 53 because "they relate to decisions that are natural for a region to make." Likewise, the Senator was advised to underscore the other paragraphs that referred to self-defense which did not fall under those articles.[78]

Even before appearing as a witness at the hearings, Austin was obliged to defend the treaty at the United Nations. The treaty was signed in Washington on April 4. The following day the General Assembly convened in New York for a spring session. A few days later, Gromyko brought up NATO during a discussion of the report of the ad hoc Committee on the Problem of Voting in the Security Council. Gromyko's short but pointed attack charged the development of NATO as an American attempt to destroy the veto. The suddenness of the Soviet outburst caught Austin by surprise, although discussion had taken place on the question of what might be done in the event the issue was raised by the Soviets.[79] Since Austin was scheduled to speak to the plenary meeting the following day, he utilized the interim to reorganize his remarks as an answer to Gromyko.

Austin opened with the comment that the Soviet charge was consistent with that country's usual line. He denounced it as nothing more than a propaganda approach that attempted to convey the idea that any international program, sponsored by the United States in an effort to assist free nations and to protect its own security, was a danger to peace. Austin then launched into the background of the reasons for NATO. Speaking of the Marshall Plan as a "great cooperative effort towards economic recovery and political and social stability," he said the United States supported that effort because it helped to strengthen the United Nations and the cause of peace. NATO was analogous to the Marshall Plan because it, too, was not an aggressive instrument. The treaty's employment as such was unthinkable because it was "rooted in the purposes and principles of the United Nations Charter."

Austin conceded that the United States gave consideration to its own security interests, but equally important was the American obligation to support the United Nations. All the signatories were well aware, Austin argued, that by signing the Atlantic pact they were not relieved of any responsibilities or obligations under the Charter. He cited the Act of Chapultepec as the basis for the establishment of a regional self-defense system, and argued that the San Francisco conference acknowledged regional pacts for self-defense as long as they remained compatible with the universal system. Raising a question about what action any regional group might take, Austin succinctly answered: "Enforcement action did, indeed, require authorization from the Security Council; self-defense did not."

By now Austin was warmed up as he explained the need for such a pact. He cited previous incidents of invitations extended to Russia to join with the West: in the economic sphere through the Marshall Plan, in the cultural area through the exchange of students, professors, artists, books and scientific investigation, and in political relations through the United Nations and even multilaterally through a proposed twenty-five to forty year pact against future German or Japanese aggression. The Soviets rejected all these proposals, he charged. Along with Soviet abuse of the veto, these actions forced nations to find other means within the framework of the Charter to ensure their own security and "to safeguard the purposes and principles of the Charter." Austin declared the signatories designed the North Atlantic Treaty for just that purpose.[80]

This public defense of NATO revealed Austin's changed attitude in coping with what had become immediate, real problems. The administration had moved publicly in this direction through the Truman Doctrine in 1947. But Austin required two more years before conceding reluctantly that the Soviet threat exceeded the United Nations' capability to manage the situation under its present organization. A few days after his speech in the plenary meeting, Austin answered a critic's letter which suggested that NATO would foster bloc voting in the United Nations and would intensify the global division of the two rival camps. Austin wrote that the schism was already present and it would not widen even though he envisioned continuation of Soviet intransigence and Charter violation toward neighboring countries. He could see no alternative other than "group organization for defense." NATO, Austin wrote, was the most "important stimulant of the influence of the U.N. which we have since its origin."[81]

Nonetheless, Austin still clung to his long-range hope for the United Nations. In his *Harper's* article, he told the more idealistic readers that development and progress "demand concentration on gains that are immediately possible while maintaining direction toward perfection."[82] Although not specifically mentioning NATO in his piece, it was evident that he saw regional organization among immediate possible gains.

On April 28, the Senator traveled to Washington to testify before the Senate Foreign Relations Committee. Austin enjoyed a happy reunion with his former colleagues and he drew polite laughter when he told the group he was not accustomed to the role of administration witness in this type of hearing. The Committee treated him kindly, listened attentively and did not ask embarrassing questions. Most of Austin's statements and answers were short and to the point. The reception given him reflected the bipartisan work of administration and Senate leaders to gain a swift and overwhelming passage of the treaty.[83]

In his formal opening statement, Austin told the Senators that the North Atlantic Treaty would move the world nearer to the goal of the United Nations in that it would substitute peaceful settlements in place of force. NATO would act as a part of a protective shield behind which the United Nations could implement those goals. If NATO was not available, Austin said, the fear of aggression would not abate, but would "continue to deplete the energies and confidence of peoples."

Austin argued that the Cold War forced the West to develop measures to oppose the Soviet threat. The Senator accepted the Truman Doctrine and Marshall Plan as two earlier steps in this direction. Now America's joining the Atlantic pact further advanced containment. He was certain the move would demonstrate that the United Nations Charter meant what it said and that the majority of nations were determined to uphold it.[84]

Austin related NATO to the Marshall Plan. The new agreement recognized the Marshall Plan's premise that

European economic recovery would bring peace and security. NATO would strengthen that promise by eliminating fear of aggression. In his characteristic, rhetorical language, Austin stated that the treaty would establish a "needed preponderance of moral and material power for peace." That power would aid Europe and support the United Nations. Since member nations were bound through the Charter not to use force except in self-defense, Austin argued that self-defense treaties like NATO increased the merit of the nonaggressive ideals of the Charter.

Continuing in a positive role, Austin brought up the questions about the feasibility of a general article 51 treaty that a number of revisionist groups advocated. All states could join this universal self-defense pact, which in theory was a means of circumventing misuse of the veto in the Security Council. Austin expressed doubt that this would work. He assumed that most of the nations belonging to the United Nations would be unwilling to undertake such commitments. Of greater concern to Austin, however, was the risk of splitting the United Nations by forcing out any nations who might consider an article 51 treaty directed against them. He obviously had the Soviet Union in mind.[85]

Although Austin regarded NATO as a realistic instrument to stop the Soviet threat, he maintained hope for his ideal of a functioning United Nations. Nonetheless, he admitted there was room for some concessions. For example, he saw no need for unanimity among all members of the United Nations at all times on every question related to the maintenance of peace. According to Austin, only "reasonable cooperative spirit" was essential to allow the organization to progress. This would involve pacific settlement of disputes in the "interest of peace and not in the interest of some national idea." Austin sounded almost pathetic when he said: "If we could only have that cooperative spirit . . . if it could only extend to the five permanent members, we could make more progress than we are making now."[86]

Senator Forrest C. Donnell of Missouri showed the only hostility during the Austin testimony. Neither he nor Senator Arthur V. Watkins of Utah were formal members of the Foreign Relations committee, but they had requested permission to attend the hearings as invited guests. Both opposed the treaty. Donnell questioned Austin in the legality of NATO as a regional group under the United Nations Charter. Austin found himself on solid ground on this matter since it was an aspect with which he was most familiar. His long-time interest and study in international law and its interpretation stood him well. Austin answered that the proposed treaty had characteristics of a regional group defined under the Charter as well as the aspect of a collective self-defense arrangement under article 51. Since it had characteristics common to both types, it was not interpreted solely as a regional arrangement. Austin readily conceded this, but he contended that the treaty did comply with the terms of the regional chapter. Consequently, as a regional group, it was restricted in that the organization could not employ enforcement measures unless the Security Council gave its approval. Because of that, the provisions of article 51 were incorporated to move around this obstacle.

Although NATO was a multilateral defense arrangement, Austin emphasized that it firmly adhered to the fundamental principles of the United Nations. Article 2 of the treaty reaffirmed those principles, and Austin considered this a means to reach one of the objectives of the world body — achievement of universal peace and cooperation. Under questioning from Senator Donnell, Austin pointed out that article 2 dealt specifically with that part of the United Nations Charter concerned with the removal of the causes of war, poverty, ill health, economic warfare, inadequate housing and crowded conditions.[87]

As Austin reaffirmed his belief in the world body his testimony reluctantly conceded that direct confrontation was necessary to stop the scourge in Europe. This was a strong indication of how much his thinking had changed over the course of his tenure at the United Nations. In reaching this position Austin varied from other early Cold War figures. Two points of difference should be made. First, his genuine, though naive, earlier belief in a universal international organization as a functional peacekeeper was different from other Cold Warriors who held little value in such a concept. Austin never lost his faith in the United Nations in spite of international adversity. Second, Austin's conversion was quite late in the developing Cold War. Others either converted earlier or else left the administration. Austin converted but remained to fight as both a Cold Warrior and as an advocate of peace through a functional United Nations.

Austin, then, was unwilling to capitulate totally to reality. In the Mission office, NATO continued as a subject of discussion. For example, Austin asked Porter McKeever to answer a defeatist article on NATO written by James Warburg for *Harper's*. He thought that such articles could not go unanswered because they did a "great deal of harm." McKeever expressed continued concern to Austin in July. He suggested that his boss make a strong statement in the Security Council "on the intent of the Treaty to bolster the objectives of the United Nations." In a penciled notation, Austin wrote that he was aware that something needed to be done to counter the anti-United Nations efforts of various United States groups and that he regarded the McKeever suggestion as a possible approach.[88]

Austin prepared for an expected Soviet attack on NATO in the Security Council meetings, but it never materialized. The Soviet Union's propaganda peace campaign, begun in early 1949, explained this apparent change in Soviet strategy. In April, the Soviet-supported World Peace Conference attempted to give legitimacy to a new Soviet effort to bolster its world image. While an attempt in the spring General Assembly session to limit the use of the veto was a direct attack against the Soviet Union's use of the privilege, it began to appear that they were extremely sensitive to the subject. Consequently, whatever propaganda value they could gain from a continued attack on the treaty was overshadowed by greater concern for a peaceful image in the eyes of the world.[89]

The continuing secret negotiations on the Berlin blockade provide another aspect of this question. On April 25, Tass News Agency announced that since February 15 Jacob Malik and Philip Jessup had conducted talks on the Berlin issue at the United Nations. These talks were among the best-kept diplomatic secrets and not even Austin nor his staff knew of them. After the report was confirmed by the State Department, negotiations continued between Malik and

Jessup at both the Soviet and United States Mission offices in New York. Agreement on the lifting of the blockade was formally announced on May 4, and the blockade ended May 12.[90]

These Berlin negotiations indicated again the overall strategy of the Soviet Union to pursue a less recalcitrant attitude toward the West. By March and April of 1949, it was evident that the counterblockade had an adverse effect on the East German economy and the airlift had shown that the West was determined to hold Berlin. In the arena of world opinion the Soviets could gain little with a continuation of the blockade. These developments, coupled with the fact that Russia constantly found itself in the minority on most issues at the United Nations, account for the lack of a sustained attack on NATO. After the Gromyko outburst on April 13 in the General Assembly, Soviet spokesmen practically ignored the pact.

Austin still hoped for developments that would substitute cooperation for conflict in the world at the same time that he accepted the administration's hard-line approach to Soviet tactics in the Cold War. The fourth session of the General Assembly opened in September and over the course of the next two and a half months, Austin found himself engaged in another direct confrontation with the Soviets which bolstered his growing conviction that compromise was nearly impossible. This time the specific issue centered around contrary Soviet and American "peace" resolutions, but it was framed in the larger context of other events. On September 23, President Truman announced the Soviet detonation of an atomic device, which heralded the arrival of the world's second nuclear power. Furthermore, on October 1, Mao Tse-tung established the People's Republic of China on mainland China, signaling America's failure to maintain Chiang Kai-shek's Nationalist government as China's ruling regime. These two developments helped convince Western policy makers that they could not drop their guard in ongoing diplomatic maneuvers with the communists.

In his opening speech to the plenary session, Soviet Foreign Minister Vishinski cut loose with an invective-filled speech directed specifically at the United States and Great

Britain. He contrasted the Soviets' "peace" program with the warlike preparations of his opponents. Vishinski capped his speech with the introduction of a three-point propaganda resolution entitled "Condemnation of the Preparation for a New War and Conclusion of a Five Power Pact for the Strengthening of the Peace." For the first time in the history of Soviet-United Nations resolutions, it identified the United States and Great Britain by name.[91] The proposal was referred to the First Committee.

Defeat of the Soviet resolution was uppermost in the minds of the United States delegates. Moreover, because of the devastating nature of the Soviet attack, the State Department decided that more than mere defeat of the resolution was essential, that a substitute positive statement must be passed. Austin worked vigorously to reach this objective. He initiated behind-the-scenes conferences to determine how most effectively to eliminate the Soviet resolution. After discussing plans with Britain's representative, Deputy Foreign Minister Hector McNeil, the two decided that the United States and Britain should introduce and lead a fight for a counterresolution, since the Soviet charge had specifically cited these two nations.[92]

Strategy for adoption of the joint British-American counterproposal, entitled "Essentials of Peace," included the broadest possible support from other delegations. For maximum impact, Austin and his colleagues thought that the resolution, once introduced, should not receive amendments or competing resolutions. Consequently, they contacted and informed other delegations of the resolution in advance; furthermore, the Americans lined up several representatives to speak on various points in support of the resolution. For example, plans were developed for Belgium, Norway, Colombia, Iceland and El Salvador to speak on the rationale of the Rio and NATO treaties. They would emphasize why such pacts were necessary and why the Soviet proposed Five Power Pact was not. Argentina, whose representative would describe abuse of the pledge of restraint by Russia, would shoulder the veto question. Other points included presentation of the armament impasse by Denmark, Norway and Pakistan; human rights by Lebanon,

Australia and Chile; and Soviet warmongering by Canada and New Zealand.[93]

As the time approached for introduction of the British-American proposal, Austin arranged a consultation dinner in his Waldorf suite to discuss the resolution. Present were representatives from Canada, Australia, Pakistan, Norway, Lebanon, Chile, Belgium, Colombia, Iceland, Argentina, France, Great Britain, New Zealand and El Salvador. The draft of the proposal was distributed during cocktails, but no formal discussion of it took place until after the meal. Austin then told the group that this issue loomed as one of the most momentous thus far in the Cold War. The representatives present were asked to participate in the drafting and preliminary procedures even though the only sponsors were the United States and the United Kingdom. On that point, the group reached quick agreement. They also agreed on arrangement of the debate, including the sequence of the speakers. Finally, they agreed not to amend the Soviet proposal, but rather to defeat it completely.[94]

This maneuvering by Austin displayed not only his own tactical skills but also left no doubt about his conversion to the standard American Cold War policy. The Soviet Union would no longer receive the benefit of the doubt in any of its actions. Austin was convinced that the Soviets made no contribution to world peace by such resolutions as Vishinski proposed. The Senator called for overwhelming defeat of the proposal while at the same time he enunciated a legal and moral position backed by his recruited support in order to focus public attention on the righteousness of American policy. Within this framework, Austin's long-held ideas on international cooperation meshed with the hard-line policy of his government. If the defeat of Soviet propaganda could bring the world a step nearer to his ideal of cooperation and self-discipline among nations, he favored it. The basic principle of the United Nations Charter was of greatest concern to the Senator. He was determined to uphold it, preferably through reliance on the moral courage of all nations, but, if that failed, to rely on temporary measures until the world advanced to his cherished moral plane. The "Essentials of Peace" debate amounted to a symbol of that determination.

Austin's remarks to the First Committee emphasized the need for rejection of the Soviet proposal — "an artificial olive branch surrounded by thorns" — and for the passage of the joint United States-United Kingdom resolution. He attacked Soviet behavior in the United Nations by charging that the Russians disregarded the principle of unanimity. The world needed peace, he said, without more commitments such as the Soviets proposed in their Five Power Pact. If treaties were made, they should be instruments of "inviolable law and not instruments of propaganda." Austin said the Soviets asked the General Assembly to condemn efforts at peace of the kind embodied in the Rio and NATO treaties. In doing so, that nation ignored the reality that those agreements served both the cause of the United Nations and that of individual nations whose primary purpose was the pursuit of peace.

Austin charged the Soviets with starting the Cold War and continuing it to the present. No one could believe any present Soviet "professions of pacifism," when one recalled the broken promises for free elections in the Eastern European states, the partition of Korea, guerrilla warfare in Greece, the Czech *coup d'etat* and the Berlin blockade. Only when Soviet force was checked by firm stands of the Western nations was aggression halted.

Austin insisted that the basic requirement for peace in the world remained a moral one. To fulfill the obligations of peace, sweeping gestures were not required. Peace was the product of a continuing process that required "respect for international obligations, respect for the rights of others, faith in human rights, non-interference in the internal affairs of other states through indirect aggression." The joint resolution that Austin proposed reiterated those principles. By adopting it, Austin said, the General Assembly would serve notice that any disregard of those principles would be a primary cause of international tension.[95]

Austin's hard work met success on December 1. The "Essential of Peace" proposal was adopted by a vote of fifty-three to five with Yugoslavia abstaining. The Assembly rejected the Soviet resolution paragraph by paragraph with only the states in the Soviet bloc voting in favor.[96] The results satisfied Austin. He had expended great effort to mobilize United Nations opinion in support of the counter-propaganda measure. He believed in the symbolism of "Essentials of Peace," and the resolution reflected his continuing faith in the principles of the United Nations. But to the critical observer, the resolution, like so many phrases expressed by Austin in support of United States policy, juxtaposed a cloak of seeming legality and morality with the tough policy of containment. Austin now accepted and promulgated both in good faith.

CHAPTER FIVE

THE COLD WARRIOR

In late June 1950, summer doldrums settled over Washington and New York. For many Americans the vacation period had arrived, and even the nation's leaders allocated a few extra hours at their favorite retreats. The last weekend in June found President Truman at home in Independence, Missouri, while Dean Acheson left Washington early Saturday morning for what he hoped would be a quiet two days at his nearby Harewood Farm in Maryland. In New York, Austin also had looked forward to a long weekend. He departed by plane on late Thursday, June 22, for Burlington, where he anticipated spending the next few days dividing his time between United Nations homework in his spacious study and outdoor activity in his backyard orchard. Back in Washington, Assistant Secretary of State for United Nations Affairs John D. Hickerson remained on duty in the State Department, while in New York, United States Mission affairs were left in the able hands of Deputy Ambassador Ernest Gross.[1]

At 9:26 p.m. on June 24, John Muccio, the American Ambassador to South Korea, cabled the State Department from Seoul to report a seemingly all-out attack by North Korean forces across the 38th parallel dividing North and South Korea.[2] Hickerson called Acheson, who, in turn, ordered his Assistant Secretary to contact both Secretary-General Lie and Ambassador Gross at the United Nations in order to arrange a special meeting of the Security Council to discuss the situation. After alerting other officials in the Department, Acheson called the President in Independence to advise him of the matter. He recommended that Truman not risk a "hurriedly arranged night flight" back to Washington but to wait until the next day for a more complete report of the developing crisis. Meanwhile, Hickerson immediately called Lie and Gross and asked that they arrange the Security Council meeting. Lie, in turn, requested an immediate estimate of the Korean military situation from the United Nations Commission that was on duty in Korea. After a sleepless night of telephone calls and consultations, the Secretary-General set the time for the Security Council meeting at two o'clock on Sunday afternoon, June 25.[3]

Austin was not present when the Council met on Sunday afternoon. Gross called the Senator early on Sunday morning to inform him of the happenings. Austin kept in touch with the Mission as well as the State Department while he postponed his return to New York until Tuesday, June 27. Gross proceeded to hammer out a resolution with the aid of John Ross and the United Nations desk officer, David Wainhouse, who had flown to New York from Washington for that purpose. After clearing the final wording of the proposed resolution with Acheson, Gross was ready for the meeting.[4]

Like other Council meetings since January 1950, the June 25 session was characterized by the absence of a Soviet representative. Jacob Malik, the permanent Soviet ambassador to the United Nations, had staged a celebrated walkout at the January 13 Council meeting to emphasize a Soviet campaign, which had started in the autumn of 1949, to oust the Nationalist government of Chiang Kai-shek from legal representation at the United Nations and to replace it with Mao Tse-tung's victorious People's Republic. Malik left with a declaration of further nonparticipation until "the representative of the Kuomintang group" was removed.

Despite this continuing boycott on June 25, the Council proceeded immediately to the task at hand. Two documents were before it: the American request for the meeting and an up-to-date report from the United Nations Commission in

Korea sought earlier by Lie. The latter document gave details concerning the outbreak of hostilities and suggested that the Secretary-General consider bringing the matter to the attention of the Council. Gross presented the American draft resolution. It called upon the authorities in the north to withdraw their armed forces to the border. In addition, the resolution called for all members of the United Nations to render assistance to the United Nations in carrying out the resolution and requested them not to provide aid to the North Koreans. The proposal passed unanimously although Yugoslavia, courting both the Soviet Bloc and the West, requested a more detailed investigation and abstained from the vote. The next meeting was set for June 27.[5]

This resolution must be set in the context of two aspects of the outbreak of the war. First, on January 12, 1950, Secretary Acheson told the National Press Club that South Korea was excluded from America's "defense perimeter" in the Far East. Critics of American policy have subsequently pointed to this address as an invitation to the North Koreans to attempt their later southern attack. But it also should be noted that Acheson, in the same speech, said that if South Korea was attacked, the United States was prepared to invoke "the commitments of the entire civilized world under the Charter of the United Nations." In their study of the Korean crisis, George and Smoke have pointed out that this second passage did not "relieve the administration from the main burden of the criticism that its public statements weakened rather than strengthened deterrence of a North Korean attack."[6] But it certainly cannot be overlooked as part of a contingency plan if an attack occurred.

The second aspect springs from the first one. It is the revisionist charge that the State Department's United Nations contingency plan was so well developed by June 1950 that it was, in fact, part of an overall American conspiracy to provoke the North Korean attack. So the thesis goes, the administration then could use this provocation to assist in globalizing its recently developed policy of containment of world communism. The most noteworthy supporting evidence is Hickerson's later testimony before the Senate Appropriations Committee that the State

Department had drawn up a draft resolution for use at the United Nations prior to the events of June 25. At best, however, it is thin evidence and must be twisted out of context if it is to be utilized as part of the larger conspiracy thesis. In fact, there is no indication that State Department contingency planning went beyond this sort of general diplomatic response. Rather, the attack itself should be viewed both as a surprise and as a catalyst that allowed the administration to take subsequent steps toward a globalized containment policy.[7]

Austin was in close contact with the State Department. On Monday morning, he informed Hickerson that he would return to New York the next morning; in the meantime Gross would go to Washington to obtain further instructions and a briefing on the situation. Hickerson promised Austin every "scrap of information we have." The Assistant Secretary warned Austin, however, against making any comments that might imply Soviet involvement in the invasion. He said such an assumption was difficult to document at that time. Austin replied that it was logical that the North Koreans were prodded by the Soviets and said that this was in the "mind of the world as the cause of our tribulation." But Austin understood the Department's concern for discretion and that he should not make any unsupportable charges.[8]

Austin undoubtedly recognized the challenge this new threat posed to his own belief in collective security. In his mind the United Nations faced open aggression. If the United States had failed to initiate United Nations action on June 25, it would have lost the hope for peace through united action — a hope which Austin had seen undermined by previous unilateral acts of the United States. For Austin as well as other United Nations supporters, the organization came of age.

On June 26, while President Truman publicly announced his authorization to have General Douglas MacArthur furnish military supplies and other assistance in accordance with the June 25 United Nations resolution, Gross flew to Washington for instructions. From 3:00 to 7:00 p.m. he conferred separately and in groups with various members of the State Department. These included Ambassador-at-Large

Philip Jessup, Deputy Undersecretary Dean Rusk and Assistant Secretary Hickerson.[9]

Throughout the day, news from Korea reported a deteriorating situation which induced a sense of urgency in the timing of the next move by those present at the Department. A consensus was building that strong action by the United States probably would be necessary to repel the aggression and to bring compliance with the resolution of the Security Council. Department leaders regarded the aggression as a Soviet-directed threat to world peace. What the United States should do to meet the threat remained a presidential decision which would be made that evening.[10]

Hickerson outlined for Gross the alternatives faced by the United States. The first choice was full-scale involvement to restore the status quo. Hickerson cited an American report from Moscow that analyzed the Soviet position as one not favoring war at that time, with the strong possibility that it would withdraw support of the North Korean aggression in the face of stern measures by the free nations. The Assistant Secretary said that he strongly favored such action but he realized the difficult position in which the President found himself in attempting to make the correct decision. The second alternative was to abandon Korea and to take a firm stand at other places such as Formosa, Japan and Southeast Asia. Gross commented that such action would mean scuttling the United Nations and that it could also split apart the free world. Hickerson agreed.

Hickerson then analyzed the possible explanations for the North Korean action. One interpretation was the development in the Republic of Korea of a situation that was progressively unfavorable to the communists. In part it was due to the outcome of the May 30 elections in South Korea, which strengthened the noncommunist elements there. A second explanation was that the Soviets believed the United States would negotiate the terms of a peace treaty with Japan without including the Soviets. The action in Korea was meant as a Russian warning of strength and reaction. A military explanation was the third possibility. South Korea presented a difficult defense problem to the United States where the communists hoped to gain a military advantage.[11]

Discussion turned next to action in the United Nations. David Wainhouse handed Gross a draft resolution, which the President had not yet approved, for possible use in the June 27 Council meeting. Summarized, it charged noncompliance by North Korea with the Security Council resolution of June 25. Based on this noncompliance, the document recommended that all members furnish the necessary assistance to meet the attack from the north. In addition, a second resolution was discussed. It directed the Council President to advise the Soviets that failure of their representative to attend the meeting of the Council and the noncompliance of North Korea with the June 25 resolution required the Security Council to bring the matter directly to the attention of the Soviet government. It further requested the Security Council President to ask the Soviet Union for a statement of intention pertaining to the June 25 resolution.

The second approach was rejected — a move dictated by the desire to avoid directly involving the Soviet Union at that moment. At one of the Department meetings, Jessup asked for reaction to a suggestion of instructing the United States ambassador in Moscow to seek a Soviet disavowal of responsibility on the Korean action and request the Soviet Union to use its influence with the North Koreans to have them withdraw. Dean Rusk told him that such an approach appeared to involve the United States in a unilateral action. Gross favored a combination: use the second resolution and couple it with instructions to the Moscow Embassy to follow a direct approach with the Soviets. That course of action, however, was suspended. Gross noted in his memo to check with Hickerson before acting on this resolution. Later it was discarded, as it was not even brought up in the Security Council. Nonetheless, the United States sought Soviet cooperation despite misgivings about unilateral action. The American ambassador asked the Russians to influence the North Koreans to return north of the 38th parallel. The expected Soviet reply came back. It accused South Korea of starting the hostilities and stated that the Soviet Union would adhere to the principle of noninterference in the internal affairs of other states.[12]

Concern over American unilateral action continued to receive much attention in the Department discussions.

Jessup suggested a United States statement at the June 27 Council meeting that would reaffirm the Truman Doctrine and expand it to include American armed support in Korea. The general feeling was that this would make Korea a United States matter rather than a United Nations affair. Gross made a countersuggestion that the Security Council adopt a paraphrase of the Truman Doctrine. No answer was readily given to that proposal, and apparently it was dropped.

Jessup posed another interesting question. He asked if the proposed first resolution was legally necessary. The general consensus was that it was not; however, it was politically desirable because it would find North Korea in noncompliance with the June 25 resolution. This confirmed the ultimate position of the administration that the whole matter was a United Nations problem with maximum United States support.[13] Moreover, it placed on Austin's shoulders the responsibility for presenting American policy favorably at the United Nations.

Postponement of the June 27 meeting from morning to afternoon in order for the Indian and Egyptian delegates to receive final instructions did not dampen Austin's energetic first public performance of the Korean crisis at Lake Success. His enthusiasm for the renewed life given to the United Nations by the situation seemed to overshadow all else. "With the calmness of a Vermont lawyer reading a brief," quoted *Time*, Austin opened his remarks at 3:16 p.m. by declaring that the United Nations faced the "gravest crisis in its existence." He stated it was difficult to imagine a more glaring example of disregard for the United Nations and all its principles and that his nation believed it was the Council's duty to invoke "stringent sanctions to restore international peace." He submitted the draft resolution brought to him from Washington by Gross and read a copy of President Truman's statement ordering United States air and sea forces to give South Korean troops cover and support. In his concluding remark, Austin said that the keynote of the draft resolution, his statement, and the action taken by Truman were "support of the United Nations purposes and principles — in a word: 'peace.'"

Yugoslavia's representative, Alois Bebler, next presented a counterresolution. He warned against the present trends in international relations and suggested that the Council seek a renewed appeal for the cessation of hostilities, initiate mediation with the help of the Council and invite North Korea to send a representative immediately to the United Nations. The resolution received little support from the Western nations. The American-led decision to meet the aggression was firm. Austin had received no instructions to explore an alternative political policy.[14]

Several governments supported the American position, but the Egyptian and Indian members indicated some reluctance to follow such a provocative course of action. A five hour delay of the meeting ensued while these two representatives awaited new instructions on the two proposed resolutions. Finally, the meeting was reconvened and a vote was taken on the American proposal. It passed by a seven-to-one majority with only Yugoslavia dissenting. Egypt and India, pleading their lack of instructions, did not vote. Subsequently, the Yugoslavian proposal was defeated by a vote of seven to one. Again, Egypt and India abstained. The meeting adjourned.[15]

Austin and his staff next implemented American policy by organizing as much collective assistance as possible against the North Koreans. From the beginning it was apparent that only a great amount of United States support would turn the tide of battle, but it was necessary to show that it was a collective action rather than a mere cover-up for a strong American response. To accomplish this, the United States used the Secretary-General as a cover. The Department advised Austin to make sure that Trygve Lie draft his request for aid in such a manner as to avoid embarrassment to member governments unable to contribute. Hickerson also ordered the Mission not to get involved in actual use and control of offers of assistance. Acting on these instructions, the Mission staff developed a position that emphasized the United Nations aspect of United States assistance. This position paper explicitly stated that, under the June 27 resolution, nations were invited to take joint action rather than ordered to do so. So the United States must employ caution in applying pressure on other countries, particularly the smaller nations. Out of this, Lie's subsequent request had a mixed response; certainly it was not spectacular. At week's end, for example, Sweden promised to send an ambulance unit; Israel refused to send ground troops "because our neighbors still obstinately refuse to make peace"; Norway offered merchant shipping; and Egypt offered nothing at all.[16]

Austin found himself engulfed by these fast-moving events. Within three days, the Security Council, directed by the United States, had taken quick action to attempt to halt an aggressor. The Senator followed that up by actively seeking the support of as many smaller states as possible to approve the United Nations-United States action. On June 29, Austin gave a statement to the press showing his personal optimism and conviction that the United Nations was a vigorous, peace-keeping organization. The world body, he noted, was "writing a thrilling chapter in the history of man's organized efforts to abolish war." He pointed out that the issue was not merely between two nations; instead, it was between an aggressor and the United Nations.[17] The Korean aggression had a salutary aspect for Austin in that it endowed the United Nations with a unifying trait he had never seen before. Here was an issue that really tested the reaction capacity of the United Nations. And since it reacted so well, Austin was delighted.

Austin's performance during those early days of the crisis disclosed another facet of his character. At no point did he disagree with the President on the decision to move into Korea. Like most American officials, he accepted the fact that some action was necessary. Even if he had found himself in disagreement, he was in no position to oppose the decision. Once again Austin acquiesced in a major decision of the administration without any input on his part. With very few exceptions throughout this tenure at the United Nations, Austin exhibited this willingness to conform to the policies of the President and the State Department. At the same time, he rationalized administration actions to fit his own scheme of how the United Nations must operate.

If there might have been room for disagreement, it hinged on whether the responsibility for South Korean defense was that of the United States or of the United Nations. Yet there was no lack of agreement between Austin and his staff and the administration on this point. Austin's strong faith in the United Nations made him see the measures taken in Korea as first and foremost a United Nations action supported in full by the United States. Truman, of course, reiterated his belief in the United Nations on this issue.

Even though the Korean action allowed the most acceptable diplomatic maneuver in the light of world opinion to act under the United Nations, it dovetailed neatly with United States interests so that it accomplished two purposes. First, the action gave increasing support to the fading image of the world organization as a peace-keeping unit. American policymakers realized that if United Nations involvement was not pursued in this case, the subsequent loss of prestige for that organization could be fatal. Second, the action served as a means by which the United States could gain substantial world support for its own position. While this latter reason was the most important priority for Washington policymakers, it was not for Austin. He viewed the Korean affair as a significant means to bolster the United Nations as a viable collective security group. So while he could believe this he found it also dovetailed with the lower priority Washington position. This allowed him to operate effectively and sincerely in leading the American cause at the United Nations.

The Security Council met on June 30 for the third time since the outbreak of hostilities. The meeting was scheduled to hear a report on Trygve Lie's activities in coordinating aid for the Korean reaction and to discuss future moves. After listening to the report, Austin used his best rhetoric in commenting that the contributions of member nations exemplified their interest, initiative and devotion to peace. It was a laudable chapter in the history of collective security, he noted. By making contributions, the states overcame the fear they would violate some technicality or some "strict construction raised solely for the purpose of paralyzing or even killing collective action by the United Nations to attain its noble purposes." The Senator saw the world reaction to North Korean aggression as promoting the moral power of a united public opinion, and he hoped "that may be strong enough to bring peace without more shedding of blood."[18]

The Korean situation stood as a perfect example to Austin of what he had envisioned in 1945 as a solution for world security problems. Certainly, this was the way the planners, when they wrote the Charter, had hoped to block future aggression. Now because the Soviet representative was not present, the Security Council had unanimity and was able to take quick action. In praising the Council's role, Austin nostalgically reverted to the ideal world seen in the war years. While there was a measure of hope in the quick action on Korea, Austin also appeared unrealistic in generalizing that this situation offered a typical example of the manner in which the United Nations would meet aggression. Even though the Soviet Union had outmaneuvered itself in the Security Council by use of its boycott, this development should not have nurtured Austin's faith in his ideal; the problems still persisted, almost certain to reassert themselves with the reappearance of the Soviet delegate in the Security Council.

One of the important July accomplishments came early when the Council established a unified command. France and Great Britain presented the resolution authorizing it. Again, like the earlier request for troops, the lack of an American direct connection to the resolution provided evidence of the continuing policy of leaving room for other nations to initiate publicly the United Nations policy on collective action. Certainly many Western nations eagerly wanted to participate in the Korean episode in order to dispel the haunting appeasement image of the 1930s. While other evidence indicates that the unified command idea originally came from the State and Defense Departments, the "hands off" public attitude made the move appear as genuine collective action.[19]

Throughout July, even though the battlefield situation was bleak for the United Nations forces, there was optimism that, under the leadership of General Douglas MacArthur, the situation would slowly improve. At this time the United Nations forces were being pushed into the Pusan perimeter. Yet Trygve Lie indicated in mid-July that while the Security Council must decide whether United Nations forces should drive north of the 38th parallel, he recalled that the United Nations had repeatedly urged unification of Korea. And at the State Department an internal dispute developed over what course to follow in this matter, although no decisions were made.[20]

The Soviets, although not officially represented at the Security Council meetings, verbally attacked the United States. In mid-July Malik circulated a statement from Deputy Foreign Minister Andrei Gromyko placing blame for the Korean aggression on the United States. Russian propaganda also was aimed at Austin. Charging him as a "conceited and eloquent fool," one statement claimed he spoke about "progress and true democracy" while at the same time subjecting parts of the world to "gangster type" methods. In a most bitter criticism, the author claimed that Austin demanded contributions from the members of the United Nations in order to disguise American intervention in Korea under a "fig leaf of joint action."[21] Austin bore such attacks in stride.

The stage was set for formal diplomatic confrontation when Malik told Lie on July 27 of his intended return to the Security Council on August 1 to assume his duties as president. Evidence of expected fireworks came on July 31 when Austin introduced to the Council a draft resolution condemning the North Korean authorities for continued defiance. It called upon all nations to use their influence to induce North Korea to halt the aggression. In his introduction of the proposal, he remarked that several nations were giving moral, if not material, support to North Korea and it seemed propitious to "reinforce the efforts of the Security Council to keep the conflict localized."[22] The resolution was tabled for discussion at the next meeting on August 1.

New Yorkers trooped to Lake Success in great numbers on August 1 in hope of catching a glimpse of the expected verbal tussle between big, blond Jacob Malik, the career Soviet diplomat with a clean-cut, almost American-like face, and Austin, the portly, heavy-jowled, dedicated United Nations advocate. Over 23,000 requests for tickets to the session were refused; however, the increasing use of television brought the debates live, not only to New Yorkers, but to many Americans across the land. Through fourteen August meetings of the Council, accentuated by inflammatory emotional outbursts and parliamentary maneuver, Malik fired away at the West in general and at the United States in particular. One student of those sessions depicted them using the analogy of an international court, with the plaintiff cast as the United States Far Eastern policy: "Malik was prosecuting attorney; Ambassador Austin, ably seconded by Sir Gladwyn Jebb and Jean Chauvel of France, was chief counsel for the defense. Judge and jury were the peoples of the world."[23]

The fireworks did not explode immediately; it was three days into August before Austin could unleash an onslaught against Malik's tactics. On the first day of the month, the Russian, in the role of president, attempted to pick up where he left off in January by placing the question of Red Chinese representation on the agenda. Furthermore, he offered a suggestion changing the title of the American resolution involving Korea from "Complaint of aggression upon the Republic of Korea" to "Peaceful settlement of the Korean question." The Russian move obviously attempted to thwart the Council's work. More importantly, however, the tactic linked Red Chinese representation to the Korean question in order to force the United States to reject the substance of both items. A vote against admission of Red China would be a vote against that regime, and a vote against the title change would be a vote against peaceful settlement. Then the Soviets could utilize the West's votes as propaganda to show that the United States was in fact opposed to a fruitful settlement of the conflict.[24]

On the agenda item, Austin established the American point that Chinese representation was not related to Korean aggression. The firm opposition of the United Nations to the use of force, said Austin, "has given strength and encouragement to all free peoples." Disillusionment with the United Nations could result if the question of Chinese representation were allowed to preempt the discussion on Korea. The free world would not tolerate this disenchantment, he contended.

In the matter of the Soviet-proposed title change, Austin considered it inappropriate. The implication was, Austin said, that the Soviet Union was the only nation interested in a peaceful settlement of the Korean question. The Council, he recommended, should reject this erroneous impression.[25]

Debate heated up on the second day when Austin again rejected any "deals" — a reference to the Malik proposed agenda items — for the settlement of the Korean war. "So long as men are dying on the battlefield in defense of the United Nations," Austin said in a short statement, "this Council will not wish to cheapen their suffering or sully their heroism by seeming to engage in the consideration of deals."[26] The Council adjourned with no apparent progress.

The following day, the tempo of debate increased considerably. Malik moved and charged the United States with "flagrant, open and active aggression against the people of Korea." Turning red-faced and obviously angry, Austin waved his arms and shook his forefinger at his Soviet adversary as he made a heated, emotional rebuttal. Austin said that Malik spoke on a matter that was irrelevant while representatives of member states were fighting in Korea "under the flags of their own nationalities and countries and fighting also under the blue and white banner of the United Nations." Austin lashed out at Malik's propaganda tactics as a perversion of the facts. He told the Russian that the whole world was tired of the "shameless travesties of the realities with which we . . . are supposed to deal." The whole Korean question was too tragic and too real, Austin shouted, to be served "by any preoccupation with propagandistic distortions which were properly referred to here yesterday as 'upside-down' language."[27]

That stormy session finally brought a procedural vote on the items. The Council rejected the two proposed by the Soviet Union while adopting the original United States proposition charging aggression upon the Republic of Korea. In a sense, the vote was a Pyrrhic victory for the United States. The agenda remained unchanged, but Russia gained substantial material for propaganda purposes. Yet, had a reversal of the vote taken place, the United States and its allies would have suffered an even greater loss.

Austin used twofold debating tactics on these issues. First, he always argued from a United Nations point of view. This downplayed the Soviet charge that United Nations action was a puppet move of the United States. By doing this, the Senator gained a desired effect in appearing more as a representative of the United Nations than as the representative of the United States. Second, Austin sought to refute Soviet charges as propaganda and lies. On both points he was successful. His basic faith in the United Nations, supported in this case by the fact that the Soviet absence had allowed an immediate response, enabled Austin to argue from a moral, idealistic point of view. At the same time, he demonstrated his skill in the art of refutation. One student who studied Austin's speaking ability pointed out that he used emotionalism much more in the Korean debates than he did in previous United Nations sessions. Prompted by greater use of television and radio, Austin adapted his speeches to a worldwide audience in order to beat the Soviets at their own game. He refuted Soviet arguments publicly and immediately and almost never allowed his personal feelings to overshadow his logic. The Senator was always well prepared. He knew hundreds of documents by heart and cited them with success in debate.[28]

Yet Malik was far from being defeated. During the second week of August, the Soviet diplomat continued his delay and obstruction tactics. At the August 8 meeting, he was pressed for a ruling on the seating of a South Korean representative. Malik curtly answered that he had no firm basis for a ruling on that question and then quickly proposed a vote on a Soviet motion on the seating of a North Korean representative.[29] Tension mounted in the chamber as Western diplomats perceived the nature of the Malik tactic.

When Malik recognized Austin, the Council chamber hushed. In contrast to his flamboyant manner of the previous week, the Senator employed restraint as he met the latest Malik challenge. "When the President, as such, or as the representative of the Soviet Union — it makes no difference which hat he wears while he is doing it," Austin slowly began, "undertakes to persuade this great audience here present, and all the world outside, that the United States is an aggressor in Korea, I should like to ask whose troops are attacking deep in the country of somebody else?" He paused before answering his own question: "the North Koreans."

The tension in the room eased somewhat as Austin deliberately continued to make his point. "Whose country is being overrun by an invading army? The Republic of Korea. Who is assisting the Republic of Korea to defend itself? The United Nations, with the support of fifty-three out of fifty-nine members." Then Austin followed with a jab at the Soviet Union. "Who has the influence and power to call off the invading North Korean army? The Soviet Union. Who then is supporting the United Nations Charter and working for peace? The fifty-three members of the United Nations which are assisting the Republic of Korea. Is the USSR one of the fifty-three? No. What member of the Security Council is assisting the invaders in the Security Council? The Soviet Union."[30]

Throughout Austin's remarks, the grim faces around the council table became more relaxed and pleased, with the exception of Malik. As Austin concluded, Trygve Lie and Sir Gladwyn Jebb were smiling broadly. The pro-Western audience in the packed visitor's gallery — against the rules of the Council — applauded for a full minute. Malik pounded his gavel for silence and threatened to expel the public from the room. In the minds of the partisan majority of those present, Austin had given a good performance. In addition, he was seen by a wide American television audience.[31]

After receiving approval from Washington to continue to hit hard, Austin resumed his attack on August 10 in the longest speech of that session. He reviewed all aspects of Korean history since the end of World War II and noted no diminution in the effort by the United Nations to keep Korea free and independent.[32] At the August 17 meeting, Austin spoke as if he were representing the United Nations. He outlined United Nations objectives in Korea. He avowed the United Nations acted on the belief that, by protecting one small country, the organization guaranteed all countries freedom from political oppression and military invasion. He again challenged the Soviet Union to use its influence to stop the fighting. In doing so, Austin said, it would act as a dutiful member of the United Nations.

In the debate following, Austin wondered aloud if it was possible for the Soviets to believe that no country threatens them in Korea or "anywhere else around their vast perimeter." In raising this question, the Senator reflected his long-held security psychosis theory about the Soviet Union. In a facetious way, he asked if the Soviets needed some assurance that a tiny, independent Korea would not threaten the security of Russia. If so, such assurance was possible if the Soviets would cooperate to develop the United Nations as a major safeguard against attack.[33]

While private consultations were held among the major powers, the Security Council resumed the public debate on August 22. For the observer, boredom set in quickly as all the main arguments were stated once more by the delegates of the Soviet Union and Great Britain. Austin was last to speak after listening to a ringing tirade of denunciations by Malik. The Senator's rejoinder employed a masterful use of rhetoric designed to expose the Soviet propaganda.

The Soviets, Austin said, distorted the facts by tricks. The first of these Austin called the "false label trick," which he defined as making falsities sound like fact. For example, Malik had charged that the United States had resorted to intervention because the Syngman Rhee government was collapsing. Austin countered that the reverse was true. It was obvious, he said, when the North Korean government found that it could not destroy the Republic of Korea from within, it attacked it. The second trick Austin cited involved "concealing guilt by accusation." The Soviets attempted this maneuver to show that the North Koreans were defending themselves from an attack by South Korea. Austin stated the Soviet tactic charged the United States with starting the aggression as an extension of American imperialism. Likewise, the Soviets used this approach to discredit the objective testimony of the United Nations Commission on Korea. They dismissed the Commission's findings on the ground that they were fabrications by United States representatives passed off as fact.

Austin labeled the third Soviet trick as a tactic similar to Hitler's "Big Lie." He cited examples such as statements that the United States was guilty of aggression, that America proposed to continue and to extend the war, and that all of Korea was to become an American monopoly. Austin refuted these charges by asking if Russia had brought a complaint to the Security Council on June 25 that the United States had made an armed attack on North Korea? He then asked if the Soviet Union had complained that the Republic of Korea had invaded North Korea? Since answers to both questions were negative, Austin pointed out that the Soviet's failure to do so only proved more conclusively that the aggressors were North Koreans.[34] Austin was masterful in debate with such rhetorical tactics. He was forceful and incisive, while at the same time his sincerity for the United Nations' cause permeated the debate.

Relief was largely in evidence around Lake Success as the August presidency of Malik closed. The fourteen public meetings and many more private consultations had netted little in the way of decisions. The Soviets gained little in their public propaganda battle. Austin effectively countered the wily Malik. At the last meeting of the month, the Vermonter stated that the four weeks were a waste of time due to the Soviet Union's "colossal contempt for the simple rules of the game of life, disregard of good morals and good behavior, and the use of this great forum to heap contumely upon men of honor, character and dignity, and upon great nations which love freedom and which have gained it at great expense."[35] But if nothing more, the August debate delineated again the two power blocs. While the United States attempted to limit the conflagration to Korea, it was insistent on the right to take a stand there. The Soviets, thwarted initially by their blundering, self-imposed boycott, attempted to regain lost ground by placing many impediments in the way of a peaceful solution unfavorable to themselves. With Gladwyn Jebb of Great Britain assuming the presidency of the Council for the month of September, Western leaders now hoped for progress.

While the propaganda war in the Security Council commanded most of the August headlines, Austin's position also was utilized to clarify two major phases of United States policy in the Far East. The first related to the unification of Korea; the second pertained to American policy toward Formosa.

The military situation in Korea was bleak for the United Nations throughout July and into early August. However, by the second week in August, the United Nations forces had established and held the Pusan perimeter, thus halting the farthest advance of the North Koreans into South Korea. Meanwhile, MacArthur readied plans for a bold counteroffensive, spearheaded by an amphibious assault landing far behind enemy lines at Inchon, some thirty-five miles west of Seoul. If successful, it could return United Nations troops to the 38th parallel within a short period of time. It also would create the context for a political decision that might possibly sanction the crossing of the parallel. Of course there were valid military reasons to pursue the North Koreans into their own sector to eliminate the sanctuary from which they might again strike. Politically, however, there were more serious implications. How would the Soviet Union and Communist China react? Under what authority would the United Nations forces move into North Korea — the June 25 resolution merely called for the *status quo ante bellum.* And tactically, could the United States maneuver a change of policy through the United Nations now that Malik was again present in the Security Council?

To seek answers to these questions, Austin was instructed to loft a trial balloon in the Security Council.[36] His August 17 comments to the Council were intended to draw reaction to a veiled idea of uniting Korea — presumably based on the 1948 United Nations decision to do so. Austin deliberately avoided any direct reference to a United Nations objective of creating a unified and independent nation because his major emphasis centered on the cessation of hostilities. But Austin hinted at the idea of crossing the parallel when he suggested ending the fighting in such a way that "no opportunity is provided for another attempt at invasion." He went on to say that "Korea's prospects would be dark if any action of the United Nations were to condemn it to exist indefinitely as 'half slave and half free' or even one-third slave and two-thirds free." Then he raised the possibility of United Nations action: "The United Nations had consistently worked for a unified country, an independent Korea. The United Nations will not want to turn from that objective now." Response to his remarks was guarded, but it was generally favorable. Even Malik's comment was not exceedingly strong as he said that Austin's statement "makes it clear the United

States wants to extend the scope of the war."[37] As a result, the American government continued its planning.

Meanwhile, MacArthur had created a major stir in public as well as in the high echelons of the American government with his unilateral actions and remarks toward Formosa. A speech Truman delivered to Congress on July 19 partially assured the world that, by placing the Seventh Fleet in the Formosa Straits, the nation had no designs on that island and did not seek a wider war. But a much publicized, unauthorized MacArthur trip to Formosa at the end of July raised the specter of widening the war. It prompted the dispatch to Korea of Presidential Assistant W. Averell Harriman to ameliorate the matter.

To lessen misunderstandings among America's allies, on August 24 Truman directed Austin to write a public letter to Trygve Lie outlining clearly the American policy toward Formosa. The subsequent letter, drafted by Austin and his staff, spelled out the limited nature of the Korean struggle and the effect the neutralization of the Formosa Straits by the United States had in limiting the conflict. The letter also reaffirmed the position that the United States had no designs on Formosa.[38]

MacArthur continued his independent course by composing a lengthy statement for the Veterans of Foreign Wars which he made public without approval from his Washington superiors. He outlined the strategic importance of Formosa and claimed a catastrophe if that island fell into hostile hands. Truman received a copy on August 26. He was furious; he directed the Secretary of Defense, Louis Johnson, to order MacArthur to retract the message. MacArthur complied; but already it was too late to prevent publication.[39]

Concerned over the effect the MacArthur statement would have on the previous Austin clarification of American policy to Lie, Undersecretary of State James Webb suggested to Truman through presidential aide George Elsey that the President should consider receiving Austin at the White House. This would amount to a show of support for the Austin position at the United Nations as opposed to what MacArthur was doing. Truman decided against this "on the grounds that he was not going to engage in dramatics."

However, he did speak to Austin by phone and followed that call with a public letter to the Senator reiterating American policy in regard to Formosa. Truman also dispatched to MacArthur a copy of Austin's recent letter to Lie.[40]

These events confused United Nations observers of American policy. On the one hand, Austin hinted at crossing the parallel and uniting Korea, thus broadening the scope of the war. On the other hand, he was publicly stating a policy of limited war by excluding Formosa from the fray. And at the same time, he was conducting a full-scale verbal war across the Security Council table against Jacob Malik. Where was the real American policy? September loomed as an important month at Lake Success, for perhaps it would bring an answer to this question.

On September 1, with Truman's approval, the National Security Council concluded that the United Nations should employ military operations north of the 38th parallel under terms of the June 27 United Nations resolution. The subject was under discussion for several weeks, but battlefield conditions had not allowed a final decision until this time. Intelligence reports, along with MacArthur's already approved counteroffensive scheduled for mid-September, provided enough optimism to approve the policy.[41]

In conjunction with the decisions, the State Department had to consider the relation of future policy in Korea to the present United Nations policy. Standing instructions required American policy to seek collective United Nations approval. Accordingly, work went forward on a plan which actually resulted in two separate United Nations actions: the first involved the well-known "Uniting for Peace" resolution, while the second resulted in General Assembly approval of a plan to cross the 38th parallel as well as to create a "unified, independent and democratic government" in Korea. In retrospect, both resolutions appear as short-sighted, but in the context of the situation in 1950, both fit the developing long-range situation quite well.

Austin's August experience in the Security Council added considerably to the development of those plans. The month-long encounter with Malik convinced Washington policy-makers that with the Soviets again seated in the Security

Council, they would continue to stop any action there which the American-led bloc might wish to pursue in Korea. While assumption of the Council presidency in September by Britain's Gladwyn Jebb smoothed the procedural process, it did not eliminate the Soviet veto or provide substantial optimism for progress. Yet Austin's August 17 reference to a future unified Korea showed enough of a favorable diplomatic and public reception to encourage the plan to cross the parallel. Then the subsequent successful Inchon invasion served to bolster the policymakers' convictions that brighter days were ahead.[42]

Encouraged by Far Eastern desk officers Rusk and John Allison and United Nations desk chief Hickerson, the Department developed plans to utilize the fall General Assembly session, scheduled to open on September 19, to declare that, if a veto paralyzed the Security Council, the General Assembly should assume responsibility and authority in maintaining international peace. After working a resolution out, Acheson placed it before the Assembly in his opening speech to the gathering. Entitled "United Action for Peace," its provisions included (1) power to call an emergency session of the General Assembly on a 24-hour notice if the Security Council was prevented from acting because of a veto; (2) establishment of observation teams to provide immediate inspection and reports from any area; (3) provision under which each member would designate a United Nations unit within its national forces; (4) establishment of a Collective Measure Committee composed of representatives of fourteen states to study and report on methods which might be used collectively to maintain and strengthen international peace and security.[43]

The proposal amounted to an amendment of the rules of procedure of the General Assembly. Contrary to what is often assumed, it did not amend the Charter or transfer power from the Security Council to the General Assembly. Acheson later recalled that during the planning for the proposal he was forewarned by the British Foreign Office that there was future danger in the idea, specifically if the 1950 "majority in the United Nations should give way to one holding contrary views." But the Secretary disclosed that "present dangers outweighed possible future ones," and he allowed his planners to continue their work.[44]

John Foster Dulles, a member of the United States delegation, was given major responsibility to carry the resolution through the committee and plenary debates. Dulles was qualified for the task because of his background, both at previous United Nations sessions and at the San Francisco conference in 1945. As head of the delegation, Austin supported Dulles's efforts, but he devoted his main efforts to the concurrent meetings of the Council. Shortly after its passage on November 3, Austin noted that after five years article 43 still remained a matter of words. He realized that a unique set of circumstances allowed the establishment of a unified command in Korea, and the availability of that solution was limited. Thus he saw the best interest of the United Nations and the world in development of adequate available machinery should another emergency arise. For this reason, the "Uniting for Peace" resolution was of paramount importance.[45]

"Uniting for Peace" was planned as the basic foundation for a policy declaration by the Assembly on the Korean question. The rapid change in the military situation, however, forced adoption of a Korean policy statement by the Assembly prior to final passage of the "Uniting for Peace" resolution. The MacArthur-planned counteroffensive in mid-September was so successful that it brought the United Nations forces to the 38th parallel by the end of the month. The State and Defense Departments had already decided a move across the parallel would be legal under the terms of the June 27 Security Council resolution. Nonetheless, the United States did not want to cross the parallel without new collective approval by the United Nations. The military circumstances now presented an opportunity to seek a broader mandate based on the 1947-48 Assembly attempt to create a unified Korea.[46]

In late September, much behind-the-scenes discussion took place among the Assembly delegations. Secretary Acheson carried the burden of negotiations within the American delegation although all members participated. The United States policy — based on the assumption that the opposing forces had disintegrated — advocated the United Nations cross into North Korea unless the North Koreans agreed to a ceasefire, turned over their arms to United Nations forces and accepted the authority of the United Nations until an independent Korea was established. A resolution was hammered out, cosponsored by Great Britain, Australia, Brazil, Cuba, the Netherlands, Norway, Pakistan and the Philippines. Kenneth Younger, British Minister of State, introduced it on September 30. It provided for conditions of stability throughout Korea; that the United Nations hold elections and that United Nations forces not remain in any part of Korea except as necessary for the achievement of these objectives.[47] While not explicitly authorizing United Nations forces to cross the parallel, it clearly implied that they could.

Austin represented the United States in the committee debate on the resolution. His presentation on September 30 — Acheson later said it was "almost a naive view of what was likely to happen" — emphasized both the military necessity of crossing the line and the more expansive unification policy. Toward the latter, Austin called for the erection of a "living political, social and spiritual monument to the achievement of the first enforcement of the United Nations peacemaking function." He went on to say that the "question whether the artificial barrier of the 38th parallel should remain removed, and whether Korea should be united now, must be determined by the United Nations."[48]

In addition to expected opposition from the Soviet bloc, another group composed mostly of Asian and Arab states led by India and Yugoslavia opposed the measure. These states held varying degrees of concern; foremost, however, was the risk of bringing Communist China or the Soviet Union directly into the conflict. As a result, three major viewpoints developed in the committee debate. The majority view advocated the total defeat of North Korea as expressed by Austin and in the eight-power resolution. The Soviet bloc wanted an immediate cease-fire and withdrawal of troops. The growing neutral nations remained opposed to both plans and insisted that United Nations forces not cross the parallel. The final vote on the eight-power resolution was along these lines. It passed, forty-seven to five, with seven abstentions. In the plenary meeting on October 7, the same voting pattern occurred on the final adoption of the resolution.[49] By November, United Nations forces stretched across the northern frontier of Korea, with advanced troops encamped on the banks of the Yalu River dividing Korea from Manchuria.

Before proceeding to events precipitated by the expansion of ground war into North Korea, a brief return to the role Austin played in the September Security Council meetings is in order. The delaying and inflammatory tactics of Malik within that body have already been observed. Austin's standing instructions dictated that he continue to thwart any Soviet abuses with verbal counterattacks of his own. Typical was the colloquy on September 11, after Malik charged, the day before, that the United States had bombed the territory of China and asked for a Security Council censure of the United States. The complaint was coupled with a renewed demand to seat a representative of Red China on the Security Council to hear the discussion.

Austin and his colleagues viewed the Soviet demand in behalf of Red China as a waste of time which prevented a quick decision on the bombing matter. Austin charged that this Soviet move was a deceptive ruse to gain United Nations admittance for Communist China as well as a propaganda move directed at America. He asserted again that the Security Council should not discuss the issue of representation collaterally, but as a second and independent issue. As to the bombing, Austin said the United States sought further investigation and he proposed a commission to ascertain the facts in the alleged incident. The Senator stated, however, that he believed the Chinese Communists were more interested in gaining a seat at the Council than in determining guilt on the bombing issue.[50]

In the debate the following day, on the agenda item of the American resolution of July 31 that condemned the North Koreans for continued defiance of the United Nations, Austin again met the Soviets head-on. He charged that the Soviet Union's mission divided the Council: "to destroy its solidarity and to enervate its power to resist Soviet

aggression." The Soviets feared facing the entire United
Nations, said Austin; therefore, they singled out one member
for attack. Austin emphasized that this approach, if allowed
to go unchallenged, could result in brutal attacks against
country after country. Despite Soviet misuse of the veto,
Austin told his audience, the objectives of the United
Nations still remained intact and would grow in strength.
But Malik had his instructions. Despite Austin's arguments,
he beat down the American resolution with the forty-seventh
Soviet veto.[51]

Austin displayed more dramatic ability at the Council
meeting on the 18th. Malik earlier rejected a charge that the
Soviet Union had supplied arms to North Korea after the
Soviet withdrawal from that nation in 1948. To discredit that
denial, Austin produced, while presenting a report of the
United Nations Command to the Council, a Soviet-made
submachine gun with 1950 markings on it. It caused Malik to
walk out of the meeting. Later, he denounced Austin's
gesture as "a provocation designed for simpletons."[52]

While Austin displayed this hard-line rhetorical style, he
could not forsake his lifetime belief in cooperation and in
international organization as the best hope for the world.
Whenever he could, he expressed optimism for the future of
the Security Council. He pointed out that the Council had
resolved some questions by pacific means. In the absence of
such action war might have resulted, and even in cases
where the problem was not immediately solved, it was at
least "transferred from the battlefield to the conference
table." He claimed that the Security Council never failed
completely, and he had faith that it never would. If nothing
more, it proved itself as an effective voice "for the conscience
of mankind."[53]

Austin is open to criticism for this naivete. His own
experience in the Council since the return of Malik should
have removed any doubts in his mind about the further
possibility of utilizing that body to strengthen collective
action in Korea. In addition, the United States' decision to
utilize the General Assembly under the "Uniting for Peace"
resolution, if Security Council actions were hindered by a
veto, indicated the real situation. Both these developments
underscored the futility of Security Council action. There is,

of course, a logical answer for his optimism even in those trying months. His position at the United Nations necessitated his presentation of this image and that alone is enough to explain his rhetorical outbursts. But underlying that there also was expressed a deep sincerity for the work of the United Nations as well as a faith in what the organization may one day accomplish. Being a United Nations advocate made his task there much easier.

From the beginning of the Korean conflict various pieces of intelligence indicated Red China's anxiety over the peninsular war. The first concern appeared over the United States' action in the Straits of Formosa, seen by Red China as designed to thwart a final military decision between Mao's forces and those of Chiang Kai-shek. But by mid-August, evidence showed a decided turn on the part of the Chinese Communists toward the struggle in Korea. Warning statements, directed at foreign audiences by Mao and Chou En-lai, massive military movements into North China and Manchuria, and domestic Chinese communications about developments in Korea increased throughout late August and into September. In the immediate post-Inchon phase of the war, the intelligence indicated the increasing seriousness of a Chinese intervention in Korea. However, it was not until after the Chinese saw the United Nations ignoring their warnings, through the authorization for the crossing of the parallel, that the decision for intervention was made. Throughout all this, United States policymakers placed low priority on the evidence and relied mainly on MacArthur's intelligence sources and estimates. The General thought there was little chance the Red Chinese would come into the fray.[54]

The first Chinese "volunteers" crossed the Yalu River a week after the United Nations forces crossed the 38th parallel. Between mid-October and November 1, from 180,000 to 228,000 Chinese troops entered Korea. The United Nations Command officially announced the presence of these troops on November 5 in its report to the Security Council.

The State Department requested an urgent meeting of the Council, and, in conjunction with the British, approved a proposal made by Gladwyn Jebb that the Security Council

invite a representative of Communist China to discuss the
MacArthur report of Chinese involvement. Austin was
furious over this newest affront to United Nations authority.
At the November 8 Council meeting, he said that, since
China was the aggressor, it should receive a "summons"
rather than an invitation. Malik would not let Austin's
objection go unchallenged. He snapped back: "When a
colonial power speaks to a colonial slave, it may summon
him, but in the present case, the term should be to invite."
The vote on the invitation was favorable by an 8-2 count.
Nationalist China and Cuba opposed it, Egypt abstained;
the Soviets and Americans voted in favor.[55]

Constant consultation with Washington resulted in a
decision that Austin should set the stage for what was
expected to be a renewed, acrimonious public debate. He was
directed to submit a resolution calling on the Chinese to
cease their activities in Korea. President Truman thought
this necessary in order to maintain United Nations support
for any further action in Korea, just as the June 25 resolution
had when the North Koreans invaded. Subsequently, on
November 10 Austin submitted the resolution with a blunt
statement that China's intervention must stop. While the
resolution made it clear that the United Nations sought
peace through amicable settlement, Austin stressed that it
also provided for the use of force to prevent any new
assault.[56]

Delays ensued before Red China's General Wu Hsiu-chuan
arrived in New York and attended his first Security Council
meeting on November 28. An atmosphere similar to that of
August 1 surrounded his appearance because four days
earlier General MacArthur had launched a new "home by
Christmas" offensive. Quickly the Red Chinese forces
unleashed a vicious counterattack all along the line; this
stopped the United Nations troops by the very day General
Wu first sat in the Council chamber. Thwarted in his quest
for victory, MacArthur cabled that day that the United
Nations forces faced an "entirely new war." Thus the
continuing conflict of interpretation between Washington
and MacArthur created this superheated situation that
brought tension to Lake Success and also to America's

European allies, who became gravely concerned that the United States was abandoning its paramount European strategy for a wider adventure in Asia.[57]

The resulting Security Council debate, for which Austin spent long hours in preparation, proved short-lived. Immediately, Wu Hsiu-chuan addressed the group to state his country's position on Korea. With great invective, he condemned the United Nations forces and said that his nation's entrance into Korea came at the request of North Korea. All the troops, he said, were "volunteers."

When Austin received his turn to speak, he fired twenty questions at the Chinese general. His staff had prepared these to downplay the expected propaganda value of the Chinese claims. The Senator opened by speculating whether the aggression was really in the interests of the Chinese, or in favor of the Soviet Union. By the very nature of the intervention, Austin said, it appeared that Red China had prepared for this move for some time. He asked for an explanation of the manner in which supplies had crossed the border in such an organized fashion. This bothered him, Austin said, since General Wu claimed the action voluntary. Turning to the subject of aircraft, Austin jabbed his adversary. He said he could not comprehend how "volunteer" private Chinese citizens were able to come into the possession of jet aircraft!

The Senator turned to the proposed United States resolution. While he believed that a Soviet veto would kill its chance of passage, Austin said the measure represented the conscience of the people of the world and he thought that was a consideration to which the Peking government should give attention. The United Nations needed some assurance of peaceful intent by Communist China. But even more important, it sought deeds from Peking that would demonstrate that Red China's interest in peace was genuine.[58] Despite Austin's efforts, on November 30 the Soviet Union defeated the United States resolution.

In turn, the West defeated, by identical 9-1 votes, two resolutions sponsored by the Soviet Union. The first, submitted by General Wu, called on the United States to get out of Korea and Formosa. The second, submitted back on

September 2, demanded that the United States leave
Formosa. After these bitter proceedings, the Council adjourned. Action shifted to the General Assembly where it was
bolstered by the "Uniting for Peace" resolution.

Austin's brief but sarcastic encounter with the Red
Chinese in the Security Council attested again to his
developing hard-line attitude toward communist defiance of
the United Nations. Dean Acheson later called the Austin-
Wu debate a charade: "this ridiculous puppet show."[59]
Austin viewed it as holding the line against attack. In either
case, it helped set the stage for his upcoming energetic,
impatient role in condemning the Chinese for their actions.

MacArthur's public call for a wider war to stop the new
Chinese onslaught, combined with President Truman's
misconstrued press conference statements on November 30
concerning use of the atomic bomb, caused great anxiety
among the Western European nations and members of the
Arab-Asian bloc. British concern over these events was
acute. While Britain had cosponsored the defeated Security
Council resolution directed at Red China, its leaders were
unenthusiastic about the hardening position taken by the
United States. They still hoped to persuade the Chinese to
adopt a more reasonable attitude. To offset this anxiety, the
Department directed Austin to assure the British delegation
that MacArthur would work only through United Nations
channels. In addition, the administration clarified Truman's
press conference comments and the State Department
directed further assurances toward the British through
regular diplomatic channels. Despite these assurances,
Prime Minister Clement Atlee made a sudden visit to the
United States to discuss the deteriorating situation with
Truman and his aides.[60]

The "state of panic" that developed at the United Nations
among the various delegations did not provide an ideal
situation in the General Assembly to attempt passage of a
resolution condemning Communist China as an aggressor.
Acheson had always believed that such a proclamation
would serve as a countermeasure to the Soviet proposals
attacking the United States and would open the way for
future collective action by the Assembly. But demands from

other nations for American support for a cease-fire also were heard constantly. Most American officials regarded this as a case in which the weaker element was appealing to the stronger side as long as the United Nations forces were retreating in Korea. Yet failure to support a peaceful solution of the Korean war, as a cease-fire proposal generally implied, could produce charges of warmongering and would place the Americans in an untenable diplomatic position. Lack of American cease-fire support could also further alienate the Arab-Asia bloc and cause division in the developing NATO alliance. Complicating these matters, heavy domestic political pressure, particularly from MacArthur supporters and the China Lobby, advocated a firm stand against the renewed Chinese onslaught.[61]

American tactics in the General Assembly were devised within this context. To meet the dilemma, the American position sought to conduct a holding action at the United Nations throughout December and early January. Austin and Gross constantly consulted with Acheson and his staff in developing an early consensus that the United States would demonstrate to its allies that it was prepared to exhaust the cease-fire procedures in which the allies were interested. To do that, the United States would passively support any proposals for a cease-fire resolution at the United Nations. This decision was based on two assumptions. One, the proposals would not involve any political commitments on the part of the United States. Two, the Chinese would reject all overtures. Then as the climate of opinion changed, it would allow support for the original American position, which would censure the Chinese.[62]

On December 12, in the Political Committee, India's Benegal Rau introduced a resolution sponsored by his nation and twelve other Arab-Asian states that requested a cease-fire and called for a general conference on the Far East. The proposal specifically called for a three-man group to determine the basis for a cease-fire and to make recommendations for its implementation. The plenary session adopted this resolution on December 14. General Wu, still in New York, refused to meet with the cease-fire group and indicated his government's belief in the futility of the plan by calling it a "trap." In spite of a United States initiative that it would go along with the plan, the end came on December 22 when Chou En-lai issued a lengthy statement reiterating the political demands of Red China as a basis for a cease-fire. American assumptions were correct; the December proposal was lost.[63]

The British and Canadians made another cease-fire attempt in January. The proposal contained more specific conditions than the December initiative in order to attract the Chinese. Following the established American strategy, Austin agreed to leave the door open for negotiations. But delay by the cease-fire negotiators irritated Austin. Lester Pearson, a member of the cease-fire committee, reported on January 5 that "Austin is more impatient about delay than the people in Washington and will explode if he is not permitted to make a tough speech before long." However, publicly, the Senator exhibited calm and waited for the proposal to run its course.[64]

In the Political Committee, the United States supported the subsequent cease-fire resolution that stemmed from this January initiative. Although the Chinese rejected the overture two days later, American support of it created, according to Acheson, an "unholy row" in the United States. Charges of appeasement came from both Republican and Democratic politicians. Stimulated by the increasing frustrations of the war, the 1951 Great Debate was on, and it accelerated as events progressed.[65]

Seething inside, Austin outwardly remained calm as he helped prepare his nation's case against Communist China. As the British and Canadians readied the latest cease-fire proposal for attempted Assembly passage, Austin asked the Department for clearance to discuss the American position regarding the condemnation of Communist China with the delegations of the Latin American nations. He was convinced that Chinese rejection of any cease-fire attempt would shift opinion that would help assure the branding of Red China as an aggressor. Austin employed "almost a crusading attitude" in both his public pronouncements and corridor discussions to win support for the United States' position.[66]

The day following Chou's second rejection of the British-Canadian cease-fire attempt, Austin opened his nation's argument for condemnation. He asked for renewed consideration of the purposes and principles of the Charter. Based on past action against North Korea, the United Nations could not now tolerate the application of two standards: one for North Korea and another for Communist China. Since the Charter was designed to outlaw aggression, Austin said, the United Nations should now prove that "no power could defy that principle with impunity." Broadening the subject, he viewed communism as a monolithic structure, and charged that the intervention in Korea by China was part of a world plan directed by Soviet imperialism that did not serve legitimate Chinese interests. While the Soviets used the pretext of helping the Chinese throw out colonialism, they sought to impose an even more rigorous form of imperialism on the Asian people. He then suggested a condemnation resolution promulgated through the Assembly and the Collective Measures Committee.[67]

Before formally introducing the condemnation resolution, Austin and his staff met with other delegations to work out final details. It soon was obvious that the United States did not have enthusiastic support for its hard-line approach. Nonetheless, the American attitude remained firm: the government was prepared to pursue the resolution regardless of the support it received.[68]

These decisions were based on larger dimensions of American Far Eastern policy that hoped to prevent further consolidation of the communist regime on mainland China. In February 1951, Dean Rusk told the Canadian ambassador that American intelligence sources in China indicated internal difficulties in Mao's ruling group over Moscow-Peking relations. Based on this, American policy dictated that outside pressure — through such matters as condemnation of Chinese aggression and continued recognition of Chiang Kai-shek's Nationalists as the legitimate government of China — might aid in nurturing a split between the two camps.[69]

In this context, Austin now fully accepted his government's hard line. He gave no quarter in pursuing the condemnation of Red China. On January 20, he presented the resolution. In comparison to the tension-filled air of the June 1950 resolutions, Austin's rallying efforts were reflect-

ed in an atmosphere of disillusionment. He appeared glum
and solitary in giving his brief presentation. The failure of
America's major allies to support the resolution readily made
the situation depressing. The United States appeared all
alone in this effort.[70]

After taking Sunday off, Austin returned to the fray the
following day. Angered by an Indian request for a 48-hour
adjournment to pursue another fleeting possibility for a
cease-fire, he leveled a searing attack on those who appeared
not to support the United States. Austin particularly insulted
the representatives of India and Egypt in what Lester
Pearson called "one of the worst performances of his career."
His rancor — obviously manifested by his growing impatience with events — brought defeat on this issue for the
United States. The motion for postponement was approved
by a 27 to 23 vote; most of America's allies voted in favor of
the item.[71]

Throughout the remainder of the debate on the resolution,
Austin remained calm, but he continued his hard-line
approach. On January 24, he declared that a solution to the
problem of Chinese intervention required a formula acceptable to both sides, not solely to Peking. He thought the
United Nations had offered liberal terms to Communist
China in the cease-fire attempts, but now the organization's
patience was tested. Three days later, Austin commented
that the intervention posed two problems for the United
Nations. First, he remarked, the intervention questioned
whether the United Nations was capable of pronouncing a
moral judgment on Red China. Second, the United Nations
must evaluate its capability to take measures based on that
judgment.[72] Austin's greatest concern related to the matter
of moral judgment. Since United Nations troops already
were fighting against the Chinese, moral condemnation was
the only action possible. Short of a United Nations decision
to alter the geographical limits of the war — which the
United States opposed — basically little else could be
accomplished in the matter of collective measures. The
resolution passed the committee on January 30 and the
plenary meeting passed it two days later. However, that vote
reflected the moderating course of many nations. Sweden,

Yugoslavia and seven Arab and Asian states abstained; the usual five-vote Soviet bloc was joined by India and Burma in opposition to the resolution.

Korean events at Lake Success slowed during the next few months at a time that saw them intensify on the Washington front between President Truman and General MacArthur. Austin was somewhat familiar with the problems between the two commanders. He could recall the necessity of his public clarification over Formosa in August 1950 as well as the reassurances he delivered to the British delegation in late November. Nonetheless, no evidence, public or private, is available on any commentary Austin made concerning the growing cleavage prior to April 11, 1951, when Truman relieved MacArthur of his command.

Austin, as a leading Republican in the Truman administration, was immediately queried and pressured on his own position in the controversy. Congressman Lawrence Smith sent a telegram asking Austin if there had been any action by the United Nations to remove MacArthur. Austin replied that the matter was entirely within the jurisdiction of the United States. One strong MacArthur supporter, Senator William F. Knowland, suggested publicly that Austin resign in protest against the MacArthur removal. Speaking to a group of Princeton University students two days later, Austin, fully aware of the scope of Republican opposition to the dismissal of the General, answered the Knowland suggestion with his own personal statement of support for the present United States policy in Korea.[73]

On two more occasions within the following week, he spoke publicly in favor of Truman's stand. To the delegates of the American Association of University Women, Austin emphasized the limiting nature of the Korean action. He disclaimed any military objective related to China or Asia; the entire action was designed merely to suppress a breach of peace in Korea. Talking to a visiting Vermont youth group at Lake Success the following day, the Senator noted how impossible it had become for the United Nations Unified Command, working under a resolution that limited its activities to Korea, to continue with a commander who held a completely different view.[74]

As American public opinion reacted to the Truman-MacArthur controversy by raging against nearly everything connected with the Truman administration, Austin continued faithful to the United Nations principle as embodied in the Korean resolution. In a major speech on May 1, he reiterated United Nations policy in Korea. It amounted to a direct rejoinder to MacArthur's argument for an expanded war. Austin stressed the political objective in Korea and said it was not necessarily achieved by military means alone. Even though the United Nations branded the Chinese Communists as aggressors, it held open the possibility of a peaceful settlement. He again emphasized that the action was limited to Korea.[75]

The willingness to speak out on a controversial issue of such magnitude once again revealed a life-long Austin characteristic. Although the particular position was unpopular, the Senator was unhesitating in its support if he thought the stand was correct. In this case, he placed himself above political considerations. Austin viewed the matter as more than a conflict between superiors. He regarded it as an attack on a just action the United Nations had taken. Deeply committed to that course, he felt obligated to defend it against any attack.

For all practical purposes, the United Nations debate on Korea ended at this point. The armistice talks and ultimate weary military and diplomatic stalemate that was to persist over the next two years did not directly involve Austin. Diplomatic maneuvers centered outside the United Nations.

Korea had profound meaning for Austin. He thought the action represented the most salutary demonstration of collective security witnessed in the world to date. He remained convinced that the world was ready to employ collective security even though many problems still remained. The Korean action disclosed to Austin two vital elements for a workable system of collective security. First, he saw that man's mind must perceive the defense of a principle, not merely a people or a territory. That the challenger confronted the whole world in the Korean situation was the essence of his argument. Second, he saw the necessity of workable plans in order to provide a quick

response to any challenge to that principle.[76] Austin
recognized the United Nation's good fortune in the Soviet
Union's boycott of the organization in June 1950. Yet he
viewed the Korean conflict as a catalyst that moved the
United Nations to adopt the "Uniting for Peace" resolution.
Even though that resolution reflected the inability of the
Security Council to act, it now appeared to Austin that
progress was evident for the first time in nearly five years.

Austin believed in the domino theory: if the United
Nations had not stopped the North Korean aggression,
Japan, Hong Kong and Southeast Asia eventually would
have fallen to the communists. More important to Austin,
this action was taken after due consideration in full view of
the world. Austin saw the entire episode as a "triumph of
higher ethics," as he claimed it was the spirit of the whole
man and not the letter of the law that made the collective
action possible. He considered the incident a brilliant
chapter in man's efforts to rid the world of aggression.[77]

Korea confirmed Austin as a Cold Warrior. He no longer
was willing to give the Soviets the benefit of his doubt. He
told a gathering of reporters in May that the "movement in
the world today is that of Communist imperialism." Austin
saw the Soviets pressing their advantage on all fronts. At the
United Nations, Austin cited Soviet propaganda in the
creation of doubt and division among members in order to
develop a pretext for withdrawal that would splinter the
organization and cause division in the free world.[78]

The Korean episode was a watershed for Austin just as it
was for the Truman administration. The President's
strategy for a limited war prevailed, but the American people
quickly became disenchanted with the Korean stalemate.
They were almost eager to elect a Republican President who
promised to end the conflict. In this context, it is an
overstatement to say that the final year and a half of
Austin's United Nations tenure was anticlimactic. His
activities were in marked contrast with the hectic events that
occurred between 1946 and 1951.

Nonetheless, Austin's continued belief in the United
Nations was reflected in several ways, for example, his
proposal to Truman that the United States initiate plans for

the erection of a "tomb of the Unknown Soldier of the United Nations Unified Command under the United States" in the new plaza of the United Nations; Truman shelved that idea.[79] Another instance was his participation in the opening of the new United Nations complex. For the Senator, it was the symbolic physical example of an institution that represented the best hope for the world.

Certainly the final two General Assembly sessions, as well as the workload of the Security Council, kept Austin thoroughly occupied. However, the trying years of United Nations work had their effect on him physically. Considering his age and his serious medical setback in 1948, he was in moderately good health. But at the sixth General Assembly meeting in Paris in the fall of 1951, Austin again could not relieve a lingering cold. It developed into a severe respiratory problem that weakened his heart and necessitated his return to the United States for recuperation while the session still was in progress. The last year in office saw Austin turning more and more of the work over to his deputy, Ernest Gross.[80]

The election of Dwight Eisenhower to the presidency in 1952 necessitated a review of all appointed positions. Secretary of State designate John Foster Dulles recommended a change at the United Nations, and he strongly urged the appointment of Henry Cabot Lodge as Austin's successor. Eisenhower agreed without reservation. On November 28, Dulles went to Austin's Waldorf apartment where he told the Senator of the proposed change in the head of the Mission. Dulles explained that the main reason Lodge received the post hinged on the latter's defeat for re-election in his Massachusetts senatorial campaign. Austin simply said he thought Lodge was well qualified. Like a good politician, he accepted the turn of events without rancor.[81]

Austin received the usual laudatory comments when his retirement was announced in December. In a radio interview over the National Broadcasting Company on December 27, Austin reminisced on his mission to the United Nations. He displayed faith in the organization even though it was hampered by the tragedy of the times. He thought that peace was near, yet it eluded mankind. He felt depressed that force alone seemed necessary to maintain peace. Austin conceded that the road was much rougher in 1952 than he had hoped or visualized back in 1945. He sadly recognized that the enthusiasm of the immediate postwar years had waned, but he thought that the United Nations had slowly found its direction and was moving toward means of maintaining peace.[82]

Austin looked forward to his retirement after twenty-two years in public life. In the coldest month of 1953, he and Mildred returned to their rambling, Williams Street home in Burlington where he began immediately to organize his new life. He hoped to spend time sorting his large collection of personal papers and documents and he thought about possible publication of a memoir. He likewise hoped to devote equal time to his backyard horticultural interests and to relaxation with his beloved Mildred. Son Bob practiced law in town and the closeness of his family was a joy to the elder Austins.

The variety of seasons in Vermont seemed to complement nicely Austin's planned division of labor. In the cold winter months of early 1953, he began to renovate a lower-level room to house his collection of papers. In anticipation of the first time in many years that he could spend an entire season cultivating his apple trees, he attended an early spring apple-grower's seminar at the nearby University of Vermont.[83]

Austin did not lose his lifelong interest in international affairs. Reflecting his conversion to a Cold Warrior, he readily accepted the appointment as honorary chairman of the nationwide Committee of One Million, the public interest group organized with the avowed purpose of keeping Communist China out of the United Nations. While most of the work was carried out by others, Austin did spend a large amount of time handling correspondence.[84]

Health problems interrupted and greatly slowed the Senator's retirement years. In the early spring of 1953, he suffered cerebral complications resulting from his long-time heart problem. The hospital listed his condition as grave when he was rushed there. But his recovery was remarkable. He left the hospital on April 11, and his attending physicians described him as "completely recovered." Austin slowly resumed his gardening and reading activities carefully watched by Mildred. He remained out of the public eye.[85]

In October 1956, Austin suffered a stroke that induced severe strain on his heart and kidneys. Paralysis afflicted his left side as he again was rushed to the hospital. After several days of fretful watching by his family and physician, Dr. Wilfred Raab, slow improvement was noticed. The next two months were long and trying, as Austin remained in the hospital. On December 1, Dr. Raab released him, although the Senator would need much more time to regain his strength. Again, Mildred nursed him through that recuperating stage. Unfortunately, however, that stroke greatly hampered the last years of his retirement. He often was in bed and moved about only with great difficulty. He maintained a lively interest in all his retirement activities, but his health often prevented his participation.[86] On Christmas day in 1962, he died peacefully in his sleep at the age of 85.

Although Austin's family was buried in Highgate, he and Mildred considered Burlington their home. They both loved the wooded slopes leading to the shore of Lake Champlain. In their retirement, they had selected a family burial site in Lakewood Cemetery where the setting was both quiet and spectacular. Here Austin marked the family plot with two Grecian-inspired ionic columns carved from Vermont granite. Slightly downhill from the columns, the Senator's body was interred in the spring of 1963. His resting place was marked by a simple tombstone with his own choice of words: Warren Robinson Austin. Born November 12, 1877. Died December 25, 1962. United States Senator, 1931 to 1946. Ambassador to the United Nations 1946 to 1953.

A FINAL ASSESSMENT

Austin's lengthy public career deserves a mixed assessment. On the one hand, the Senator was a product of a notable era and the events of those times decidedly moved and shaped him. On the other hand, like most public figures, he made a limited direct impact on the movement of events.

In domestic matters, Austin was a loyal Republican. As a senator from a highly Republican, conservative state, he served his constituency well. He voted the right way — anti-New Deal — nearly all the time and was rewarded with his return to office on two occasions. His 1934 victory, eked out in the context of a national campaign where the highly popular New Deal brought defeat to many Republicans, was symbolic of Austin's frugal, honest, independent, individualistic political position. His voting record after 1934, as a member of the small Republican conservative coalition, attests to his continued attachment to conservative characteristics.

Austin always advocated a strong national defense and was among the earliest members of the Senate to call for strengthened defenses in the 1930s. When the United States entered World War II, he pursued these activities even more vigorously from his position on the Military Affairs Committee. At times his patriotism moved him so far to the right as to be frightening — for example, his support of the controversial national service legislation — but he held no

ulterior motives. He merely wanted all to share in winning
what he considered a just war.

The Senator's place in history was not determined by his
stands on domestic or national defense issues. No major
piece of permanent legislation bears his name, nor was he
significantly involved in providing leadership on major
domestic issues. On that front, throughout his elected career,
he satisfied himself as a follower within the Republican
Senate establishment. The big names of those years largely
overshadowed his: Borah, Vandenberg, McNary and Taft.

Austin made his mark in the area of foreign relations. Here
he was a lifelong internationalist and his positions on issues
were determined by his view of the United States and the
world.

To evaluate Austin's international outlook, one must
underscore his belief in an American democratic, capitalistic
mission to the world. This concept was rather obscure in his
mind and only generally sketched out prior to events leading
to World War II. As a Vermont Progressive, his political
sense of moderate reform, his China experience in the teens,
his distant view of Republican foreign policy of the 1920s and
his caution against the nation's retreat into isolation in the
1930s all nurtured this idea. Throughout those developing
years Austin never lost sight of America's importance in the
world; however, he moved away from the general Republican
view with his proviso that the nation follow a course of
independence without isolation. This outlook eventually
placed him in a minority position within the isolationist
Republican ranks of the Senate in the late 1930s.

The Senator's fight against legalized neutrality fit his
concept of an American mission. It troubled him to think
that the United States, by failing to emerge from an
isolationist stance, might not accept a new responsibility in
world affairs. Initially against seemingly overwhelming
odds, his leadership in the internationalist movement, until
1944 without benefit of membership on the Foreign Relations
Committee, provides the best example of his philosophy of
foreign affairs in action. He stood alone early in the fight and
lost his leadership only when others jumped on the
bandwagon of the growing movement. Throughout the

infighting, he maintained a belief that American acceptance of the United Nations organization was the perfect symbol of a nation emerging from isolation and that America must channel its leadership through that world body.

Overall, Austin wanted to present America's system of freedom, capitalism and democracy to the world's countries. He saw this goal accomplished if the United States fully utilized the agencies of the United Nations as a "corner-stone" of the nation's foreign policy. With his nation setting the example, other countries, by observing the value of the American system, would, he hoped, follow it.

Austin never divorced moral purpose from international political action. As a moralist, his philosophy assumed that the United Nations was an arena for the dissemination of truth. There no nation could retreat from that truth. He saw nationalistic views brought together at the United Nations under a system of moral and legal rules and restraints where world public opinion scrutinized each nation's foreign policy.

This optimistic philosophy caused Austin to misunder-stand the Soviet Union's position on issues. He thought a friendly, candid and informal approach towards the Soviets would result in eventual solution of all the conflicting issues. From his United Nations post it seems he should have discerned early the widening East-West division as a destructive factor against the effectiveness of the world body. When the Truman administration conceptualized the containment policy as its public answer to Soviet conduct, Austin's universal view was not only awkward for him but also isolated from the developing American foreign policy. Yet he accepted the American stance skillfully by rationaliz-ing the tactics of containment as a series of short-range alternatives which supported the goals of the United Nations.

Austin's acceptance of the containment policy, both publicly and privately, was not merely to allay fears that the United States had cast the United Nations adrift in favor of a unilateral policy. That would amount to a betrayal of the principles he had long enunciated and in which he strongly believed. He was much too dedicated to those convictions to accept such an attitude. Instead, Austin neatly fit American policy into his concept of United Nations development. By adopting a theme of evolutionary growth for the world body he served various constituencies. He performed as an effective mouthpiece for the administration while at the same time he neither betrayed his own belief in the United Nations nor did he reject the American containment policy. The fact that America's policy bypassed the United Nations did not discourage Austin in his work; it merely forced him to develop a different goal to which to aspire. In other words, Austin continued as a United Nations man.

This universal position benefited both Austin and the United States. By rationalizing America's position without betraying his conscience, he became the best spokesman the administration could ask for at the United Nations. Certainly Austin's views were not realistic in the context of that postwar era. Had they been, in his own mind he would have uttered nothing more than empty words in his advocacy of American positions in support of the United Nations. And the record of the United States toward the United Nations during the period showed that use of the organization was not meant as a substitute for a nationalistic American foreign policy.

Over the years between 1946 and 1952, Austin converted into a Cold Warrior. No one particular event accounts for this; rather his contact through the United Nations with the continued intransigence of the Soviets on all major issues coupled with the administration's hard-line attitude brought him to this view. The capstone of his conversion was the trying months of the early Korean conflict when Austin and the United Nations organization were taxed sorely by both the Soviet Union and the People's Republic of China. After early 1951, Austin appeared very pessimistic regarding any *modus vivendi* with the communists.

It would be incorrect to make Austin unique in going through this conversion process. Many Americans, who hoped the postwar world would fix peace between nations, were converted by the rhetorical tirade of communist ideology against the West in combination with the Soviet Union's spectacular unilateral acts. So if Austin maintained any uniqueness at all through this, it was because of his underlying continued faith in the United Nations as the ultimate problem-solving agency for the world.

This study points up Austin's legacy as ambassador to the United Nations. During his six-and-a-half year tenure he established the basic role which has remained down to the present day — that of spokesman for American policy with little influence on the policy making process. The antagonistic nature of the universal, open diplomacy, United Nations ideals as opposed to a nationalistic, unilateral American foreign policy helps account for Austin's role. As a cooperationist striving to uphold those United Nations ideals, Austin operated from a minority position throughout his stay as ambassador. The three secretaries of state with whom he served were Cold Warriors and the relationship between Austin and those men was never close. Byrnes was probably the friendliest toward Austin, but he left the Department within six months of the Austin appointment. George Marshall, secretary during the years 1947 and 1948, remained aloof and always dealt with Austin in a formal manner through Department channels. Dean Acheson, who served as assistant and undersecretary for both Byrnes and Marshall, assumed the secretary's job in 1949. He held contempt for Austin's foreign policy viewpoint. All three secretaries, however, appreciated the important relationship between America's continued support (although at times only rhetorical) for the United Nations and the foreign policy of the nation. And Austin, with his sincere, cooperationist outlook, well carried out the role of American spokesman.

Austin's effectiveness at the United Nations was substantial in spite of his philosophy, which conflicted with the course of American policy. He served when the United States was undergoing a transitional phase of not only shedding isolation, but also searching for the best way to respond to emerging conditions of the Cold War. The American government presented the United Nations organization to the public as a symbol of the nation's rejection of isolation. But the world body was oversold (and Austin must partially share responsibility for this) as the American-led answer to problems in international society. A sizeable measure of

Austin's effectiveness is the manner in which he continued to uphold America's belief in the United Nations despite a policy that moved away from major use of the world body to conduct foreign relations. Adhering to legalistic ideas and associated with a sense of moral purpose and righteousness, Austin successfully reconciled his own personal views on the conduct of American foreign relations with the realities of the situation. In doing so, he was one of the last important universal internationalists in recent American history.

NOTES

ABBREVIATIONS

AP	Warren R. Austin Papers
CF	Correspondence File
CR	*Congressional Record*
DAP	Dean Acheson Papers
EP	George Elsey Papers
FRC	Federal Records Center
FRUS	*Foreign Relations of the United States*
GA (I/2)	Official Records of the General Assembly followed by session/part
HSTP	Harry S. Truman Papers
IO	International Organization
JJP	Joseph Jones Papers
NA	National Archives
NYT	*New York Times*
RG	Record Group
SC (Second/85)	Official Records of the Security Council followed by year/meeting number
SDDF	State Department Decimal File
SF	Speech File
USUN	United States/United Nations Mission File

CHAPTER ONE

[1]Press release, June 5, 1946, OF 85A, HSTP; *NYT*, June 6, 1946; James Byrnes, *Speaking Frankly* (New York: Harper, 1947), p. 235; Harry S. Truman, *Memoirs* (2 vols., Garden City, N.Y.: Doubleday, 1956), II, 164.

[2]Austin Family, Histories and Notes, n.d., box 106, AP.

[3]Life of Chauncey G. Austin, Sr. by George M. Hogan of the Franklin County Bar Association, 1933, box 106, AP.

[4]Interview, Warren R. Austin, Jr., with the author, Burlington, Vermont, Aug. 14, 1968; *The Bugle,* Oct. 5, 26, 1894; June 18, Oct. 23, 1895, Brigham Academy Papers, University of Vermont; *Ariel* (Burlington: University of Vermont, 1897).

[5]Interview, Mrs. Mildred Austin, with the author, Burlington, Vermont, July 23, 1970.

[6]Interview, Mrs. Mildred Austin, July 23, 1970; interview, Warren R. Austin, Jr., Aug. 14, 1968.

188   *Notes*

Interview, Warren R. Austin (WRA) with Sidney Fields, Apr. 22, 1951, SF 541; SF 15, 15a, 16, 17, 19, 20, 21, 22b, 24, AP.

Burlington Free Press (hereafter cited as *Free Press*), July 2, 3, 1908; *St. Albans Messenger*, Mar. 2, 1909.

Luther B. Johnson, *80 Years of It, 1869-1949* (Randolph, Vermont: Randolph Publishing Co., 1949), pp. 222-23; Lester F. Jipp, "The Progressive Party in Vermont in 1912" (Master's Thesis, University of Vermont, 1965), pp. 4-5; Winston Allen Flint, *The Progressive Movement in Vermont* (Washington, D.C.: Government Printing Office, 1941), pp. 54-57; *Free Press*, May 12, June 12, 17, 19, 1912; Speech to As-You-Like-It Club, June 21, 1912, SF 33; campaign speech Oct. 29, 1914, SF 48, AP.

Interview, Warren R. Austin, Jr., July 31, 1970; WRA to William Kies, Dec. 31, 1916, box 6, AP; Henry W. Berger, "Warren Austin in China," *Vermont History*, 40 (Autumn 1972), 248.

Draft of report to stockholders of National City Bank Nov. 6, 1915; Vanderlip to James Stillman, Aug. 27 and Oct. 29, 1915; draft letter on AIC, Nov. 27, 1915, Frank A. Vanderlip Papers, Columbia University; *NYT*, Sept. 16, Dec. 12, 1915; see also the author's "Our New Gold Goes Adventuring: The American International Corporation in China," *Pacific Historical Review*, 43 (May 1974), 212-21.

"Draft of Cable to be sent by Mr. Carey to Peking," June 14, 1916, Vanderlip Papers; Straight to Reinsch, June 21, 1916, box 5, Willard Straight Papers, Cornell University; AIC to Hsu Shih-Ying, Aug. 29, 1916; Straight to Gregory, Aug. 2, 1916, box 5; WRA to Roy L. Patrick, Aug. 31, 1916, box 1, AP.

For a detailed analysis of the American International Corporation's China venture in 1916-1917, see the author's, "Our New Gold Goes Adventuring," and Berger, "Warren Austin in China."

Kies to WRA, Nov. 22, 1916, Feb. 13, 1917; WRA to Kies, Dec. 31, 1916, Feb. 1, 1917, box 6; Chauncey Austin to WRA, Jan. 9, 18, 24, 1917; WRA to Ezra M. Horton, Feb. 5, 1917; WRA to Chauncey Austin, Apr. 10, 1917, box 2; WRA to Straight, Feb. 1 and Mar. 27, 1917, box 6, AP.

"Memo of interview with John W. Sterling of the Firm of Sherman and Sterling," Nov. 5, 1917, box 11; WRA to F. C. Hitchcock, Jan. 21, 1918, box 6, AP; interview, Mrs. Mildred Austin, July 23, 1970.

Interview, Mrs. Mildred Austin, July 23, 1970; interview, Mrs. Frank (Hazel) Start, with the author, Aug. 14, 1968; *Boston Sunday Post*, Aug. 25, 1946; Beverly Smith, "A Yankee Meets the World," *Saturday Evening Post* (Aug. 24, 1946), 10-12.

Woodhouse v. Woodhouse et ux., 99 VT. 91 (1922); WRA to M. E. Hennessy, July 17, 1945; WRA to Gerald E. McLaughlin, Dec. 4, 1945, CF, AP.

"Senator Austin's service in the Boundary Case," Apr. 6, 1945; unpublished article by WRA to Benjamin Gates on the Vermont-New Hampshire Boundary, n.d., SF 71a; Vermont-New Hampshire Boundary Case, multiple boxes, AP; interview, Warren R. Austin, Jr., Aug. 14, 1968; *Vermont v. New Hampshire,* 289 U.S. 593 (1933).

Burlington Daily News, Apr. 8, 1926; *Free Press*, May 1, 1926; *St. Albans*

Messenger, June 12, 1928; P.O. Ray to WRA, June 17, 1928; "Warren Robinson Austin," box: Unorganized Material, AP.

[20]"Hon. Frank C. Partridge," *The Vermonter*, 36 (1931), 3.

[21]Interview Mrs. Frank B. Start, July 23, 1970; *Montpelier Evening Argus*, Dec. 20, 1930; *Rutland Herald*, Dec. 23, 1930.

[22]*Burlington Clipper*, Jan. 15, 1931; *Newport Standard*, Jan. 29, 1931; *Rutland Herald*, Jan. 30, 1931; Vrest Orton to WRA, Jan. 12, 1931; WRA press release, Feb. 5, 9, 1931, SF 78 AP.

[23]*Statements of Expenditures of Candidates for Nomination for United States Senator*, Secretary of State, Montpelier, Mar. 11 and 13, 1931; *Barre Daily Times*, Mar. 2, 1931; *Report of Canvassing Board*, Secretary of State, Montpelier, Mar. 10, 1931.

[24]WRA to Ann Robinson Austin (ARA), Mar. 23, 1931, CF, AP; *Caledonian Record*, Mar. 31, 1931; *Official Certificate of Election*, Secretary of State, Montpelier, Apr. 7, 1931.

[25]WRA to ARA, Mar. 9, Nov. 10, 1932; Jan. 14, Feb. 15, 1933, CF, AP.

[26]For both their ideas on conservatism and application thereof to practical politics, the author owes a debt of gratitude to the following scholars. Their influence is apparent throughout the discussion. Clinton Rossiter, *Conservatism in America* (New York: Knopf, 1955); James T. Patterson, *Congressional Conservatism and the New Deal* (Lexington: University of Kentucky Press, 1967); Russell Kirk, *The Conservative Mind from Burke to Santayana* (Chicago: H. Regnery Co., 1953); Richard Hofstadter, *The American Political Tradition and the Men Who Made It* (New York: A. A. Knopf, 1948), Chapters 11 and 12; Richard W. Leopold, *Elihu Root and the Conservative Tradition* (Boston: Little, Brown, 1959).

[27]WRA to ARA, Apr. 8, 1933, CF, AP; WRA to Herbert Hoover, May 3, 1933, PPF, Hoover Papers, Herbert Hoover Library; WRA to ARA, Apr. 27, 1933, CF, AP; *CR*, Mar. 30, 1933, 1042; Apr. 28, 1933, 2562; May 3, 1933, 2808-09; June 9, 1933, 5424-25; June 13, 1933, 5861.

[28]WRA to ARA, Jan. 19, 1934, CF, AP; WRA to Herbert Hoover, Jan. 2, 1934; PPF, Hoover Papers; *Free Press*, Jan. 17, 1934; John E. Weeks to WRA, Apr. 23, 1934; WRA to Weeks, Apr. 26, 1934, CF, AP.

[29]*St. Albans Messenger*, Sept. 20, 1934.

[30]*Middlebury Register*, cited in *Rutland Herald*, June 5, 1934; *Brandon Union*, Sept. 14, 1934.

[31]*Rutland Herald*, Sept. 21, 1934; *Free Press*, Sept. 26, 1934; *The Vermont Democrat*, box 29, AP.

[32]*Free Press*, Oct. 19, 1934; *Rutland Herald*, Oct. 19, 1934; *Newport Express*, Oct. 19, 1934; *Vergennes Enterprise*, Oct. 5, 1934; *Boston Advertiser*, Oct. 21, 1934.

[33]*Free Press*, Oct. 2, 18, 1934; *Montpelier Evening Argus*, Oct. 18, 1934; *Newport Express*, Oct. 19, 1934; *Waterbury Record*, Oct. 8, 1934; *Bennington Banner*, Oct. 10, 1934.

[34]Entries for Sept. 12-Nov. 5, 1934, Calendar Book, 1934, box 67; speech at Old Home Day, Sandgate, Vermont, Sept. 1, 1934; SF 140; speech at the Parker Hill Service of the Universalist Church, Springfield, Vermont, Sept. 9, 1934, SF 141, AP.

³⁵Speech at Republican State Convention, Oct. 2, 1934, SF 145C; speech at St. Albans, Vermont, Oct. 23, 1934; SF 148; speech over WDEV, Waterbury, Vermont, Nov. 5, 1934, SF 150; radio speech from Montreal, Nov. 5, 1934, SF 152, AP.

³⁶*Canvass of Votes for United States Senator,* November 1934, State of Vermont, Public Records Division, Montpelier; *Free Press,* Nov. 7, 1934. For a lengthy discussion of Austin's campaign see the author's "Vermont's Traditional Republicanism vs. the New Deal: Warren R. Austin and the Election of 1934," *Vermont History* (Spring 1971), 128-41.

³⁷WRA to John E. Weeks, Jan. 4, 1934, CF, AP. In 1935-36 conservatives from both parties acted as individuals and made no serious attempt to establish a coalition against the New Deal. They accepted no counsel except their own as they filled the conservative role of the independent legislator. Among the Democrats, five senators formed a strong conservative anti-New Deal faction: Carter Glass and Harry F. Byrd of Virginia; Thomas P. Gore of Oklahoma; Millard E. Tydings of Maryland; and Josiah W. Bailey of North Carolina. While only a tiny minority, they, not conservative Republicans, became the rallying point of a conservative coalition. Other Democrats joined the anti-New Deal position between 1935 and 1938 and by the latter year they were as irreconcilable as the original five. These "bolters" included: Ellison "Cotton Ed" Smith of South Carolina, Walter F. George of Georgia, Royal S. Copeland of New York, Edward R. Burke of Nebraska, Peter G. Gerry of Rhode Island, Bennett Champ Clark of Missouri, Patrick A. McCarran of Nevada, A. Victor Donahey of Ohio and William H. King of Utah.

On the Republican side, the staunchest conservatives came from the East: Austin and his Vermont colleague, Ernest W. Gibson; Daniel O. Hastings and John G. Townsend, Jr. of Delaware; Frederick Hale and Wallace H. White of Maine; Henry W. Keyes of New Hampshire; Jesse H. Metcalf of Rhode Island; W. Warren Barbour of New Jersey and James J. Davis of Pennsylvania. Comparatively, the progressive wing of the Republican Senate was from the West. William F. Borah, of Idaho, Hiram Johnson of California and two famous "bolters," George W. Norris of Nebraska and Robert M. LaFollette, Jr. of Wisconsin headed a group of ten senators who sometimes supported the New Deal, but opposed it if the situation presented itself. Leadership came from Charles McNary, the Minority Leader from Oregon and Arthur H. Vandenberg of Michigan. See Harry W. Morris, "The Republicans in a Minority Role, 1933-38" (Ph.D. dissertation, State University of Iowa, 1960), pp. 89-93; E. Pendelton Herring, "First Session of the Seventy-fourth Congress, Jan. 3, 1935 to Aug. 26, 1935," *American Political Science Review,* 24 (Dec. 1935), 985; Patterson, *Congressional Conservatism,* pp. 18-31, 40-51, 105-06; Joseph Boskin, "Politics of an Opposition Party: The Republican Party in the New Deal Period, 1936-1940" (Ph.D. dissertation, University of Minnesota, 1959), p. 70; C. David Tompkins, *Senator Arthur H. Vandenberg: The Evolution of a Modern Republican* (East Lansing: Michigan State University Press, 1970), pp. 60-113.

³⁸Arthur Schlesinger, Jr., *The Age of Roosevelt: The Politics of Upheaval* (Boston: Little, Brown, 1960), p. 385ff; Otis Graham, Jr., "Historians and the

New Deal, 1944-1960," *Social Studies,* 54 (Apr. 1963), 133-40; William E. Leuchtenburg, *Franklin D. Roosevelt and the New Deal, 1932-1940* (New York: Harper and Row, 1963), pp. 162-66; J. Joseph Huthmacher, *Senator Robert F. Wagner and the Rise of Urban Liberalism* (New York: Atheneum, 1968), pp. 200-01.

[39]Samuel I. Rosenman (ed.), *The Public Papers and Addresses of Franklin D. Roosevelt* (13 vols., New York: Russell and Russell, 1938), VI, 51; James MacGregor Burns, *Roosevelt: The Lion and the Fox* (New York: Harcourt, Brace, 1956), pp. 293-94; Joseph Alsop and Turner Catledge, *The 168 Days* (Garden City, N.Y.: Doubleday, Doran, 1938), pp. 54-55, 97-100; Patterson, *Congressional Conservatism,* pp. 94-101; Boskin, "Politics of an Opposition Party," p. 94; Tompkins, *Senator Arthur H. Vandenberg,* pp. 146-47.

[40]WRA to ARA, Jan. 25, Feb. 1, 1937, CF, AP; Patterson, *Congressional Conservatism,* pp. 108-09; *NYT,* Feb. 6, 1937; WRA to ARA, Feb. 8, 1937; Edward Austin to ARA, Feb. 10, 1937, CF, AP.

[41]*NYT,* Feb. 10, 1937; notes on legislation of 1930s, box 22, AP.

[42]WRA to ARA, Mar. 9, 1937; WRA to Leslie J. Freeman, Mar. 15, 1937; CF, AP.

[43]*NYT,* Mar. 11, 1937; U.S. Congress, Senate, Committee on the Judiciary, *Hearings on S. 1392, A Bill to Reorganize the Judicial Branch of the Government,* 75th Cong., 1st sess., 1937 (Hereafter cited as *Judicial Hearings.*), pp. 23-24.

[44]*Judicial Hearings,* pp. 102-04, 429-30.

[45]Alsop and Catledge, *The 168 Days,* pp. 100-05, 124-26; *Judicial Hearings,* pp. 485-99; Merlo J. Pusey, *Charles Evans Hughes* (2 vols., New York, 1951), II, 754-55.

[46]*Judicial Hearings,* pp. 176-77, 305, 1007-08.

[47]*NYT,* Apr. 6, 1937, WRA to ARA, Apr. 27 and 29, 1937, CF, AP.

[48]Burns, *Roosevelt: The Lion and the Fox,* pp. 303-06; *NYT,* May 9, 1937; WRA to Mrs. Chauncey G. Austin, Jr., May 14, 1937; WRA to ARA, May 21, 1937, CF, AP; *NYT,* June 15, 1937; U.S. Congress, Senate, Committee on the Judiciary, *Adverse Report to Accompany S. 1392,* Report Number 711, 75th Cong., 1st sess., 1937, p. 23.

[49]WRA to ARA, June 24, July 2, 1937, CF, AP; Boskin, "Politics of an Opposition Party," p. 123. Approximately 1200 pieces of constituent correspondence of this issue are located in the Austin Papers, Yale University.

[50]WRA to ARA, July 22, CF, AP.

[51]Fields interview, Apr. 22, 1951, SF 541, AP; *NYT,* Aug. 8, 15 and Sept. 1, 2, 1913.

[52]Selig Adler, *The Isolationist Impulse: Its Twentieth-Century Reaction* (New York: Abelard-Schuman, 1957), *passim.* See also Betty Glad, *Charles Evans Hughes and the Illusions of Innocence* (Urbana: University of Illinois Press, 1966), pp. 129-30, 321-27; Dexter Perkins, *Charles Evans Hughes and American Democratic Statesmanship* (Boston: Little, Brown, 1956), pp. 89-90; Pusey, *Charles Evans Hughes,* II, 437-39; Leopold, *Elihu Root and the Conservative Tradition,* p. 124; Philip C. Jessup, *Elihu Root* (2 vols., New York: Dodd, Mead and Company, 1938), II, 372-79; Arthur Link, *Wilson the Diplomatist, a Look at His Major Foreign Policies* (Baltimore:

Johns Hopkins Press, 1957), p. 119. For a critique of the legal-moral philosophy, the best examples are: George F. Kennan, *American Diplomacy 1900-1950* (Chicago: University of Chicago Press, 1951); J. Hans Morgenthau, *In Defense of the National Interest, A Critical Examination of American Foreign Policy* (New York: Knopf, 1951); Robert E. Osgood, *Ideals and Self-Interest in America's Foreign Relations, The Great Transformation of the Twentieth Century* (Chicago: University of Chicago Press, 1953).

⁵³Speech at Burlington, Vermont, May 3, 1918, SF 58D; WRA to Hitchcock, Jan. 21, 1918, box 6; Memorial Day Speech, May 30, 1918, SF 59; Speech at Burlington, Vermont, Dec. 24, 1918, SF 60; Notes for a speech to the Northern District of the Vermont Federation of Women's Clubs, Oct. 8, 1924, SF 62; Speech to the Massachusetts State Federation of Women's Clubs, Feb. 26, 1925, SF 63, AP.

⁵⁴WRA to Gerald P. Nye, Jan. 3, 1935; WRA to ARA, Mar. 3, 1937, CF, AP.

⁵⁵Robert A. Divine, *The Illusion of Neutrality* (Chicago: University of Chicago Press, 1962), pp. 81-85; Dexter Perkins, *The New Age of Franklin Roosevelt, 1932-1945* (Chicago: University of Chicago Press, 1956), pp. 97-98; Selig Adler, *The Uncertain Giant: 1921-1941, American Foreign Policy Between the Wars* (New York: Macmillan, 1965), pp. 157-72; *CR*, Aug. 24, 1935, 14908.

⁵⁶Adler, *Uncertain Giant*, p. 199; Divine, *Illusion of Neutrality*, pp. 180-85; Tompkins, *Senator Arthur H. Vandenberg*, pp. 126-29.

⁵⁷WRA to ARA, Mar. 3, 1937, CF, AP; *CR*, Mar. 1, 1937, 1677-83, Mar. 3, 1937, 1807.

⁵⁸Adler, *Uncertain Giant*, p. 190; see also Leuchtenburg, *Roosevelt and the New Deal*, pp. 226-27.

⁵⁹Speech to the People's Forum, Johnson, Vermont, Oct. 8, 1937, SF 189, AP.

⁶⁰Speech to American Legion, Rutland, Vermont, Nov. 11, 1937, SF 192, AP.

⁶¹Speech to Burlington, Vermont Lions Club, Jan. 1938, box 103; speech to the Executive Club of Chicago, Nov. 4, 1938, SF 207; speech to Vermont Hotel Men's Association, Oct. 7, 1938, SF 205, AP.

⁶²Rosenman, *Papers of Roosevelt*, VII, 69-71; Executive Club Speech; WRA to ARA, Apr. 27, 1938, CF, AP.

⁶³The best discussion of the failure of neutrality revision is in Divine, *Illusion of Neutrality*, pp. 229-78. Less detailed narratives are in Adler, *Uncertain Giant*, pp. 211-14; William L. Langer and S. Everett Gleason, *The Challenge to Isolation 1937-1940* (New York: Harper, 1952), pp. 136-47; Leuchtenburg, *Roosevelt and the New Deal*, pp. 291-92; Donald F. Drummond, *The Passing of American Neutrality, 1937-1941* (Ann Arbor: University of Michigan Press, 1955), pp. 87-90.

⁶⁴Divine, *Illusion of Neutrality*, pp. 278-79; *CR*, July 14, 1939, 9127-28; WRA to ARA, July 15, 1939, CF, AP.

⁶⁵WRA to ARA, July 18, 1939, CF; memo, White House Conference on Neutrality, July 19, 1939, box 10; WRA to ARA, Apr. 27, 1933, CF; McNary to WRA, July 28, 1939; WRA to McNary, July 29, 1939, box 25, AP.

⁶⁶Joseph Alsop and Robert Kitner, *American White Paper, The Story of*

American Diplomacy and the Second World War (New York: Simon and Schuster, 1940), pp. 58-59; Langer and Gleason, *Challenge to Isolation,* pp. 143-44; Divine, *Illusion of Neutrality,* pp. 280-81; Cordell Hull, *The Memoirs of Cordell Hull* (2 vols., New York: Macmillan Co., 1948), I, 649-50; memo, Neutrality Conference, July 19, 1939, AP.

[67]Memo, Neutrality Conference, July 19, 1939, AP; Hull, *Memoirs,* I, 650.

[68]Memo, Neutrality Conference, July 19, 1939, AP.

[69]Rosenman, *Papers of Roosevelt,* VIII, 387-88; memo, Neutrality Conference, July 19, 1939, AP.

[70]Rosenman, *Papers of Roosevelt,* VIII, 458, 464-78, 480; Divine, *Illusion of Neutrality,* pp. 290-92; Roosevelt, telegram to participants, Sept. 13, 1939, OF 1561, box 2, FDRP. The Democrats invited were James Garner, William Bankhead, Sam Rayburn, Sol Bloom, Alben Barkley, Key Pittman, Sherman Minton and James Byrnes.

[71]Transcript, White House Conference on Neutrality, Sept. 20, 1939, President's Personal Files (PPF) 1-P, box 263, FDRP.

[72]See constituents' letters in CF, Sept.-Oct., 1939, AP; U.S. Congress, Senate, Committee on Foreign Relations, *Neutrality Act of 1939,* Report Number 1155, 76th Cong., 2nd sess., 1939, pp. 1-14; *CR,* Oct. 24, 1939, 780-90; Divine, *Illusion of Neutrality,* p. 317; *CR,* Oct. 19, 1939, 599-601. For a very positive assessment of Austin's role in neutrality revision, see David Porter, "Senator Warren R. Austin and the Neutrality Act of 1939," *Vermont History,* 39 (Summer 1974), 228-38.

[73]WRA to ARA, May 21, 23, Sept. 4, 5, 1940, CF, AP.

[74]*CR,* May 22, 1940, 6587-88; NBC radio interview, May 27, 1940, SF 240; WRA to ARA, July 3, 1940, CF, AP; *NYT,* July 5, 1940; U.S. Congress, Senate, Committee on Military Affairs, *Hearings on S. 4164, A Bill to Protect the Integrity and Institutions of the United States Through a System of Selective compulsory Military Training and Service,* 76th Cong., 3rd sess., 1940; *CR,* July 10, 1940, 9385.

[75]*CR,* Aug. 8, 1940, 10060-62. For an example of Austin's attitude toward executive power in wartime, see the author's, "The National War Service Controversy, 1942-1945," *Mid-America,* 57 (Oct. 1975), 246-58.

[76]WRA to ARA, June 18, 23, 26, Aug. 13, Nov. 7, 1940, CF; campaign speech at St. Johnsbury, Vermont, Oct. 30, 1940, SF 246; speech over station WDEV, Waterbury, Vermont, Oct. 31, 1940, SF 247, AP; *NYT,* Nov. 7, 1940.

[77]*NYT,* Nov. 23, Dec. 24, 31, 1940; A. W. Sheldon to WRA, Jan. 24, 1941; WRA to Sheldon, Feb. 1, 1941; WRA to Roy Patrick, Jan. 30, 1941, box 14; speech over station WTAG Worcester, Massachusetts, Feb. 6, 1941, SF 251; symposium comments, station WOL, Feb. 11, 1941, SF 252; R. J. Coar to WRA, Feb. 8, 1941, CF, AP; Diary, Jan. 25, 1941, Vol. 32, Henry L. Stimson Papers, Yale University; "Lend-lease agreement, 1940-43," OF 4193, box 1-2, FDRP.

[78]Memo, "White House Conference Regarding Legislation Necessary for Extension of Time of Service of Trainees, National Guard, and Reserve Components," July 14, 1941, box 20, AP; *CR,* July 24, 1941, 6292; July 31, 1941, 6510-12; "Conferences at the White House re Neutrality Act in Oct. 1941," Oct. 7 and 8, 1941, box 20, AP; *CR,* Nov. 7, 1941, 8592, 8594-95, 8680.

⁷⁹See the author's "Warren R. Austin: A Republican Internationalist and United States Foreign Policy" (Ph.D. dissertation, Kent State University, 1969), pp. 55-93; Harley Notter, *Postwar Foreign Policy Preparation, 1939-1945* (Washington, D.C.: Government Printing Office, 1949), pp. 71-78, 263, 582-91; Hull, *Memoirs*, II, 1630-33, 1656-59; Hull to WRA, May 27, 1942; WRA to Hull, May 28, 1942; "Memorandum re Meeting of Subcommittee on Political Problems of Advisory Committee on Post-War Foreign Policy," July 11, Aug. 15, 29, Sept. 5, 1942, box 20; WRA draft recommendation of Aug. 16, 1943; "Letters and Notes;" "Record of Executive Session of Foreign Policy Committee with Whole Council," box 15; WRA to Roy Patrick, Apr. 3, 1944, CF; Austin notes: "Policy of War and Peace in the Platform of the Republican Party, 1944," box 25, AP; Fred Israel (ed.), *The War Diary of Breckinridge Long* (Lincoln, Nebraska: University of Nebraska Press, 1966), pp. 341-42, 345, 346, 356-58; Draft of Foreign Policy Plank, June 10, 1944; Hugh R. Wilson to John F. Dulles, Sept. 18, 1944, Supplement of 1971, II, Correspondence, 1939-44, John Foster Dulles Papers, Princeton University; CR, Mar. 21, 1944, 2811; Jan. 25, 1945, 474; WRA to Edward Lindsay, Oct. 25, 1944, box 24; WRA to Rupert Lucas, Oct. 28, 1944, CF; radio speech, Nov. 2, 1944, SF 315, AP.

⁸⁰Senators Arthur Vandenberg, Robert Taft, Hiram Johnson and Gerald Nye composed the vanguard of the isolationists, and they were moderately supported by several others including Styles Bridges of New Hampshire, James Davis of Pennsylvania and John Danaher of Connecticut as well as Minority Leader Charles McNary. The 1940 election brought new personalities into the Senate, but it was difficult to stamp them as isolationists or internationalists. Joseph H. Ball of Minnesota, Harold Burton of Ohio and George Aiken of Vermont were among this group. In any case, Austin certainly was not the typical Republican presented in Donald McCoy's essay, "Republican Opposition During Wartime, 1941-45," *Mid-America*, 44 (1967), 174-89. Charles McNary to WRA, Dec. 26, 1940; Memo: "Republican Conference for the 78th Congress," Jan. 8, 1943, box 25, AP; *New York Herald Tribune*, Dec. 25, 1942; Frank McNaughton to James McCohaughy, Mar. 13, 1943, Frank McNaughton Papers, Harry S. Truman Library.

⁸¹The best indicators are the Fulbright Resolution, which passed the House by an overwhelming 360 to 29 vote, and the Senate vote on the Connally Resolution, which was 85 to 5. The standard study of the internationalist movement is the excellent one by Robert A. Divine, *Second Chance, The Triumph of Internationalism in America During World War II* (New York: Atheneum, 1967).

⁸²*CR*, Jan. 25, 1945, pp. 474-75; *NYT*, Jan. 18, 1945.

⁸³*CR*, Jan. 25, 1945, pp. 476-77.

⁸⁴Memo, Truman's Visit to the Capitol, Apr. 13, 1945, box 20, AP.

⁸⁵Speech to Foreign Policy Association, October 3, 1942, SF 271, AP.

⁸⁶WRA to Ernest M. Hopkins, June 18, 1945, CF, AP; *CR*, July 19, 1945, 7780, July 20, 1945, 7855; U.S. Congress, Senate, Committee on Foreign Relations, *Report to Accompany H. J. Resolution 145 on Membership of the United States in the Food and Agriculture Organization of the United Nations*, Senate Report 357, 79th Cong., 1st sess., 1945; WRA to Marquis Childs, Sept. 18, 1945, CF, AP.

[87]*CR*, Feb. 15, 1946, 1331-32; WRA to Paul D. Evans, Mar. 11, 1946, CF, AP.

[88]In varying degrees, revisionist historians have accentuated this theme in opposition to the traditional interpretation of the origins of the Cold War. They argue that United States involvement in postwar international crisis was not a reaction to Soviet political thrusts or an expanding ideology, but rather an American desire to use its power to remake the world to fit American economic objectives. The extreme revisionists argue further that American anti-communism was merely a means to that end. Anti-communism was more useful in selling the economic objective to the American people and to Congress than the use of a straight economic argument. For a sampling of revisionist writing see: William Appleman Williams, *The Tragedy of American Diplomacy* (Cleveland: World Publishing Co., 1959); *The Contours of American History* (Cleveland: World Publishing Co., 1961), especially pp. 469-78; Gabriel Kolko, *The Politics of War, The World and United States Foreign Policy, 1943-1945* (New York: Random House, 1968); Joyce and Gabriel Kolko, *The Limits of Power: The World and United States Foreign Policy, 1945-1954* (New York: Harper and Row, 1972); Stephen E. Ambrose, *Rise to Globalism: American Foreign Policy Since 1938* (London: Penguin Press, 1971); Thomas G. Paterson, *Soviet-American Confrontation, Postwar Reconstruction and the Origins of the Cold War* (Baltimore: Johns Hopkins University Press, 1974); also see the essays in Thomas G. Paterson, ed., *Cold War Critics: Alternatives to American Foreign Policy in the Truman Years* (Chicago: Quadrangle Books, 1971) as well as the revisionist diplomatic history text by Lloyd C. Gardner, Walter F. LaFeber and Thomas J. McCormick, *Creation of the American Empire: U.S. Diplomatic History* (New York: Rand McNally, 1973), chapters 23, 24. A balanced answer to the changes posed by the revisionists is in John Lewis Gaddis, *The United States and the Origins of the Cold War, 1941-1947* (New York: Columbia University Press, 1972). For a review of the current academic imbroglio over this issue, see Warren F. Kimball, "The Cold War Warmed Over," *The American Historical Review*, 79 (October 1974), 119-36.

CHAPTER TWO

[1]Henry Berger, "Bipartisanship, Senator Taft, and the Truman Administration," *Political Science Quarterly*, 90 (Summer 1975), 225.

[2]*New York Herald Tribune*, June 4, 1946; Thomas M. Campbell and George C. Herring (eds.), *The Diaries of Edward R. Stettinius, Jr., 1943-1946* (New York: New Viewpoints, 1975), pp. 470-72; U.S., Department of State, *Bulletin*, XIV (June 9, 1946), 988-89. The controversy over the role of the United States representative continues as the object of study and speculation to the present. See Donald G. Bishop, *The Administration of United States Foreign Policy Through the United Nations* (Dobbs Ferry, N.Y.: Oceana Publications, 1967); Arnold Beichman, *The "Other" State Department: The United States Mission to the United Nations, Its Role in the Making of Foreign Policy* (New York: Basic Books, 1969).

[3]Ernest A. Gross "Memoir," *Oral History Collection*, Columbia University, pp. 532-33, 535, 983-84.

[4]Truman to WRA, Aug. 3, 1946, OF 150G, HSTP; *CR*, Aug. 2, 1946, 10716; executive session, Jan. 14, 1947, Foreign Relations Committee Papers, Records of the United States Senate, RG 46, NA.

[5]*NYT*, June 6, 7, 9, 1946; *Washington Post*, June 6, 1946, box 161, Democratic National Committee Clipping File, Truman Library; WCAX (Burlington, Vermont) radio, June, 1946; *Portland Oregonian*, n.d.; *Miami* (Florida) *Daily News*, June 6, 1946; box 77; Cedric Foster broadcast, Mutual System, n.d., CF, AP.

[6]Henry Cabot Lodge followed Austin to the post. Eisenhower accorded more prestige on the position by elevating it to cabinet status. Adlai Stevenson and Arthur Goldberg carried the position down to 1968. Since then a series of lesser-known personalities have held the post although the recent appointments of Daniel P. Moynihan and William W. Scranton attest to the continued prestige given the position.

[7]U.S., Department of State, *The United States and the United Nations, Report by the President to the Congress for the Year 1947*. For the evolutionary growth of the United States Mission, see *FRUS, 1946*, I, 1-50; *The Federal Register*, XII, No. 84, Apr. 29, 1947 (Washington, 1947), 2765; "Brief Report of Items Transacted in Washington, D.C. on Jan. 27, 28 and 29, 1947" box 65, AP. (Hereafter cited as "Austin Report.")

[8]Lincoln P. Bloomfield, "The Department of State and the United Nations," *Department of State Bulletin*, 23 (Nov. 20, 1950), 807-09; Beichman, *The "Other" State Department*, pp. 88-103.

[9]Robert Riggs, *Politics in the United Nations: A Study of United States Influence in the General Assembly* (Urbana: University of Illinois Press, 1958), pp. 13-15.

[10]Riggs, *Politics in the United Nations*, pp. 810-11; Channing B. Richardson, "The United States Mission at the United Nations," *International Organization*, 7 (Feb. 1953), 22-34; George Barrett, "Our Global Embassy on Park Avenue," *New York Times Magazine*, Nov. 27, 1949, 14-15; *FRUS, 1946*, I, 40-42.

[11]Eleanor Roosevelt, *On My Own* (New York: Harper, 1958), pp. 71-72.

[12]John C. Ross to WRA, July 16, 1947, CF; Thomas F. Powers, Jr. to WRA, Sept. 4, 1947, box 64, AP.

[13]Memo of telephone conversation, Aug. 27, 1946; minutes of meetings on General Assembly preparations with Senator Warren R. Austin, Sept. 12, 1946, *FRUS, 1946* I, 35-37; memo for Matthew Connally, Sept. 9, 1946, OF 20, HSTP; draft of statement upon resignation from Senate and acceptance of United Nations appointment, June 6, 1946, SF 342, AP.

[14]Speech to Foreign Policy Association, June 26, 1946, SF, AP.

[15]Draft of radio interview, July 16, 1946, SF 342, AP.

[16]Speech to American Association for the United Nations, Oct. 25, 1946, SF 347, AP.

[17]Gross, "Oral History Memoir," p. 982.

[18]Beichman, *The "Other" State Department*, pp. 24-31; Robert Riggs, *US/UN: Foreign Policy and International Organization* (New York: Appleton-Century-Crofts, 1971), pp. 3-16, 33-81; John G. Stoessinger, *The*

United Nations and the Superpowers, United States-Soviet Interaction at the United Nations (New York: Random House, 1965), pp. 13-19; Franz B. Gross, "The US National Interest in the UN," *Orbis*, 7 (July 1963), 367-85.

¹⁹See Stoessinger, *The United Nations and the Superpowers*, pp. 5-13, 16-19.

²⁰Beichman, *The "Other" State Department*, pp. 19-24; William A. Scott and Stephen B. Withey, *The United States and the United Nations, The Public View 1945-1955* (New York: Manhatten Publishing Co., 1958), pp. 11, 16, 32.

²¹See Thomas Paterson, "Introduction: American Critics of the Cold War and their Alternatives," in *Cold War Critics*, pp. 3-17.

²²For details of these problems see, U.S., Department of State, *U.S. and U.N., 1947*, pp. 8-9, 104-07; Francis O. Wilcox and Carl M. Marcy, *Proposals for Changes in the United Nations* (Washington: Brookings Institution, 1955), pp. 310-21; *FRUS, 1946*, I, 251-92.

²³Memo to Matthew Connally, Sept. 9, 1946, OF 20, HSTP; minutes of meetings on General Assembly preparations with Senator Warren R. Austin at the Department of State, Sept. 6, 9, 10, 11, 12, 1946, IO Files, FRC.

²⁴Minutes of meeting on General Assembly preparations with Senator Austin, Sept. 11, 1946, IO Files FRC; position paper: "United States Position on General Assembly Agenda Items Dealing with Voting in Security Council." Oct. 22, 1946, *FRUS, 1946*, I, 298-312.

²⁵Memo, Bernard Bechoefer to Joseph Johnson, Oct. 23, 1946, SDDF 501.BB/10-2446, NA.

²⁶Minutes of Delegation Meeting, Oct. 28, 1946, *FRUS, 1946*, I, 315-17.

²⁷GA (I/2), *Plenary*, Oct. 29, 1946, 832-47.

²⁸Memo of conversation by Lincoln Gordon, Oct. 28, 1946, *FRUS, 1946*, I, 969-71; WRA to Byrnes, Oct. 29, 1946, SDDF 501.BB/10-2946; John Ross to Byrnes, Oct. 30, 1946, SDDF 501.BB/10-3046, NA.

²⁹GA (I/2), *Plenary*, Oct. 30, 1946, 893-908.

³⁰Truman to WRA, Oct. 31, 1946, PPF 322, HSTP; *NYT*, Oct. 31, 1946.

³¹Comments on Austin's speech, Nov. 1, 1946, CF, AP; Vincent Sheehan, "Molotov and Austin," *The New Republic*, 115 (Nov. 1, 1946), 616.

³²Howard Schwartz, "Warren Robinson Austin: International Orator" (unpublished ms., The University of Vermont, 1967), p. 11; Robert D. Murphy, *Diplomat Among Warriors* (Garden City, N.Y.: Doubleday, 1964), p. 366.

³³GA (I/2), *Plenary*, Dec. 14, 1946, 1557-59; 231-50.

³⁴WRA to R. Hoppock, Nov. 27, 1946, box 58; WRA to J. Ashton Oldham, Nov. 20, 1946, box 64, AP.

³⁵WRA to Truman, Dec. 18, 1946, CF, AP.

³⁶John Jay Iselin, "The Truman Doctrine: A Study in the Relationship Between Crisis and Foreign Policy-making" (Ph.D. dissertation, Harvard University, 1964), p. 33.

³⁷Draft of radio interview, box 63; John Ross to WRA, Dec. 30, 1946, CF; speech to Council of State Governments, Jan. 16, 1947, SF 354, AP.

³⁸State Department to United States-United Nations, Jan. 17, 1947, box 58; "Austin Report," box 65, AP.

³⁹John C. Campbell, *The United States in World Affairs 1947-48* (New

York: Harper, 1949), pp. 409-15; Wilcox and Marcy, *Proposals for Changes in the United Nations*, pp. 34-39, 57-81; Ernest M. Patterson (ed.), "World Government," *The Annals of the American Academy of Political and Social Science*, 264 (July 1949), 1-31.

[40]WRA to Gregory E. Shinert, Nov. 3, 1947, box 64, AP.

[41]WRA to Mrs. J. Anderson Lord, Jan. 21, 1948; WRA to Cord Meyer, Jr., Feb. 10, 1948, box 64, AP.

[42]Memo of conversation, WRA and Porter McKeever, Apr. 28, 1948, box 35, AP.

[43]U.S. Congress, House, Committee on Foreign Affairs, *Hearings on the Structure of the United Nations and the Relations of the United States to the United Nations*, 80th Cong., 2nd sess., pp. 39-49.

[44]Hearings, *Structure of U.N.*, pp. 74-75.

[45]Hearings, *Structure of U.N.*, pp. 75-78.

[46]Hearings, *Structure of U.N.*, p. 81.

[47]Hearings, *Structure of U.N.*, pp. 83, 84.

[48]WRA to Jerry Voorhis, Jan. 26, 1949, box 64; speech to the Vermont General Assembly, Feb. 24, 1949, SF 432, AP.

[49]WRA, "A Warning on World Government," *Harper's Magazine* (May 1949), 93-97.

[50]WRA to J. Lynn Calland, Dec. 21, 1949, box 64, AP.

[51]Memo, Frederick T. Rope to WRA, Dec. 2, 1949, box 64; report to the State Department from United States Mission at the United Nations, re Policy on World Government legislation, Jan. 26, 1950, box 66, AP.

CHAPTER THREE

[1]Harrison J. Conant to WRA, May 11, 1945; WRA to Conant, May 16, 1945, CF; memo of meeting with James F. Byrnes, box 20, AP. See also Thomas G. Paterson, "Potsdam, the Atomic Bomb, and the Cold War: A Discussion with James F. Byrnes," *Pacific Historical Review*, (May 1972), 225-30.

[2]WRA to Francis X. C. Balling, Aug. 22, 1945; WRA to Irving F. Carpenter, Sept. 26, 1945; WRA to Henry A. Milne, Oct. 17, 30, 1945, CF, AP.

[3]*CR*, Mar. 14, 1946, 2257. Austin's point is one which was stressed by that era's critics of the administration as well as the current school of revisionists. See Barton J. Bernstein, "Walter Lippmann and the Early Cold War," and Ronald Radosh and Leonard P. Liggio, "Henry A. Wallace and the Open Door," in Paterson, *Cold War Critics*, pp. 18-53, 76-113; Gar Alperovitz, "How Did the Cold War Begin?" *The New York Review of Books*, 8 (March 23, 1967), 6, 8, 9, 11; Fred Warner Neal, "The Cold War in Europe: 1945-1967" in Neal D. Houghton (ed.), *Struggle Against History: U.S. Foreign Policy in an Age of Revolution* (New York: Washington Square Press, 1968), pp. 23-30.

[4]Speech at Johnson State Teachers College, Mar. 29, 1946, SF 335; speech at Middlebury College, Mar. 30, 1946, SF 336, AP.

[5]Unused notes for radio interview with Tom Connally, Apr. 1946; transcript of radio interview, Apr. 5, 1946, SF 338, AP.

⁶Kennan to Byrnes, Feb. 22, 1946, *FRUS, 1946*, VI, 696-709; Clark Clifford, "American Relations with the Soviet Union," Sept. 24, 1946, White House Central Files, Truman Library. George Kennan's analytic February 22 cable on Soviet motives was reported as a widely disseminated and eagerly accepted document in the State and Navy Departments. See George F. Kennan, *Memoirs 1925-1950* (Boston: Little, Brown, 1967), pp. 292-95, 354-55; Walter Millis (ed.), *The Forrestal Diaries* (New York: Viking, 1951), pp. 135-40; Gaddis, *Origins of the Cold War*, pp. 290, 304; Kolko and Kolko, *Limits of Power*, pp. 42-46. Also see Thomas G. Paterson, "The Search for Meaning: George F. Kennan and American Foreign Policy," in Frank J. Merli and Theodore A. Wilson (eds.), *Makers of American Diplomacy, From Benjamin Franklin to Henry Kissinger* (New York: Scribner, 1974), pp. 264-68; Kennan to Acheson, July 18, 1946, *FRUS, 1946*, I, 860-65; John Davies to Bedell Smith, Nov. 18, 1946, *FRUS, 1946*, VI, 806-08; Dean Acheson, *Present at the Creation, My Years in the State Department* (New York: Norton, 1969), p. 219; Joseph M. Jones, *The Fifteen Weeks* (New York: Harcourt, Brace and World, 1955), pp. 139-42; Arthur M. Schlesinger, Jr., "Origins of the Cold War," *Foreign Affairs*, 46 (October 1967), 22-52.

⁷Acheson, *Present at the Creation*, p. 217; U.S. Congress, Senate, Committee On Foreign Relations, *Legislative Origins of the Truman Doctrine* (Executive Session Hearings before the Senate Committee on Foreign Relations, 80th Cong., 1st sess.; made public Jan. 12, 1973), Mar. 13, 1947, pp. 3-4; Acheson, Princeton Seminar, July 2, 1953, DAP; Truman to Eleanor Roosevelt, May 7, 1947, box 4560, A. E. Roosevelt Papers, Roosevelt Library; Jones, *Fifteen Weeks*, p. vii; John Lewis Gaddis, "Was the Truman Doctrine a Real Turning Point?" *Foreign Affairs*, 52 (Jan. 1974), 386-408; "Harry S. Truman and the Origins of Containment," in Merli and Wilson, *Makers of American Diplomacy*, pp. 506-08. See also his *United States and the Origins of the Cold War*, pp. 282-352; Geoffrey Warner, "The Truman Doctrine and the Marshall Plan," *International Affairs*, 50 (Jan. 1974), 87-88.

⁸Report of the Committee Appointed to Study Immediate Aid to Greece and Turkey, n.d.; minutes of meeting of the Secretaries of State, War and Navy, Feb. 26, 1947; memo, Marshall to Truman, Feb. 27, 1947, *FRUS, 1947*, V, 47-55, 56-57, 60-62; Jones to Benton, Feb. 26, 1947, box 1, JJP; Acheson, *Present at the Creation*, pp. 218-19.

⁹Jones, *Fifteen Weeks*, p. 160; Acheson, *Present at the Creation*, p. 223.

¹⁰Arthur H. Vandenberg, Jr. (ed.), *The Private Papers of Senator Vandenberg* (Boston: Houghton Mifflin, 1952), pp. 340-41.

¹¹Minutes of SWNCC subcommittee on foreign policy information, Feb. 28, 1947, box 1, JJP.

¹²Memo, John C. Ross to Joseph E. Johnson, Mar. 6, 1947; memo of conversation between Acheson and WRA, Mar. 6, 1947, USUN, RG 84, NA; Trygve Lie, *In the Cause of Peace: Seven Years with the United Nations* (New York: Macmillan, 1954), p. 104; Acheson to WRA, Mar. 11, 1947, box 30, AP.

¹³Acheson, *Present at the Creation*, p. 223; WRA copy of Truman Doctrine Speech, box 30, AP.

[14]U.S. Senate, *Legislative Origins of the Truman Doctrine*, Mar. 13, 1947, pp. 13-17, 22-24.

[15]*NYT*, Mar. 14, 1947; Lie, *In the Cause of Peace*, p. 104.

[16]Jones, *Fifteen Weeks*, pp. 179-80; Lie, *In the Cause of Peace*, p. 104.

[17]*New York Herald Tribune*, Mar. 18, 22, 1947; *NYT*, Mar. 19, 1947; Childs quoted in Denna F. Fleming, *The Cold War and Its Origins* (2 vols., Garden City, N.Y.: Doubleday, 1961), I, 452. The FAO studied the Greek situation for four months and recommended a twenty-five year plan of rehabilitation sparked by a $1,000,000,000 loan from the World Bank. However, the recommendations would not have helped the immediate situation.

[18]Owens quoted in Jones, *Fifteen Weeks*, p. 180; *NYT*, Mar. 13, 1947; Thomas G. Paterson, "The Dissent of Senator Claude Pepper" in Paterson, *Cold War Critics*, pp. 129-30.

[19]Vandenberg, *Papers*, pp. 344-45; Acheson, *Present at the Creation*, pp. 223-24; C. David Tompkins, "Bipartisanship: Senator Arthur H. Vandenberg and the Truman Administration," paper delivered at the Pacific Coast Branch of the American Historical Association, Aug. 1974 (copy in possession of author); see U.S. Senate, *Legislative Origins of the Truman Doctrine*, passim.

[20]Vandenberg, *Papers*, pp. 344-45; U.S., Department of State *Bulletin*, 16 (May 4, 1947), 866-95.

[21]U.S. Congress, House, Committee on Foreign Affairs, *Hearings on H.R. 2616, A Bill to Provide for Assistance to Greece and Turkey*, 80th Cong., 1st sess., 1947, p. 4; U.S. Congress, Senate, Committee on Foreign Relations, *Hearings on S. 938, A Bill to Provide for Assistance to Greece and Turkey*, 80th Cong., 1st sess., 1947, p. 8.

[22]Jones, *Fifteen Weeks*, pp. 183-84; Walter Millis, *The Forrestal Diaries*, pp. 258-59; Acheson, *Present at the Creation*, p. 224.

[23]SC (Second/123), Mar. 28, 1947, 620-22.

[24]Jones, *Fifteen Weeks*, p. 184; *NYT*, Mar. 30, 1947.

[25]Vandenberg, *Papers*, p. 346; McNaughton to Don Bermingham, Apr. 5, 1947, box 11, McNaughton Papers.

[26]David E. Lilienthal, *The Atomic Energy Years* (New York: Harper and Row, 1964), p. 166-67, 132.

[27]SC (Second/128), Apr. 10, 1947, 746-48.

[28]SC (Second/131), Apr. 18, 1947, 801, 803.

[29]"Concluding Section of Mr. Acheson's Talk Before the ASNE," Apr. 18, 1947, box 1, JJP; *NYT*, Apr. 19, 1947; speech to American Society of Newspaper Editors, Apr. 19, 1947, SF 361, AP.

[30]Speech to ASNE, SF 361, AP.

[31]Campbell, *The United States in World Affairs 1947-1948*, pp. 360-61.

[32]Acheson, Princeton Seminar, July 2, 1953, DAP; speech to United States Associates, International Chamber of Commerce, May 6, 1947, SF 363, AP.

[33]Speech to Chamber of Commerce, SF 363, AP.

[34]Material Relating to State Department Conference on Foreign Policy; memo, Williams to WRA, May 26, 1947, SF 365; speech at MIT, June 13, 1947, SF 366, AP.

[35]Speech at MIT; speech at Bates College, June 15, 1947, SF 367; speech at the University of Vermont, June 16, 1947, SF 368, AP.

36Jones to Francis Russell, June 30 and July 2, 1947, box 1, JJP; Charles E. Bohlen, *The Transformation of American Foreign Policy* (New York: Norton, 1969), p. 87; Frank McNaughton to Don Bermingham, July 11, 1947, box 12, McNaughton Papers; Gaddis, "Harry S. Truman and the Origin of Containment," pp. 506-07.

37Speech to ASNE, SF 361, AP.

38Speech to Chamber of Commerce, SF 363, AP.

39Ross to WRA, July 17, 1947, USUN, RG 84, NA; copy of July 1947 *Foreign Affairs,* box 96, AP.

40Memo, Porter McKeever to Dean Rusk, Nov. 25, 1947, box 60, AP. The above memo opens with the following comment: "Ambassador Austin wishes to leave open for the moment the question of whether or not the United Press questions should be answered and to submit for your consideration and comment the following observations which he would be inclined to make if it were decided to reply to these questions." "Memorandum Briefly Outlining Accomplishments of the United Nations to Date," Dec. 3, 1947, box 30, AP.

41Memo of conversation with Byron Price, June 17, 1947; memo of conversation with James Shotwell, June 17, 1947; memo of conversation with Clark Eichelberger, June 16, 1947, CF, AP.

42Transcript of radio interview, June 30, 1947, CF; speech at Alfred E. Smith Memorial Fund Dinner, Oct. 14, 1947, SF 373, AP.

43Summary of discussion on problems of relief, rehabilitation and reconstruction of Europe, May 24, 1947, *FRUS, 1947,* III, 236; memo, George Elsey to Clark Clifford, Sept. 22, 1947, box 4, Clark Clifford Papers, Truman Library.

44Acheson, Princeton Seminar, July 2, 1953, DAP; Frank McNaughton to Don Bermingham, July 11, 1947, box 12, McNaughton Papers; Campbell, *The United States in World Affairs 1947-1948,* p. 364; Bohlen, *Transformation of American Foreign Policy,* pp. 90-91; Paterson, *Soviet-American Confrontation,* pp. 215-20.

45GA (II/84), *Plenary,* Sept. 18, 1947, 86-88; memo of conversation by G. Hayden Raynor, Oct. 16, 18, 1947, *FRUS, 1947,* I, 84-86; minutes of 24th and 26th meetings of United States Delegation, Oct. 21, 24, 1947, IO Files FRC; GA (II), *First Committee,* Oct. 22-Oct. 27, 1947, 179-248; GA (II/108), *Plenary,* Nov. 3, 1947, 745-48.

46WRA to Oswaldo Aranha, Nov. 24, 1947, CF, AP.

47U.S. Congress, Senate, Committee on Foreign Relations, *Hearings on United States Assistance to European Economic Recovery,* 80th Cong., 1st sess., 1948, pp. 486, 559, 588, 938.

CHAPTER FOUR

1A survey of the literature on American policy toward Palestine must include the still excellent, though written 25 years ago, J. C. Hurewitz, *The Struggle for Palestine* (New York: Norton, 1950). Herbert Feis has written a brief interpretive account, *The Birth of Israel, The Tousled Diplomatic Bed* (New York: Norton, 1969), while the Kolkos emphasize economic aspects of

American policy in the Near East in their *The Limits of Power*, pp. 420-26. Other literature places the Palestine issue in a larger context. See Grant S. McClellan (ed.), *The Middle East in the Cold War* (New York: H. W. Wilson Co., 1956), pp. 16-19, 30-33; Walter Laqueur, *The Soviet Union and the Middle East* (New York: Praeger, 1959), pp. 146-48 and *The Struggle for the Middle East, The Soviet Union in the Mediterranean* (New York: Macmillan, 1959), pp. 5-13; George Lenczowski (ed.), *United States Interests in the Middle East* (Washington: American Enterprise Institute for Public Policy Research, 1968), pp. 14-17; John C. Campbell, *Defense of the Middle East, Problems of American Policy* (New York: Harper, 1960), pp. 35-38; Samuel Halperin and Irwin Oder, "The United States in Search of a Policy: Franklin D. Roosevelt and Palestine," *Review of Politics*, 24 (1962), 320-41. John Snetsinger's *Truman, The Jewish Vote and the Creation of Israel* (Stanford: Hoover Institution Press, 1974) is an important study that analyzes American policy as it was affected by Jewish political pressure in the United States.

²Hurewitz, *Struggle for Palestine*, pp. 17-93.

³Hurewitz, *Struggle for Palestine*, pp. 94-111; Rony E. Gabbay, *A Political Study of the Arab-Jewish Conflict: The Arab Refugee Problem, a Case Study* (Geneva: E. Droz, 1959), p. 37; William R. Polk, *The United States and the Arab World* (Cambridge: Harvard University Press, 1965), pp. 173-74.

⁴Elie Kedourie, "Britain, France and the Last Phase of the Eastern Question," in J. C. Hurewitz, ed., *Soviet-American Rivalry in the Middle East* (New York: Columbia University Press, 1969), pp. 192-93.

⁵Hurewitz, *Struggle for Palestine*, pp. 174-76, 216, 226; Snetsinger, *Truman, The Jewish Vote*, pp. 4-10.

⁶Hurewitz, *Struggle for Palestine*, pp. 176-78; Polk, *United States and the Arab World*, pp. 288-89; Snetsinger, *Truman, The Jewish Vote*, pp. 13-15; Ephraim A. Speiser, *The United States and the Near East* (Cambridge: Harvard University Press, 1947), pp. 125-33; Raymond S. Mikesell and Hollis B. Chenery, *Arabian Oil, America's Stake in the Middle East* (Chapel Hill: University of North Carolina Press, 1949), pp. 44-70; Grant S. McClellan, "Palestine and America's Role in the Middle East," *Foreign Policy Reports*, 21 (July 1, 1945), 100, 104-05; James M. Landis, "Middle East Challenge," *Fortune*, 32 (Sept. 1945), 161-64; Bartley C. Crum, *Behind the Silken Curtain, A Personal Account of Anglo-American Diplomacy in Palestine and the Middle East* (New York: Simon and Schuster, 1947), pp. 36-37; Acheson, *Present at the Creation*, pp. 169-71; Sumner Welles, *We Need Not Fail* (Boston: Houghton Mifflin Co., 1948), pp. 74-76; Chief of Petroleum Division memo, Feb. 5, 1946; George Wadsworth to Byrnes, May 29, 1946; Joint Chiefs of Staff, memo to State-War-Navy Coordinating Committee, June 21, 1946, *FRUS, 1946*, VII, 18-22, 616-17, 631-33.

⁷Snetsinger, *Truman, The Jewish Vote*, pp. 26-33; Lie, *In the Cause of Peace*, pp. 160-61; Hurewitz, *Struggle for Palestine*, pp. 282-85.

⁸Loy Henderson to Acheson, Oct. 21, 1946, *FRUS, 1946*, VII, 710-13.

⁹Gordon Merriam to Henderson, Dec. 27, 1946, *FRUS, 1946*, VII, 732-35.

¹⁰"Memorandum Re Meeting of Subcommittee on Political Problems of Advisory Committee on Post-War Foreign Policy," Aug. 29, 1942, box 20, AP.

[11]"Memorandum, Political Problems," Aug. 29, 1942, AP; *Time*, Feb. 5, 1951, p. 16.

[12]Campbell, *United States in World Affairs 1947-48*, p. 311; "Report of the Subcommittee to Consider Resolutions on Palestine," Dec. 11, 1945, Foreign Relations Committee Papers, Records of the United States Senate, RG 46, NA; Austin to Irving Carpenter, Nov. 23, 1945, CF, AP; *CR*, 79th Cong., 1st sess., Dec. 17, 1945, 12165-89.

[13]Acheson to Truman, July 15, 1946, *FRUS, 1946*, I, 414-16; Acheson telegram, Mar. 19, 1947; memo, Rusk to Acheson, Apr. 3, 1947, box 8, Palestine Reference file of Robert McClintock (cited hereafter as McClintock File), RG 59, NA.

[14]Ivar Spector, *The Soviet Union and the Muslim World*, 1917-1956 (Seattle: University of Washington Press, 1956), pp. 112-30; Yaacov Ro'I, "Soviet-Israel Relations, 1947-1954," in Michael Confino and Shimon Shamir (eds.), *The U.S.S.R. and the Middle East* (New York: Wiley and Sons, 1973), pp. 124-25; Loy Henderson, "American Political and Strategic Interests in the Middle East and Southeastern Europe," in John A. Draft (ed.), *Proceedings of the Academy of Political Science*, 22 (1946-1948), 451-59; Welles, *We Need Not Fail*, p. 75; J. C. Hurewitz, *Middle East Politics: The Military Dimension* (New York: F. A. Praeger, 1969), pp. 69, 71.

[15]Marshall to WRA, Apr. 7, 9, 1947, SDDF 501.BB/4-427; SDDF 501.BB/4-447; memo, Loy Henderson, Apr. 15, 1947; memo, Acheson to Henderson, Apr. 17, 1947; memo of conversation with WRA, Apr. 18, 1947, box 8, McClintock File, RG 59; memo of conversation between Elwood Thompson and Ross, Apr. 30, 1947, USUN, RG 84 NA.

[16]Acheson, *Present at the Creation*, p. 181; memo, Marshall to Truman, Apr. 17, 1947, *FRUS, 1947*, V, 1070-72; memo, Acheson to Henderson, Apr. 17, 1947, box 8, McClintock File, RG 59; memo of conversation, Acheson, Henderson, Moshe Shertock, Apr. 23, 1947, SDDF 867N.01/4-2347; memo, Rusk to Acheson, May 27, 1947, SDDF 501.BB/5-2747; memo of conversation between Rusk and Ross, May 4, 1947, USUN, RG 84, NA; United Nations, Department of Public Information, *Yearbook of the United Nations 1946-47* (Lake Success: United Nations Department of Public Information, 1947), pp. 294-301; Jean Caldwell, "Zionist Pressure Groups and the Palestine Policy of the Truman Administration" (unpublished M.A. thesis, University of Kansas, 1967), pp. 62-63; Campbell, *United States in World Affairs 1947-48*, pp. 320-21. UNSCOP consisted of Australia, Canada, Czechoslovakia, Guatemala, India, Iran, Netherlands, Peru, Sweden, Uruguay and Yugoslavia.

[17]WRA to Marshall, May 22, 1947, SDDF 501.BB Palestine/5-2247 NA.

[18]Memo, McClintock to Rusk, May 21, 1947, box 9, McClintock File, RG 59; memo, Rusk to Acheson, May 27, 1947, SDDF 501.BB/5-2747; "Possible Forms of International Machinery for Carrying Out United Nations Responsibilities Toward Palestine," June 3, 1947, box 8, McClintock File RG 59, NA.

[19]Marshall to WRA, June 13, 1947; "A Plan for the Future Government of Palestine," June 4, 1947; Henderson to Marshall, July 7, 1947, *FRUS, 1947*, V, 1103-05, 1096-1101, 1120-23.

[20]U.S., Department of State *Bulletin*, 16 (June 15, 1947), 1154; Marshall to Diplomatic Officers, June 13, 1947, *FRUS, 1947*, V, 1103.

[21]Minutes of meeting of U.S. Delegation, Sept. 15, 1947, IO File, FRC. Excerpts of the meeting are printed *FRUS, 1947*, V, 1147-51.

[22]Delegation meeting, Sept. 15, 1947, IO File, FRC. For advice to Marshall, see "Comment on the UNSCOP Report" by W. A. Eddy, Sept. 13, 1947, box 8, McClintock File, RG 59, NA.

[23]Delegation meeting, Sept. 15, 1947, IO File, FRC. For confirmation of Austin's opposition to partition, see Eleanor Roosevelt to Truman, Mar. 22, 1948, box 4560, A. E. Roosevelt Papers.

[24]GA (II/82), *Plenary*, Sept. 17, 1947, 20; "U.S. Position with Respect to the Question of Palestine," Sept. 30, 1947, Palestine "Reference Book" of Dean Rusk, RG 59; memo, Henderson to Marshall, Sept. 22, 1947; memo, John Hildring to Johnson, Sept. 24, 1947, box 8, McClintock File, RG 59, NA.

[25]Truman, *Memoirs*, II, 162. This is corroborated in Merle Miller's *Plain Speaking, An Oral Biography of Harry S. Truman* (New York: Berkley Publishing Corp., 1973), pp. 215-16; Snetsinger, *Truman, The Jewish Vote*, p. 59. See also Ian Bickerton, "President Truman's Recognition of Israel" (unpublished M.A. thesis, Kansas State University, 1966), pp. 46-49; Caldwell, "Zionist Pressure Groups," pp. 64-68; Millis, *Forrestal Diaries*, pp. 344-47.

[26]Memo, Henderson to Robert Lovett, Oct. 6, 1947; memo, Harley Notter to Johnson, Oct. 7, 1947, Palestine "Reference Book" of Dean Rusk; memo, Gordon Knox to Johnson, Oct. 9, 1947, box 8, McClintock File, RG 59, NA.

[27]Robert Lovett, memo of conversation, Oct. 15, 1947; Bedell Smith to Marshall, Nov. 14, 1947, *FRUS, 1947*, V, 1183, 1263-64. See also Nadar Safran, "The Soviet Union and Israel, 1947-1969," in Ivo J. Lederer and Wayne S. Vucinich (eds.), *The Soviet Union and the Middle East, The Post World War II Era* (Stanford: Hoover Institution Press, 1974), pp. 161-62.

[28]United Nations, *United Nations Weekly Bulletin*, 3 (Nov. 18, 1947), 655-57; memo, Gordon Knox to Johnson, Nov. 4, 1947, IO Files, FRC; Gordon P. Merriam to Fraser Wilkens, Nov. 5, 1947, SDDF 501.BB Palestine/10-2547; memos, WRA to Marshall, Nov. 7, 1947, SDDF 501.BB Summaries/11-747; Nov. 11, 1947, SDDF 501.BB Palestine/11-1147, NA.

[29]Memo, Green to Rusk, Nov. 15, 1947, Palestine "Reference Book" of Dean Rusk, RG 59, NA.

[30]*Yearbook of the United Nations, 1947*, pp. 244-45; memo, Henderson conversation, Oct. 22, 1947; Robert Meminger to Marshall, Nov. 10, 1947, McClintock File, RG 59; memo, Lovett conversation Nov. 24, 1947, SDDF 501.BB/11-2447; Lovett to U.S. Embassy in Chile, Nov. 28, 1947, SDDF 501.BB Palestine/11-2847; Lovett to Truman, Dec. 10, 1947, SDDF 501.BB Palestine/12-1047; Truman to Lovett, Dec. 11, 1947, SDDF 501/12-1147 NA; Kermit Roosevelt, "The Partition of Palestine: A Lesson in Pressure Politics," *Middle East Journal*, 2 (Jan. 1948), 1-16; Feis, *The Birth of Israel*, pp. 45-46; Truman, *Memoirs,* II, 158; Caldwell, "Zionist Pressure Groups," pp. 71-74; Snetsinger, *Truman, The Jewish Vote*, pp. 66-71.

[31]Memo, McClintock to Merriam, Nov. 13, 1947; "Forthcoming Procedures and Policy on Palestine," Nov. 18, 1947; memo, McClintock to Lovett, Nov. 25, 1947, Palestine "Reference Book" of Dean Rusk, RG 59, NA; memo,

Henderson to Lovett, Nov. 24, 1947, *FRUS, 1947*, V, 1281-82; Editorial Note, *FRUS, 1947*, V, 1283, 1313-14; Millis, *Forrestal Diaries*, pp. 360-62; *NYT*, Jan. 27, 1948; Eleanor Roosevelt to Truman, Mar. 22, 1948, box 4560, A. E. Roosevelt Papers.

[32]Lillie Schultz, "Conspiracy Against Partition," *Nation* (Jan. 31, 1948), 121-22; see also "Excerpts from Daily Summary of Opinion Development," Palestine, EP; memo, Gordon Knox to WRA, Feb. 2, 1948, USUN, RG 82, NA.

[33]Memo, Ross to WRA, Feb. 12, 1948, USUN, RG 84, NA; *NYT*, Feb. 21, 24, 1948; Freda Kirchwey, "If America Scuttles Partition," *Nation* (Feb. 14, 1948), 173-74; "Excerpts," EP.

[34]SC (Second/253), Feb. 24, 1948, 264-67, 269.

[35]*Nation* (Feb. 28, 1948), 225; "Excerpts," Feb. 25, 26, 1948, EP.

[36]SC (Second/255), Feb. 25, 1948, 294-95; (260), Mar. 2, 1948, 299-401; (263), Mar. 5, 1948, 40.

[37]Lie, *In the Cause of Peace*, p. 169; Andrew W. Cordier and Wilder Foote (eds.), *Public Papers of the Secretaries-General of the United Nations*, Vol. I, *Trygve Lie* (New York: Columbia University Press, 1969), 106; *NYT*, Mar. 13, 1948; memo, Rusk to Marshall, Mar. 15, 1948, box 13, Clifford Papers; memo, Knox to Louis Lipsky, Apr. 20, 1948, USUN, RG 84, NA.

[38]*NYT*, Mar. 20, 22, 1948; Lie, *In the Cause of Peace*, p. 170; Snetsinger, *Truman, The Jewish Vote*, p. 87.

[39]*NYT*, Mar. 20, 1948; memo, Clifford to Truman, Mar. 6, 1948, box 13, Clifford Papers; Snetsinger, *Truman, The Jewish Vote*, p. 87; Truman, *Memoirs*, II, 161-63.

[40]Truman to Eleanor Roosevelt, Mar. 25, 1948, box 4560, A. E. Roosevelt Papers, *NYT*, Mar. 25, 1948; executive session, Mar. 24, 1948, Foreign Relations Committee Papers, RG 46, NA. A note dated Dec. 4, 1973, states that no transcript was made of Marshall's testimony on Palestine.

[41]SC (Second/271), Mar. 19, 1948, 167; memo from MLH [?], Mar. 29, 1948, box 13, Clifford Papers.

[42]SC (271), Mar. 19, 1948, 171-72; Lie, *In the Cause of Peace*, pp. 170-71.

[43]Lovett to WRA, Mar. 27, 1948, box 14, Clifford Papers; GA (Special/135), *Plenary*, May 14, 1948, 36-47.

[44]Memo by Donald Blaisdell, Mar. 15, 1948, USUN, RG 84, NA; *NYT*, May 15, 1948; Joseph P. Lash, *Eleanor: The Years Alone* (New York: Norton, 1972), p. 134.

[45]United States/United Nations efforts to exclude the Soviets continued. When the Security Council adopted the U.S. proposal to establish a truce commission in April 1948, it was composed of "representatives of those members of the Security Council which have career consular officers in Jerusalem." This excluded the Soviets. See SC (Third/287), Apr. 23, 1948, 32-33.

[46]For the domestic priority, see Snetsinger, *Truman, The Jewish Vote*.

[47]"Summary of Proposals for American Policy in Palestine," n.d., box 13, Clifford Papers, Internal evidence indicates these notes were prepared early in 1948.

[48]See the essays in Hurewitz, *Soviet-American Rivalry in the Middle East* and in Confino and Shamir, *The U.S.S.R. and the Middle East*. For the dynamics of later Arab policy, see Malcolm Kerr, *The Arab Cold War, 1958-*

1967, A Study of Ideology in Politics (2nd ed., New York: Oxford University Press, 1967); see also the perceptive commentary of Freda Kirchwey in "America and Israel," *Nation* (May 22, 1948), 565-66.

[49]"Walter Reed Hospital Notebook," 1948, box 69, AP.

[50]W. A. Mills to Mrs. Frank Start, Nov. 10, 1948; Mildred Austin to WRA, Jr., Nov. 11, 1948, CF, AP; *NYT*, Nov. 11, 1948; "Walter Reed Hospital Notebook" AP.

[51]WRA to Collin M. Graves, Dec. 19, 1948, CF, AP; Truman to WRA, Nov. 10, 1948; WRA to Truman, Jan. 19, 1949, PPF 322, *HSTP; NYT*, Jan. 19, 1949.

[52]Leland M. Goodrich and Edward Hambro (eds.), *Charter of the United Nations: Commentary and Documents* (2nd ed., rev., Boston: World Peace Foundation, 1949), pp. 309-10.

[53]Hans Kelsen, "Recent Trends in the Law of the United Nations," Supplement to *The Law of the United Nations, A Critical Analysis of Its Fundamental Problems* (New York: F. A. Praeger, 1951), p. 922.

[54]See *FRUS, 1947*, VIII, 41-77, for memos of conversations of the Marshall meetings. See also, Campbell, *The United States in World Affairs 1947-1948*, pp. 113-19, Vandenberg, *Papers*, pp. 366-71; Rio Conference Notebook, 1947, box 69, AP.

[55]Rio Notebook, AP.

[56]Notes for speech over Columbia Broadcasting System, Sept. 18, 1947, SF 369, AP.

[57]Notes for Chicago speech to Council on Foreign Relations, Nov. 24, 1947, SF 381, AP.

[58]Executive session, Dec. 4, 1947, Senate Foreign Relations Committee Papers, RG 46, NA; *FRUS, 1947*, II, 811, passim; *FRUS, 1948*, III, 1-12; U.S. Congress, Senate, Committee on Foreign Relations, *Executive Session Hearings on the Vandenberg Resolution and the North Atlantic Treaty*, 80th Cong., 2nd sess.; 81st Cong., 1st sess. (made public Aug. 1973), May 11, 1948, pp. 3-5. (Cited hereafter as *Exec. Sessions Hearings: NATO*.); WRA, "A Pincer Movement for Peace," *The American Foreign Service Journal*, 25 (Jan. 1948), 7.

[59]Memo of conversation, Williams and Aake Ording, Mar. 8, 1948, box 65, AP.

[60]Dean Rusk, Princeton Seminar, Mar. 14, 1954, DAP.

[61]SC (3/268), Mar. 17, 1948, 102-10; SC (273), Mar. 23, 1948, 225-29.

[62]SC (303), May 24, 1948, 28-29; Dept. to WRA, Apr. 1, 1948, USUN, RG 84, NA.

[63]Memo of conversation, WRA and Porter McKeever, Apr. 28, 1948, box 35, AP.

[64]U.S. Congress, House, Committee on Foreign Affairs, *Hearings on the Structure of the United Nations*, May 5, 1948, p. 84.

[65]Executive sessions, Apr. 6, 9, 13, 20, 1947, Senate Foreign Relations Committee Papers, RG 46, NA; *Exec. Session Hearings: NATO*, May 11, 1947, p. 1.

[66]Memo, Blair House Meeting, Apr. 27, 1948, I, G, Folder 1948, Dulles Papers.

67Press Conference, May 11, 1948 with Senator Arthur H. Vandenberg, Senate Foreign Relations Committee Papers, RG 46, NA; *Exec. Session Hearings: NATO*, pp. 2-83.

68Speech over Columbia Broadcasting System, Sept. 7, 1948, SF 415; speech at Westminster, London, Oct. 24, 1948, SF 425, AP.

69Notebook, Paris Third Assembly, Sept. 26, 1948, box 43, AP; SC (3/361), Oct. 4, 1948, 9-30; SC (362), Oct. 5, 1948, 1-21; Philip Jessup. "The Berlin Blockade and the Use of the United Nations," *Foreign Affairs*, 50 (Oct. 1971), 163-70.

70SC (364) Oct. 6, 1948; (366) Oct. 15, 1948; (368) Oct. 19, 1948; (370) Oct. 22, 1948, 5-6; (372) Oct. 25, 1948; 13-14; Jessup, "The Berlin Blockade," 170.

71Princeton Seminar, July 8, 9, 1953, DAP.

72Notebook Paris, Oct. 13, 1948; "Walter Reed Hospital Notebook," Dec. 31, 1948, AP.

73Memos, Gilbert Stewart to WRA, Jan. 31, Feb. 21, 1949, box 61, AP.

74"A Proposed Program for Implementation Through the United Nations and the Specialized Agencies of the President's Program for Technical Assistance," Jan. 31, 1949; "Draft of the Objectives and Nature of the 'Point Four' Program," Feb. 21, 1949, box 62, AP.

75Office of Special Political Affairs to WRA, Jan. 6, 1949, box 35, AP.

76Speech to the Vermont Historical Society, Feb. 24, 1949, SF 433, AP.

77Memo, Ross to WRA, Mar. 25, 1949, box 54, AP.

78Memo of conversation between Ross and William Sanders, Mar. 28, 1949, USUN, RG 84, NA; Office of Special Political Affairs to WRA, re Senate Foreign Relations Committee Hearings on Atlantic Treaty, n.d., box 54, AP.

79GA (III/194), *Plenary*, Apr. 13, 1949, 65; memo of conversation between Ross and Sanders, Mar. 22, 1949, USUN, RG 84, NA.

80GA (195), Apr. 14, 1949, 124-27.

81Raymond Dennett to WRA, Apr. 10, 1949; WRA to Dennett, Apr. 18, 1949, box 54, AP.

82WRA, "A Warning on World Government," 96.

83See *Exec. Session Hearings: NATO*, pp. 85-251, 363-66.

84U.S. Congress, Senate, Committee on Foreign Relations, *Hearings on North Atlantic Treaty*, 81st Cong., 1st sess., 1949, pp. 90, 91. (Cited hereafter as *NATO Hearings*.)

85*NATO Hearings*, pp. 92-99.

86*NATO Hearings*, p. 115.

87*NATO Hearings*, pp. 137, 139.

88WRA to McKeever, June 6, 1949, box 41; memo, McKeever to WRA, July 27, 1949, box 54, AP.

89Richard P. Stebbins, *The United States in World Affairs 1949* (New York: Harper, 1950), p. 35; Kolko and Kolko, *Limits of Power*, pp. 502-03; Lawrence S. Kaplan, "The United States, the NATO Treaty and the United Nations Charter," *NATO Letter*, 17 (May 1969), 22-26.

90*NYT*, Apr. 19, 26, 27, May 5, 1949; W. Phillips Davison, *The Berlin Blockade, A Study in Cold War Politics* (Princeton: Princeton University Press, 1958), pp. 268-70; Jessup, "Berlin Blockade," 172; Acheson, *Present at*

the Creation, pp. 269-74; Princeton Seminar, July 8, 9, 1953, DAP.
   ⁹¹GA (IV/226), *Plenary*, Sept. 23, 1949, 36-39.
   ⁹²Stebbins, *United States in World Affairs 1949*, p. 305; "Notes on Austin meetings with representatives of foreign governments re Soviet resolution," Oct. 6, 1949, box 41, AP.
   ⁹³WRA notes: Points for development in speeches, Nov. 1949, box 41, AP.
   ⁹⁴WRA notes on consultation dinner on Soviet resolution, Nov. 7, 1949, box 41, AP.
   ⁹⁵GA (IV), *First Committee*, Nov. 14, 1949, 265-66.
   ⁹⁶GA (IV, 261), *Plenary*, Dec. 1, 1949, 438-39.

CHAPTER FIVE

   ¹Truman, *Memoirs*, II, 331-32; Acheson, *Present at the Creation*, pp. 402-04; WRA Desk Calender, box 69, AP.
   ²The documentation of the history of post-World War II Korea is found in the following: Arthur L. Grey, Jr. "The Thirty-Eighth Parallel," *Foreign Affairs*, 24 (Apr. 1951), 482-83; U.S. Department of State, *The Conflict in Korea: Events Prior to the Attack of June 25, 1950.* No. 4266 (Far Eastern Series 45) (Washington, 1951), pp. 2, 6-7; Leland M. Goodrich, *Korea: A Study of United States Policy in the United Nations* (New York: Council on Foreign Relations, 1956), pp. 7-41, 57-59; Tang Tsou, *America's Failure in China, 1941-50* (Chicago: University of Chicago Press, 1963), pp. 556-57; U.S., Department of State, *North Korea: A Case Study in the Techniques of Takeover.* No. 7118 (Far Eastern Series 103) (Washington, 1961); *The Record on Korean Unification.* No. 7084 (Far Eastern Series 101) (Washington, 1960), p. 14. An exceptionally good analysis of the developing situation in 1949-50 is made in Alexander L. George and Richard Smoke, *Deterrence in American Foreign Policy: Theory and Practice* (New York: Columbia University Press, 1974), pp. 140-48.
   ³Memo by George Elsey re Korean crisis, June 25, 1950, June 29, 1950, box 71, EP; Princeton Seminar, Feb. 13, 1954, DAP; U.S., Department of State, *The United States Policy in the Korean Crisis.* No. 3922 (Far Eastern Series 34) (Washington, 1950), p. 1; Acheson, *Present at the Creation*, pp. 402-04; Lie, *In the Cause of Peace*, pp. 327-28; Gross, "Oral History Memoir," pp. 536-37; Philip Hamburger, "Letter from Lake Success," *The New Yorker*, 26 (July 29, 1950), 41-45.
   ⁴Gross, "Oral History Memoir," p. 537; Princeton Seminar, Feb. 13, 1954, DAP; WRA Desk Calendar, AP.
   ⁵SC (5/461), Jan. 13, 1950, 9-10; (5/473), June 25, 1950, 7-8. Of the many accounts of the June 25 meeting, one of the best is in Glenn D. Paige, *The Korean Decision, June 24-30, 1950* (New York: Free Press, 1968), pp. 116-21.
   ⁶U.S. Department of State, *Bulletin*, XXII (Jan. 23, 1950), 116; George and Smoke, *Deterrence in American Foreign Policy*, p. 147.
   ⁷NSC-68: A Report to the National Security Council by the Executive Secretary on United States Objectives and Programs for National Security, Apr. 14, 1950, reprinted in *Naval War College Review*, 27 (May-June 1975),

51-108; Ambrose, *Rise to Globalism,* p. 195; U.S. Congress, Senate Appropriations Committee, *Hearings on State, Justice, Commerce and the Judiciary Appropriation for 1952,* 82nd Cong., 1st sess., June 5, 1951, p. 1086; Walter F. LaFeber, *America, Russia, and the Cold War, 1945-1975* (3rd ed., New York: Wiley, 1976), pp. 97-100, 107-27; George and Smoke, *Deterrence in American Foreign Policy,* pp. 178-80.

⁸"Notes on conversation between Austin and Hickerson, re policy in Korean situation, June 26, 1950," box 51, AP. The 1961 State Department study, *North Korea: A Case Study in the Techniques of Takeover,* stated that the projected offensive into South Korea was important to the Soviet Union because, if successful, it would give the Soviets control over that area without direct employment of Soviet troops. The study went on to confirm what Austin and Hickerson assumed: "Even in the absence of explicit documentary evidence, the nature of Soviet controls in the area attests to the fact that the decision to attack South Korea could never have been taken without Soviet approval if not inspiration" (p. 5.) The Kolkos' work, *Limits of Power,* utilizes "absence of explicit documentary evidence" to argue that the Soviets were "probably quite as surprised as anyone by the events of June." (pp. 585-87.) The Kolko book is a more sophisticated treatment of a similar thesis earlier subscribed to by I. F. Stone in his 1952 *The Hidden History of the Korean War* (Monthly Review Press ed., New York: Monthly Review Press, 1971), pp. 1-13. George and Smoke refute the Kolkos' argument in their work, *Deterrence in American Foreign Policy,* pp. 173-80.

⁹Memo, Gross to WRA, June 27, 1950, box 51, AP.

¹⁰Memo, Gross to WRA, June 27, 1950. Many have reconstructed and analyzed the top level decisions in Washington during the week of June 24-30. Two early journalistic accounts are Albert L. Warner, "How the Korean Decision was Made," *Harper's Magazine,* 202 (June 1951), 99-106, and Beverly Smith, "The White House Story: Why We Went to War in Korea," *The Saturday Evening Post,* 224 (Nov. 10, 1951) 22-23. The latter story was written in collaboration with White House officials and Acheson later referred to it as a "very accurate account" (Princeton Seminar, Feb. 13, 1954, DAP). Alexander L. George reconstructed the period in detail, utilizing mostly newspaper accounts and interviews in "American Policy-making and the North Korean Aggression," *World Politics,* 7 (Jan. 1955), 209-32. Richard C. Snyder and Glenn D. Paige analyzed the situation through a conceptual study of the decision-making process in "The United States Decision to Resist Aggression in Korea: The Application of an Analytical Scheme," *Administrative Science Quarterly,* 3 (Dec. 1958), 341-78. In Edwin C. Hoyt's "The United States Reaction to the Korean Attack: A Study of the Principles of the United Nations Charter as a Factor in American Policy-making," *The American Journal of International Law,* 55 (Jan. 1961), 45-76, the author discussed the legal principles involved in the decision to utilize the United Nations. The most detailed account is Paige, *The Korean Decision,* and George and Smoke examined the period from the standpoint of deterrence theory and practice in their *Deterrence in American Foreign Policy,* pp. 140-82.

¹¹Memo, Gross to WRA, June 27, 1950, AP; see A. George, "American Policy-making and the North Korean Aggression," pp. 211-15.

[12]Memo, Gross to WRA, June 27, 1950, AP; *U.S. Policy — Korea*, 7; Acheson, *Present at the Creation*, p. 410; Alan G. Kirk to Acheson, June 29, 1950, box 71, EP.

[13]Memo, Gross to WRA, June 27, 1950, AP; Acheson, *Present at the Creation*, p. 408; Truman, *Memoirs*, II, 335-39.

[14]*Time*, July 10, 1950; SC (5/474), June 27, 1950, 3-7; A. George, "American Policy-making and the North Korean Aggression," p. 224.

[15]SC (5/474), June 27, 1950, 7-21.

[16]"Minutes of Truman Meeting with Congressional Leaders," June 30, 1950, box 71, EP; Lester B. Pearson, *Mike, The Memoirs of the Right Honorable Lester B. Pearson* (2 vols. New York: Quadrangle, 1972, 1973), II, 155-56; memo of conversation between Ross and Hickerson, June 28, 1950; "Proposed Policy with Respect to Coordination of Action of Members of the United Nations in Response to a Security Council Resolution," June 28, 1950, box 51, AP; Richard P. Stebbins, *The United States in World Affairs, 1950* (New York: Harper, 1951), p. 214; Lie, *In the Cause of Peace*, p. 33; *Time*, July 24, 1950.

[17]Press Release No. 900, United States Mission to the United Nations, June 29, 1950, box 51, AP.

[18]SC (5/475), June 30, 1950, 11-12.

[19]Lie, *In the Cause of Peace*, p. 333; Truman, *Memoirs*, II, 347; "Minutes of Truman Meeting with Congressional Leaders," June 30, 1950, box 71, EP. See also Richard S. Kirkendall, *Harry S. Truman, Korea and the Imperial Presidency* (St. Charles, Mo.: Forum Press, 1975), pp. 24-25.

[20]*Time*, July 24, 1950; Acheson *Present at the Creation*, p. 451; memo, George Elsey to James Lay, July 12, 1950, box 72, EP.

[21]K. Simonov, "The Bloodstained Fools," *Literaturnaya Gazeta*, reprinted in *USSR Home Service*, July 13, 1950, box 64, AP.

[22]SC (5/470), July 31, 1950, 7.

[23]*Time*, Aug. 14, 1950; Stebbins, *The United States and World Affairs, 1950*, p. 233.

[24]*NYT*, Aug. 3 and 4, 1950.

[25]SC (5/480), Aug. 1, 1950, 14-15.

[26]SC (5/481), Aug. 2, 1950, 15; *Washington Post*, Aug. 3, 1950, box 10, Democratic National Committee Clipping File.

[27]SC (5/482), Aug. 3, 1950, 13-14, 20, 22-23; *Washington Post*, Aug. 4, 1950, box 10, Democratic National Committee Clipping File; *Time*, Aug. 14, 1950.

[28]Schwartz, "Warren Robinson Austin: International Orator," pp. 13-14.

[29]SC (5/484), Aug. 8, 1950, 4-16.

[30]SC (5/484), Aug. 8, 1950, 17.

[31]*Time*, Aug. 21, 1950.

[32]SC (5/485), Aug. 10, 1950, 3-9; *Washington Post*, Aug. 11, 1950, box 10, Democratic National Committee Clipping File.

[33]SC (5/488), Aug. 17, 1950, 5-8.

[34]SC (5/489), Aug. 22, 1950, 26-34.

[35]SC (5/493), Aug. 31, 1950, 23.

[36]Acheson, *Present at the Creation*, p. 454.

[37]SC (5/488), Aug. 17, 1950, 6-7; *Washington Post*, Aug. 18, 1950, box 10,

Democratic National Committee Clipping File; *NYT*, Aug. 20, 1950; Acheson, *Present at the Creation*, p. 454.

[38]WRA to Lie, Aug. 25, 1950, box 42, AP.

[39]Memo by George Elsey, Aug. 26, 1950, box 72, EP; Stebbins, *The United States in World Affairs, 1950*, pp. 239-40.

[40]Memo by George Elsey, Oct. 2, 1950, box 72, EP; Truman to WRA, Aug. 27, 1950, OF 150 G, HSTP.

[41]Acheson, *Present at the Creation*, p. 452.

[42]*Time*, Sept. 4 and 25, 1950; *NYT*, Sept. 9, 1950; Walter Lippmann in the *Washington Post*, Sept. 26, 1950, box 10, Democratic National Committee Clipping File.

[43]John D. Hickerson, oral history memoir, Oct. 11, 1965, 11-12, John Foster Dulles Oral History Collection, Princeton University; GA (V/279), *Plenary*, Sept. 20, 1950, 24.

[44]Gross, "Oral History Memoir," p. 575; Acheson, *Present at the Creation*, p. 450.

[45]Gross, oral history memoir, May 3, 1966, pp. 11, 13-14, Dulles Oral History Collection; WRA to Dulles, Oct. 19, 1950, IX, Folder; Uniting for Peace, Correspondence, Memos, Telegrams, Dulles Papers; Speech to American Academy of Political Science, Nov. 8, 1950, SF 514, AP.

[46]Acheson, *Present at the Creation*, p. 450; Goodrich, *Korea, A Study of United States Policy*, p. 126.

[47]Pearson, *Mike*, II, 158-60; Princeton Seminar, Feb. 13, 1954, DAP; *NYT*, Sept. 26, 27, and 28, 1950; GA (V), *First Committee*, Sept. 30, 1950, 11-12.

[48]Princeton Seminar, Feb. 13, 1954, DAP; GA (V), *First Committee*, Sept. 30, 1950, 12-14.

[49]Goodrich, *Korea, A Study of United States Policy*, pp. 127, 131-32; GA (V), *First Committee*, Oct. 4, 1950, 57; (294), *Plenary*, Oct. 7, 1950, 231. The abstentions were from the nations opposed to crossing the parallel: India, Lebanon, Egypt, Syria, Yugoslavia, Yemen and Afghanistan.

[50]SC (5/499), Sept. 11, 1950, 10-12.

[51]SC (5/501), Sept. 12, 1950, 22-23, 28.

[52]SC (5/502), Sept. 18, 1950, 17-27; *Time*, Oct. 2, 1950.

[53]WRA, "The Security Council Acts Against War," *The Rotarian*, 77 (Sept. 1950), 9, 53; speeches to American Association for the United Nations, Sept. 15, 1950, American Veterans Committee, Sept. 22, 1950, University of Michigan Alumni, Oct. 2, 1950, SF 504, 505, 507, AP.

[54]Allen S. Whiting, *China Crosses the Yalu, The Decision to Enter the Korean War* (New York: Macmillan, 1960), pp. 79-115. John W. Spanier, *The Truman-MacArthur Controversy and the Korean War* (Cambridge: Belknap Press, 1959), pp. 84-87, 92-93; George and Smoke, *Deterrence in American Foreign Policy*, pp. 184-216; J. H. Kalicki, *The Pattern of Sino-American Crisis: Political-Military Interactions in the 1950s* (London: Cambridge University Press, 1975), pp. 43-62; *NYT*, Sept. 3, 24, Oct. 2, 3, 1950; Truman, *Memoirs*, II, 366; Acheson, *Present at the Creation*, p. 454, 456; Pearson, *Mike*, II, 162; Princeton Seminar, Feb. 13, 1954, DAP.

[55]Whiting, *China Crosses the Yalu*, p. 118; SC (5/520), Nov. 8, 1950, 1-2, *Time*, Nov. 20, 1950.

⁵⁶Truman, *Memoirs*, II, 374; SC (5/521), Nov. 10, 1950, 22-23.

⁵⁷Spanier, *Truman-MacArthur Controversy*, pp. 124-27; George and Smoke, *Deterrence in American Foreign Policy*, pp. 222-31; Princeton Seminar, Feb. 14, 1954, DAP.

⁵⁸SC (5/526), Nov. 28, 1950, 20-25.

⁵⁹Princeton Seminar, Feb. 13, 1954, DAP.

⁶⁰Pearson, *Mike*, II, 165-66; Princeton Seminar, Dec. 11, 1953, DAP; memo, Hickerson to WRA, Nov. 28, 1950, box 52, AP; Acheson, *Present at the Creation*, p. 479.

⁶¹Pearson, *Mike*, II, 166; Princeton Seminar, Feb. 14, 1954, DAP; Acheson, *Present at the Creation*, pp. 472-73; Stebbins, *The United States in World Affairs, 1950*, pp. 420-21; Spanier, *Truman-MacArthur Controversy*, pp. 192-93.

⁶²Princeton Seminar, Feb. 14, 1954, DAP; *Time*, Dec. 11, 1950; Acheson, *Present at the Creation*, p. 513; Truman, *Memoirs*, II, 517-18.

⁶³Stebbins, *The United States in World Affairs, 1950*, pp. 422-23; U.S. Congress, Senate, Committee on Armed Services and Committee on Foreign Relations, *Hearings on the Military Situation in the Far East*, 82nd Cong., 1st sess., 1951, pp. 3509-13; Pearson, *Mike*, II, 166-68, 279-87.

⁶⁴Acheson, *Present at the Creation*, p. 513; Pearson, *Mike*, II, 290, 291-95.

⁶⁵Princeton Seminar, Feb. 14, 1954, DAP.

⁶⁶Memo, T. J. Cory to WRA, Dec. 5, 1950, box 50, AP; Gross, "Oral History Memoir," pp. 937-39, 983.

⁶⁷GA (V/426), *First Committee*, Jan. 18, 1951, 502-03.

⁶⁸Pearson, *Mike*, II, 298-99.

⁶⁹Pearson, *Mike*, II, 175-79; see also Acheson, *Present at the Creation*, pp. 328-56.

⁷⁰GA (V/428), *First Committee*, Jan. 20, 1951, 517; *Time*, Jan. 29, 1950; Pearson, *Mike*, II, 299.

⁷¹GA (V/429), *First Committee*, Jan. 22, 1951, 531-32; Pearson, *Mike*, II, 301-02.

⁷²GA (V/430), *First Committee*, Jan. 24, 1951, 539; (433), Jan. 27, 1951, 569.

⁷³Lawrence H. Smith to WRA; WRA to Smith, Apr. 11, 1951, box 53, AP; *NYT*, Apr. 14, 1951.

⁷⁴Speech to National Delegates to AAUW, Apr. 16, 1951, SF 539; Speech to Youth Fellowship League of Lake Region Parish, Vermont, Apr. 17, 1951, SF 540, AP.

⁷⁵Speech to Grand Master of the Masonic Order, May, 1, 1951, SF 544, AP.

⁷⁶Draft of *NYT* Magazine, "Is the World Ready for Collective Security?" Feb. 15, 1951, box 37; speech to Rotary District Conference, Apr. 1, 1951, SF 537, AP.

⁷⁷Speech to AAUW; Harvard Commencement address, June 21, 1951, SF 539, AP.

⁷⁸WRA to Frances Bolton, Dec. 11, 1950, box 32; transcript of press conference, May 2, 1951, SF 545; WRA to O. A. Ross, May 7, 1951, box 35, AP.

⁷⁹WRA to Truman, Aug. 22, 1951; Truman to WRA, Aug. 24, 1951, OF471B, HSTP.

⁸⁰*NYT*, Nov. 29, Dec. 16, 1951; Beichman, *The "Other" State Department*, pp. xvii, 110, 172; Gross, "Oral History Memoir," p. 550.

[81]Dwight D. Eisenhower, *The White House Years: Mandate for Change 1953-1956* (Garden City, N.Y.: Doubleday, 1963), p. 89; "Conversation First Held with Secretary of State Designate John Foster Dulles About Termination of Office of Warren Austin," Nov. 28, 1952, box 40, AP.

[82]Speech over NBC, Dec. 27, 1952, SF 592, AP.

[83]*Boston Globe*, Mar. 8, 1953.

[84]See correspondence in boxes 37-39, AP; *NYT*, June 22, 1955.

[85]*NYT*, Mar. 28, Apr. 12, 1953; interview, Mrs. Frank Start, July 23, 1970.

[86]*Free Press*, Dec. 1, 1956; Mrs. Frank Start to the American Cancer Association, Nov. 29, 1956, box 65, AP; interview, Mrs. Frank Start, July 23, 1970, interview, Mrs. Warren R. Austin, July 23, 1970.

BIBLIOGRAPHIC NOTE

The following essay highlights the significant sources and is not meant as a recapitulation of the notes.

MANUSCRIPT COLLECTIONS

This study is based primarily on the Warren R. Austin papers at the University of Vermont. During the 1930s Austin considered donating his papers to Yale University and he deposited there approximately 1200 pieces of constituent correspondence expressing approval of his opposition to the attempted reorganization of the Federal Judiciary in 1937. Other than this, his papers, a large collection of 110 linear feet, are at Vermont.

The Austin papers reflect his public life. Little of substance regarding his family affairs is revealed in the collection. Even his longtime correspondence with his mother while he was in the Senate reveals little of private matters. One of the best parts of the collection records Austin's career up to his United Nations appointment. Austin prided himself on his sense of history; consequently, during his Senate years he dictated several memos on events he thought might later be significant. This practice abruptly stopped after 1946. Undoubtedly, the press of the workload in his new job, combined with the fact he was no longer his own boss accounts for this.

For the years prior to Austin's election to the Senate, the researcher must rely mainly on his papers. Other collections are of limited use. The Brigham Academy papers, also at the University of Vermont, add some knowledge about Austin's years in attendance there. His China experience, which the Austin collection documents in detail, is supplemented by the Frank Vanderlip papers at Columbia University and the Willard Straight papers at Cornell Univesity.

In addition to Austin's own papers, many collections fill some voids in Austin's Senate career. The Vermont Secretary of State's office in Montpelier houses official reports of state campaign expenditures and the tallies of election results. These are useful in documenting Austin's 1931, 1934 and 1940 campaigns.

The Herbert Hoover papers in the Herbert Hoover Presidential Library at West Branch, Iowa, have some general material pertaining to Austin. The Franklin D. Roosevelt Presidential Library at Hyde Park, N.Y., contains bits of information in several collections. The Franklin D. Roosevelt papers are useful in regard to occasional, specific events. The Samuel I. Rosenman papers provide some material, as do the Isador Lubin papers. Disappointing are the papers of William Hassett, secretary to Roosevelt and Austin's fellow Vermonter, and the Eleanor Roosevelt papers. The latter collection, a massive lot, proved of limited use for Austin's United Nations years, when Mrs. Roosevelt also served on the General Assembly delegation. There is little there that is not available in Joseph P. Lash, *Eleanor: The Years Alone* (New York: Norton, 1972) although some correspondence relating to United Nations policy between Mrs. Roosevelt and President Truman has been declassified since the Lash publication. The Henry Stimson papers at Yale University are useful for coverage of Austin's positions on national defense.

The story of Austin's crusade for a postwar international organization relies heavily on the Austin collection and published material. It is supplemented by the Harley Notter papers at the National Archives (RG 59) and the Frank McNaughton papers at the Harry S. Truman Presidential Library at Independence, Mo. The Arthur H. Vandenberg papers at the University of Michigan reveal little that is not available in Arthur H. Vandenberg, Jr. (ed.), *The Private Papers of Senator Vandenberg* (Boston: Houghton Mifflin, 1952) and in C. David Tompkins, *Senator Arthur H. Vandenberg: The Evolution of a Modern Republican* (East Lansing: Michigan State University Press, 1970). The papers of the Senate Committee on Foreign Relations at the National Archives (RG 46) are disappointing relative to Austin's brief tenure on the committee (1944-46). The minutes of the committee's executive sessions are more useful on issues concerning the United Nations arising during the Truman administration.

Many collections fill in Austin's career at the United Nations. One of the most useful is the State Department decimal file at the National Archives. Presently open through the year 1949, it reveals the thinking of Department planners as well as the importance or lack thereof placed on the United Nations on many issues. While much material is duplicated in the decimal file, the subject file of the United States Mission in New York is important for the collective thinking of that group. Its papers, through 1949, were recently transferred to the National Archives from the Federal Records Center in New York and are labeled the United States/United Nations file (RG 84). Also important is the International Organization file, located at the Washington Federal Records Center. These records are accessible through application at the State Department. Again, there is much duplication in the decimal file, but the IO file provides a view of the issues from the Department's United Nations desk. Two important files, recently opened, on the volatile Palestine issue at the United Nations are the Palestine Reference Book of Dean Rusk and the Palestine Reference file of Robert McClintock (RG 59).

The key to these materials is the *Foreign Relations of the United States* series, published by the Historical Office of the State Department. This much-heralded, meticulously edited series (now into the year 1949) is multivolumed for the war and postwar years. Starting in 1945, volume one of each year contains materials relating to the United Nations, although other volumes supplement the issues presented therein. The series is valuable not only for the documents published, but also as a finding aid to other materials in the National Archives and the Federal Records Centers.

The Harry S. Truman Library contains much material on United Nation issues. The Official File and the President's Personal File in the White House Central Files of the Truman papers are voluminous and not altogether rewarding. More important material is located in the Library's other collections. The Clark M. Clifford papers pertain mostly to domestic matters, but there are occasional items on foreign affairs, particularly in reference to American relations with the Soviet Union and the Palestine issue. The Joseph M. Jones papers are valuable on the Truman Doctrine and the Marshall Plan in spite of the fact that much of the material is available in Jones, *The Fifteen Weeks* (New York: Harcourt, Brace and World, 1955). The George M. Elsey papers are very important for the Korean crisis. The Frank McNaughton papers, noted above, reveal the occasional nuggets that a Washington reporter can dig out. Recently opened, but largely still undergoing declassification procedures, are the papers of Dean Acheson. Transcripts of seminars conducted at Princeton University in 1953 and 1954 are open. Participants, in addition to Acheson, included such notables as George Kennan, Dean Rusk, Philip Jessup, J. Robert Oppenheimer, W. Averell Harriman and Paul Nitze. These people ranged over the issues of the Truman period and provided some revealing insights. The Democratic National Committee Clipping File is an important source that gives a national press overview.

The John Foster Dulles papers at Princeton University contribute information on Austin's relationship with the Republican hierarchy in 1943-1944. Even more important is evidence of the advisory role Dulles played in the Truman administration.

AUSTIN PUBLICATIONS

The few articles Austin published over the years reveal something of both his writing style and his philosophy of business, law, politics and international relations. See "The American International Corporation," *Far Eastern Review,* 13 (Mar. 1917), 370-71; "Law Courts in China," *Case and Comment,* 24 (May 1918), 956-61; "What Shall the G.O.P. Do?" *Guide: The Women's National Political Review,* 14 (Feb. 1940), 6-9; "Home Fronts for War Shape World Fronts for Peace," *Free World,* 3 (Aug. 1942), 205-07; "United We Stand," *Foreign Policy Reports,* 20 (Oct. 1, 1944), 166-76; "The Policy of War and Peace in the Platform of the Republican Party," *American Peace Society Bulletin* (Oct. 1944), 3-7; "The First Step, Security," *Post War World,* 1 (Oct. 16, 1944), 15-19; "A Pincer Movement for Peace," *The American Foreign Service Journal,* 25 (Jan. 1948), 7-9; "A Warning on World Government," *Harper's Magazine* (May 1948), 93-97; "The Security Council Acts Against War," *The Rotarian,* 77 (Sept. 1950), 8-10.

AUSTIN PARTICIPATION
IN GOVERNMENT HEARINGS

Austin was no exception to the life of a legislator who spends much time in committee hearings. He participated both as a questioning senator and as an administration witness while serving at the United Nations. His style, manner and preparation are shown through hearings such as the Senate Judiciary Committee, *Hearings on S. 1392, A Bill to Reorganize the Judicial Branch of the Government,* 75th Cong., 1st sess. (1937); Senate Committee on Military Affairs, *Hearings on S. 4164, A System of Selective Compulsory Military Training and Service,* 76th Cong., 3rd sess. (1940); House Committee on Foreign Affairs, *Hearings on the Structure of the United Nations and Relations of the United States to the United Nations,* 80th Cong., 2nd sess. (1948); Senate Committee on Foreign Relations, *Hearings on the North Atlantic Treaty,* 81st Cong., 1st sess. (1949).

GOVERNMENT DOCUMENTS

Austin's participation in the affairs of the nation are recorded in many of the regularly published documents of various agencies. Particularly helpful for his Senate years are the volumes of the *Congressional Record,* which give not only his remarks on the floor but also items he considered important enough to insert in the record. The *Foreign Relations of the United States* series, noted above, remains a most valuable tool for the researcher, as is the bimonthly *Department of State Bulletin.*

Although awkward to use, due to lack of an index for the period 1945-1950, the Official Records of the General Assembly and of the Security Council are mandatory reading for anyone researching United Nations affairs. There the official positions of member governments are recorded. For this study of Austin those records also revealed something of his philosophy as well as his public debating style.

Three published Congressional documents are noteworthy. The oft-quoted Senate Committee on Armed Services and Committee of Foreign Relations, *Hearings on the Military Situation in the Far East,* 82nd Cong., 1st sess. (1951) is a must to understand United States/United Nations policy re Korea and China. In 1973, the Senate Foreign Relations Committee released for publication the executive session minutes of that Committee on the *Legislative Origins of the Truman Doctrine* and the *Executive Session Hearings on the Vandenberg Resolution and the North Atlantic Treaty.* Both documents reflect United States attitudes toward the United Nations on these important issues.

NEWSPAPERS

The New York Times with its fine news coverage and index remains a key asset in any research in twentieth-century American history. The *Times* also proved its value as a substitute index to the unindexed Official Records of the United Nations.

Vermont newspapers' reaction to Austin's public positions are culled from runs of the state's dailies and weeklies located at the Vermont State Library in Montpelier. The two largest dailies, the *Burlington Free Press* and the *Rutland Herald* are the most valuable, but the other papers cannot be overlooked totally. See the *Barre Daily Times, Bennington Banner, Brandon Union, Brattleboro Reformer, Burlington Clipper, Burlington Daily News, Caledonia Record, Enosburg Standard, Montpelier Evening Argus, Newport Express, Newport Standard, St. Albans Messenger, Vergennes Enterprise* and the *Waterbury Record.*

Time magazine provides good contextual information for Austin's United Nations years.

INTERVIEWS,
ORAL HISTORY MEMOIRS

For the most part, reading oral history memoirs proved disappointing. There are collections at the Truman and Roosevelt Libraries, the Princeton Library (the John Foster Dulles Oral History Collection) and the most prestigious and comprehensive one at Columbia. Three individual memoirs are noteworthy: two by Ernest Gross (the longer, more detailed and better one is at Columbia; the other is at Princeton) and one by John D. Hickerson at Princeton. Several personal interviews with three other persons proved rewarding: Mrs. Warren R. Austin (now deceased), Mrs. Frank Start and Warren R. Austin, Jr.

MEMOIRS AND PUBLISHED
COLLECTIONS

These works have an uneven quality. Cordell Hull's two volume work, *The Memoirs of Cordell Hull* (New York: Macmillan, 1948) is stilted and self-serving. Henry W. Stimson and McGeorge Bundy, *On Active Service in Peace and War* (New York: Harper, 1947) is important for factual data on Austin's national defense role. Allen Drury, *A Senate Journal, 1943-1945* (New York: McGraw-Hill, 1963) is witty and cynical on Austin. Fred L. Israel (ed.), *The War Diary of Breckinridge Long* (Lincoln: University of Nebraska Press, 1966), is important for understanding the State Department-Congressional relationship in pursuit of a postwar international organization. *The Private Papers of Senator Vandenberg,* already noted, reveals not only the Senator, but others as well.

Important volumes by participants in the Truman years include Truman's *Memoirs* (2 vols., Garden City, N.Y.: Doubleday, 1956) which are more telling about the character of the President than they are in providing factual data. James Byrnes, *Speaking Frankly* (New York: Harper, 1947) is biting; Dean Acheson, *Present at the Creation, My Years in the State Department* (New York: Norton, 1969) contains pointed prose, much information, and proves how avid a Cold Warrior Acheson really was. George F. Kennan, *Memoirs 1925-1950* (Boston: Little, Brown, 1967) is eloquently frank. Walter Millis (ed.), *The Forrestal Diaries* (New York: Viking Press, 1951) is a key published work in understanding the foreign policy of the Truman period. David Lilienthal, *The Atomic Energy Years* (New York: Harper and Row, 1964) gives a different perspective on an important aspect.

United Nations participants have provided some good material. Eleanor Roosevelt, *On My Own* (New York: Harper, 1958) is candid. Trygve Lie, *In the Cause of Peace: Seven Years with the United*

Nations (New York: Macmillan, 1954) reveals the difficulties and frustrations of operating the world organization. The second volume of Lester B. Pearson, *Mike, the Memoirs of the Right Honorable Lester B. Pearson* (2 vols., New York: Quadrangle, 1972, 1973) looks at Austin and United States Korean policy from a different vantage point. Finally, a short reminiscence about one of the United Nations' best kept secrets is revealed in Philip Jessup, "The Berlin Blockade and the Use of the United Nations," *Foreign Affairs,* 50 (Oct. 1971), 163-70.

STUDIES ON AUSTIN

The bibliography on Austin has grown over the years. Beverly Smith wrote "A Yankee Meets the World," *Saturday Evening Post* (Aug. 24, 1946), 10-12, shortly after the Senator was appointed to the United Nations post. *Time,* 58 (Feb. 5, 1951), 16-18, ran a cover story on him at the beginning of the Great Debate over Korea. The first scholarly work on Austin was my "Warren R. Austin: Republican Internationalist and United States Foreign Policy" (Ph.D. dissertation, Kent State University, 1969). Henry W. Berger covers the Vermonter's China venture in "Warren R. Austin in China 1916-1917," *Vermont History,* 40 (Autumn 1971), 246-61. His role is viewed in a larger context in my "'Our New Gold Goes Adventuring': The American International Corporation in China," *Pacific Historical Review,* 43 (May 1974), 212-32. I also discussed Austin's early Senate career in "Vermont's Traditional Republicanism vs. the New Deal: Warren R. Austin and the Election of 1934, *Vermont History,* 39 (Spring 1971), 128-41. David Porter analyzes Austin's role in congressional foreign policymaking in "Senator Warren R. Austin and the Neutrality Act of 1939," *Vermont History,* 42 (Summer 1974), 228-38. An important memo written by Austin is cited in Thomas Paterson, "Potsdam, the Atomic Bomb and the Cold War: A Discussion with James F. Byrnes," *Pacific Historical Review,* 41 (May 1971), 225-30. Austin also figures prominently in two articles by me: one, "United States Policy Toward Palestine at the United Nations, 1947-48," *Prologue, the Journal of the National Archives* (Fall 1975), 163-76; the other, "The National War Service Controversy," *Mid-America* (Oct. 1975), 246-58. Austin's oratorical ability is analyzed in Howard Schwartz, "Warren Robinson Austin: International Orator" (unpublished manuscript, Special Collections, University of Vermont).

SECONDARY WORKS

The works of the many historians cited in the footnotes indicate the importance of their earlier and contemporary scholarship. In reading through these secondary works, I have been most impressed by James T. Patterson, *Congressional Conservatism and the New Deal* (Lexington: University of Kentucky Press, 1967); William E. Leuchtenburg, *Franklin D. Roosevelt and the New Deal, 1932-1940* (New York: Harper and Row, 1963); Robert A. Divine, *The Illusion of Neutrality* (Chicago: University of Chicago Press, 1962) and *Second Chance: The Triumph of Internationalism in America During World War II* (New York: Atheneum, 1967); James MacGregor Burns, *Roosevelt: The Lion and the Fox* (New York: Harcourt, Brace, 1956) and *Roosevelt: The Soldier of Freedom* (New York: Harcourt, Brace, Jovanovich, 1970); William Appleman Williams, *The Tragedy of American Diplomacy* (Cleveland: World Publishing Co., 1959); Gabriel Kolko, *The Politics of War, The World and United States Foreign Policy, 1943-1945* (New York: Random House, 1968); Joyce and Gabriel Kolko, *The Limits of Power: The World and United States Foreign Policy, 1945-1952* (New York: Harper and Row, 1972); John Lewis Gaddis, *The United States and the Origins of the Cold War, 1941-1947* (New York: Harper and Row, 1972); Thomas G. Paterson, *Soviet-American Confrontation: Postwar Reconstruction and the Origins of the Cold War* (Baltimore: Johns Hopkins University Press, 1973); John Snetsinger, *Truman, The Jewish Vote and the Creation of Israel* (Stanford: Hoover Institution Press, 1974); Glenn D. Paige, *The Korean Decision, June 24-30, 1950* (New York: Free Press, 1968); Leland W. Goodrich, *Korea, A Study of United States Policy in the United Nations* (New York: Council on Foreign Relations, 1956) and Allen S. Whiting, *China Crosses the Yalu, The Decision to Enter the Korean War* (New York: Macmillan, 1960). The overall historiography of the Truman administration is found in Richard S. Kirkendall (ed.), *The Truman Period as a Research Field* (Columbia: University of Missouri Press, 1967; 2nd ed., 1974). Both volumes should be consulted.

INDEX

Acheson, Dean G., 57, 70, 71-76, 81, 141-43, 162-64, 170, 172, 185
Act of Chapultepec, 131
ad hoc Committee on Palestine, 104-07
ad hoc Committee on the Problem of Voting in the Security Council, 130
Advisory Committee on Problems of Foreign Relations, 98
aggression, 150, 157, 173, 177
aggressor, 149, 168, 170, 176
Agricultural Adjustment Act, 15
aid to Great Britain, 33
Aiken, George, 194n
Albania, 62
Alling, Paul, 105
Allison, John, 162
ambassador, role as spokesman, 185
America, see United States
American Association for the United Nations, 45, 89, 90
American Association of University Women, 175
American Bar Association, Montreal meeting, 24
American Broadcasting Network, 55
American delegation to the United Nations, 97, 103, 163; see also United States delegation

American forces, 108-09
American foreign policy, 61, 65, 70; see also United States policy
American Foreign Service Journal, 120
American Hospital (Paris), 116
American International Corporation, 5
American-led bloc, 162
analysis of Korean War, 145
Anglo-American Committee of Inquiry, 97, 100
anti-communism, 195n
anti-New Deal, 181, 190n
appeasement, 172
Arab-Asian bloc, 164, 170-71
Arab-Asian states, sponsor cease-fire resolution, 171
Arab-Israeli war, 99
Arab leaders, 114
Arab League, 95
Arab nationalism, 95
Arab nations, 95, 97, 105-06, 175
Arabs, 98-99, 101-02, 108, 112, 114-15
Argentina, 100, 111, 126, 137-38
armistice talks, 176
arms embargo, 29, 31-32
"Armstrong Doctrine", 120
Armstrong, Hamilton Fish, 120
article 51 treaty, 133
Ashurst, Henry F., 19